Democracy in
Latin America

Democracy in Latin America

A History since Independence

Thomas C. Wright

ROWMAN & LITTLEFIELD
Lanham • Boulder • New York • London

Published by Rowman & Littlefield
An imprint of The Rowman & Littlefield Publishing Group, Inc.
4501 Forbes Boulevard, Suite 200, Lanham, Maryland 20706
www.rowman.com

86-90 Paul Street, London EC2A 4NE

British Library Cataloguing in Publication Information Available

Library of Congress Cataloging-in-Publication Data

Names: Wright, Thomas C., author.
Title: Democracy in Latin America : a history since independence /
   Thomas C. Wright.
Description: Lanham, Maryland : Rowman & Littlefield, [2023] | Includes
   bibliographical references and index.
Identifiers: LCCN 2022042316 (print) | LCCN 2022042317 (ebook) | ISBN
   9781538149331 (Cloth) | ISBN 9781538149348 (Paperback)
   | ISBN 9781538149355 (epub)
Subjects: LCSH: Democracy—Latin America—History. | Political
   participation—Latin America. | Economics—Sociological aspects—Latin
   America. | Distributive justice—Latin America. | Latin
   America—History—20th century—Chronology. | Latin America—Politics
   and government.
Classification: LCC JL966 .W75 2023 (print) | LCC JL966 (ebook) | DDC
   321.8098—dc23/eng/20221107
LC record available at https://lccn.loc.gov/2022042316LC ebook record available at
https://lccn.loc.gov/2022042317

for Dina

in memory of Arnold J. Bauer

Contents

Acknowledgments

I am indebted to many people for their contributions to this book. The anonymous reviewers of the original proposal made suggestions that sharpened my focus on the history of Latin American democracy. Colleagues and friends Robert Smale, Joseph A. (Andy) Fry, Vincent Peloso, and Jerry Simich smoothed the prose, offered valuable insights and interpretations, and saved me from egregious errors. The welcoming and expert staff of the Hispanic Division of the Library of Congress provided invaluable assistance. I could not have completed this project without Angela Moor's technical expertise and editorial skills. Katelyn Turner of Rowman & Littlefield offered guidance and encouragement along the way. I am grateful to all.

Acronyms*

AAA	Argentine Anticommunist Association
AD	Democratic Action (Venezuela)
ALBA	Bolivarian Alliance for the Peoples of Our America (Venezuela and affiliated countries)
APRA	American Popular Revolutionary Alliance (Peru)
CCT	Conditional Cash Transfer
CELS	Center for Legal and Social Studies (Argentina)
CIA	Central Intelligence Agency (United States)
COMIBOL	Bolivian Mining Corporation
COPEI	Independent Political Electoral Organizing Committee (Venezuela)
DINA	Directorate of National Intelligence (Chile)
ERP	People's Revolutionary Army (Argentina)
EU	European Union
EZLN	Zapatista National Liberation Army (Mexico)
FMLN	Farabundo Martí National Liberation Front (El Salvador)
FSLN	Sandinista National Liberation Front (Nicaragua)
GDP	Gross Domestic Product
ILO	International Labor Organization
IMF	International Monetary Fund
IPC	International Petroleum Company (Peru)
M-26-7	Twenty-Sixth of July Movement (Cuba)
MAS	Movement Toward Socialism (Bolivia)
MIR	Movement of the Revolutionary Left (Chile)
MNR	National Revolutionary Movement (Bolivia)
NAFTA	North American Free Trade Agreement
NSD	National Security Doctrine
OAS	Organization of American States
OPEC	Organization of Petroleum Exporting Countries

PAN	National Autonomist Party (Argentina)
PDC	Christian Democratic Party (Chile)
PN	National Party (Chile)
PRI	Institutional Revolutionary Party (Mexico)
PSP	Popular Socialist Party (Cuba)
PSUV	United Socialist Party of Venezuela
PT	Workers' Party (Brazil)
RADEPA	Cause of the Fatherland (Bolivia)
UCR	Radical Civic Union Party (Argentina)
UDEL	Democratic Liberation Union (Nicaragua)
UFCO	United Fruit Company
UN	United Nations
UP	Popular Unity (Chile)
URNG	Guatemalan National Revolutionary Union
USAID	U.S. Agency for International Development
USSR	Union of Soviet Socialist Republics (Soviet Union)

*This list includes those acronyms that appear on more than one page.

Mexico, Central America, and the Caribbean

NICARAGUA

Caribbean Sea

COSTA
RICA

PANAMA

Panama
Canal

Barranquilla
Cartagena

Valencia ★ Caracas

TRINIDAD
AND TOBAGO

VENEZUELA

Orinoco R.

ATLANTIC
OCEAN

Medellin

Georgetown

★Bogota

Cali ●

COLOMBIA

Paramaribo
SURINAME
FRENCH
GUIANA

G U I A N A
HIGHLANDS

Magdelena R.

Roraima

Quito ★

ECUADOR

Guayaquil ●

Japura R.

Manaus ●

Belem ●

Amazon R.

Santarem ●

Sao Luis ●

● Fortaleza

Maranon R.

Ucayali R.

Jurua R.

Amazonas

Madeira R.

Topajos R.

Xingu R.

Tocantins R.

Pernambuco

PERU

Porto Velho ●

B R A Z I L

● Recife

Callao ●

★ Lima

Cuzco ●

L. Titicaca

Trinidad ●

★ La Paz

BOLIVIA

★ Sucre

Charcas

Mato
Grosso

BRAZILIAN HIGHLANDS

Bahia

● Salvador (Bahia)

★ Brasilia

Cerrado

Rio Grande

GRAN CHACO

PARAGUAY

Parana R.

Parana

PACIFIC
OCEAN

Asuncion ★

Itaipu Dam
Santa
Catarina

Rio de Janeiro ●

● Sao Paulo

SOUTH

ATLANTIC

OCEAN

Rio
Grande
Do Sul

● Porto Alegre

Santiago ★

Rosario ●

URUGUAY

PAMPAS

Concepcion ●

A
N
D
E
S

C
H
I
L
E

A
R
G
E
N
T
I
N
A

Buenos Aires ★

★ Montevideo

Rio de la Plata

PATAGONIA

Falkland Islands (U.K.)
Claimed by Argentina as Malvinas

Tierra del
Fuego

Cape Horn

Drake Passage

| 0 | 500 | 1,000 | 1,500 Miles |

| 0 | 500 | 1,000 | 1,500 Kilometers |

South America

Introduction

This book relates the story of the gradual, erratic, and incomplete development of democracy in Latin America from independence to the present. Because much recent news of Latin American politics is negative, emphasizing the challenges to or failures of democracy in Venezuela, Nicaragua, El Salvador, Brazil, and elsewhere, it is easy to lose sight of the democratic progress that has occurred. Since 1990, freely elected governments have ruled almost everywhere and military coups, a historically common means of regime change, have virtually disappeared. Poverty has been reduced through extending the reach of governmental social services to broader clienteles—although recent declines in prices of Latin America's export commodities, combined with the effects of the COVID-19 pandemic, have jeopardized progress in this area. In comparison with much of the world, and including major areas of Asia, Africa, the Middle East, and most of the former Soviet republics, Latin America is a beacon of democracy.

Rather than arbitrarily select a definition of democracy from the vast literature on the topic, this book will employ a definition of democracy developed by Latin Americans themselves. That definition is embedded in the charter of the Organization of American States (OAS) and the same organization's American Declaration of the Rights and Duties of Man, both dating from 1948. Founded in April 1948 to replace the Pan American Union, which had been established in 1910, the OAS is a regional body that coordinates with the United Nations (UN) and exercises independent action on hemispheric affairs. The OAS charter was signed and ratified by all twenty Latin American countries and the United States. Within days of its founding, the OAS issued the American Declaration of the Rights and Duties of Man, which confirmed the democratic principles embedded in the OAS charter. The charter and the Declaration articulate, formally and officially, what democracy meant for twenty Latin American countries and for the United States, three-quarters of a century ago. The democratic provisions of the charter and Declaration have been reiterated in numerous OAS protocols and resolutions adopted since 1948.

The OAS charter addresses democracy in two dimensions: political and socioeconomic. Regarding political democracy, the preamble states: "Representative democracy is an indispensable condition for the stability, peace and development of the region" and calls for "democratic institutions." Article 2 lists as one of the organization's purposes "To promote and consolidate representative democracy." The Declaration's Article XX reads: "Every person having legal capacity is entitled to participate in the government of his country, directly or through his representatives, and to take part in popular elections, which shall be by secret ballot, and shall be honest, periodic, and free."

The OAS charter devotes more attention to socioeconomic than to political democracy. Article 3f calls for the "elimination of extreme poverty"; Article 3j proclaims that "social justice and social security are the bases of lasting peace." Article 34 includes: "equitable distribution of national income"; "fair wages, employment opportunities, and acceptable working conditions for all"; "rapid eradication of illiteracy and expansion of educational opportunities for all"; and "proper nutrition." Article 45 declares work "a right and a social duty" and requires the incorporation of the "marginal sectors of the population" into the "economic, social, civic, cultural, and political life of the nation." Article 45c posits "the right to collective bargaining and the workers' right to strike," while Article 34d endorses "reforms leading to equitable and efficient land-tenure systems." The last of these is particularly interesting for Latin America: Agrarian reform, or the breakup of large rural estates, would erode the political power of many countries' elites, which was anchored in rural land ownership and concomitant political control of their subaltern laborers.

At the time of the adoption of the OAS charter and Declaration, Latin America had a few dictatorships and other governments that, although elected, had not advanced far toward either political or socioeconomic democracy. To secure the charter's ratification by governments that did not intend to implement democratizing policies, language was inserted to exempt them from the envisioned democratic progress. With regard to political democracy, the charter's Article 2 commits the OAS "to promote and consolidate representative democracy, *with due respect to the principle of nonintervention*" (italics added). This principle, a reaction to and defense against the long history of U.S. political and military intervention in the region, was sacrosanct to all Latin American countries. It meant that dictatorships and socioeconomically retrograde regimes should not be forced by another country or countries to adopt the stipulated political democracy. The Declaration's Article XX, cited above, guarantees participation in elections and governance to those persons *"having legal capacity,"* (italics added)—a condition that in 1948 eliminated women in half the countries and illiterates in several of them. And referring to both forms of democracy, the charter's Article 3e guarantees every state "the right to choose . . . its political, economic, and social system."

Given these critical caveats, one must ask whether the OAS commitment to democracy was genuine. As with the UN's Universal Declaration of Human Rights, both the charter and the Declaration are statements of aspirations, not necessarily of current reality. The generalized post–World War II enthusiasm for democracy, resulting from the western democracies' defeat of the totalitarian Axis powers, inspired the Universal Declaration of Human Rights; clearly, it also influenced the OAS founders. The founders may also have reacted to the beginnings of the Cold War and rise of concern about communism in Latin America by attempting to seize the reformist agenda from the communists.

The OAS documents also reflect the recent history of both Latin America and the United States. In the United States, President Franklin D. Roosevelt's New Deal added a significant measure of socioeconomic democracy to the existing incomplete but long-established political democracy. Beginning in the early twentieth century, Latin American reformers began to challenge the elites' monopoly of political power and the exclusion of the non-elite majorities from sharing in the countries' wealth and well-being. By 1948, the great majority of Latin America's population had benefited, at least temporarily, from measures of political or socioeconomic democracy, or both, and a majority of Latin America's literate women had been enfranchised. Still excluded in some places, the majority of Latin America's middle and working classes had been incorporated into their countries' political systems. They had also benefited from the establishment of labor codes, social security systems, and expanded access to education. One country, Mexico, had undergone a thorough transformation since its 1910 revolution that included agrarian reform benefiting landless rural laborers, whose marginalization continued unabated in most of Latin America.

Thus the OAS charter and Declaration were more than statements of aspirations, reflections of enthusiasm for democracy, or attempts to preempt communists; they were grounded in Latin America's and the United States' reality—a reality that fell short of the lofty goals set forth in the two documents but that reflected progress toward them. This book will use the OAS's definition of democracy as a barometer of the progress, and lack of it, toward democracy in Latin America.

Political democracy is more than the basic requirement of fair, free, and open elections and the peaceful transfer of power from government to opposition following elections. It is about inclusion: which citizens can vote, which cannot. From a handful of wealthy literate males in the early post-independence years, the electorate gradually expanded to include every-one aged eighteen and over (sixteen in a few countries), with the exception of prisoners and active military in some cases. In examining socioeconomic democracy, we will follow the transition from the nineteenth-century norm of laissez-faire in economics and social welfare, in which each individual was responsible for his or her economic and social condition, to governments' assumption of responsibility for citizens' welfare in the twentieth century. Neither political nor socioeconomic democracy is perfect; far from it. But both have advanced far in the two centuries since independence.

The advances and setbacks of democracy have been determined by the contest between proponents and opponents of democratization. Throughout this book we will follow the appearance and evolution of several drivers of democratization: labor unions and federations, progressive political parties, university student organizations, powerful progressive leaders, intellectuals, and, in some cases, the militaries and progressive clerics. These forces of democratization constantly engaged opponents of the same: economic and social elites, the militaries in most instances, conservative political parties and interest groups, powerful conservative leaders, the United States in most cases, and on certain social issues, the Catholic Church hierarchy. The balance of these forces shifted periodically, often in waves that swept across Latin America.

In examining the evolution of democracy, this book will raise and try to answer several questions. How has democracy been able to develop in a region where, prior to independence, there was no antecedent for it? Why have Latin America's efforts at democratization, despite notable progress, fallen short of the perfect world described in the OAS definitions of democracy? What have been the major impediments to the realization of the OAS agenda? Have political and socioeconomic democracy been compatible, or was Fidel Castro right when he proclaimed, "revolution first, elections later"? Finally, how has the United States influenced the development of democracy in Latin America?

Chapter 1

From *Caudillos* to Oligarchs, 1820s–1910s

Most of Latin America achieved independence from Spain and Portugal between 1810 and 1825; Haiti had become independent of France earlier, in 1804. Brazil and Central America attained independence peacefully; in most of Spanish America, independence was won by war. Cuba and Puerto Rico remained Spanish colonies until 1898. The transition from colony to independent state is always challenging, as evidenced by the travails of most Asian and African countries that broke their colonial shackles following World War II. Latin America was no exception.

Even before the euphoria of independence subsided, leaders of the new countries began to grapple with serious economic and political challenges. In those areas where military action had been widespread and prolonged—Mexico and much of Spanish South America—an immediate task was to promote recovery from war damage to agriculture and the vital mining sector. Capital flight was another issue: Many Spaniards and Portuguese returned to their home countries with their liquid capital, exacerbating the economic problems facing the new authorities. Most of the new Spanish American countries also faced the major problem of how to demobilize the thousands of armed men who had fought in the independence wars, many of whom, given the wars' impact on the economy, had no livelihood to which to return. These rootless men constituted an implicit threat to government stability. Regionalism was another practical issue facing the new countries; for some, independence meant not only cutting ties with the colonial powers but also with the former colonial, now national capitals, as occurred when Bolivia and Paraguay split with the former viceregal capital of Buenos Aires and Central America from the jurisdiction of Mexico City. Moreover, hazily demarcated boundaries between the former colonies sometimes led to border wars between the new republics.

In addition to such practical concerns, ideological divisions made consensus on fundamental issues difficult to achieve in the new countries. The
Enlightenment had challenged the status quo in fundamental ways, and by
the time of independence there was a clear division between liberals and
conservatives that led to conflict. In general terms, conservatives stood for as
little change as possible from colonial institutions and practices. They supported authoritarian government, preserving the Catholic Church's powers
and monopoly of religion, and maintaining the colonial social order. Liberals
generally opposed authoritarian government and the Catholic Church's power
and monopoly, and some favored altering the social hierarchy by eliminating
the tribute—the colonial head tax on Indians—and abolishing African slavery.

These ideological differences between conservatives and liberals translated into dueling concepts of how to structure governments in the independent countries. Conservatives advocated a strong executive and centralized
government, similar to the colonial regime, and favored severely restricted
suffrage based on gender, property, and/or literacy. Liberals favored a strong
legislative branch to counter executive power and more inclusive suffrage,
although few advocated extending the vote to women, Indians, former slaves,
or illiterates. Some liberals embraced federalism to decentralize power away
from the capital to the provinces. Disagreement over whether to preserve or
dismantle the colonial regime and over the structure of government fueled
controversy that commonly disrupted institutional continuity and retarded the
establishment of stable and effective governments.

Lack of experience with governing was a daunting handicap facing the
former colonials. In contrast to British North America, where each colony
had its own legislative body, Spanish and Portuguese America were closely
governed by appointees of the kings: viceroys and their subordinates. The
only representative institutions, the city councils, had very limited powers,
and in the more important cities, seats were acquired by purchase rather than
by election. The great liberator of South America, Simón Bolívar, understood
the significance of this absence of practical experience with governance. He
wrote: "We were cut off and, as it were, removed from the world in relation
to the science of government and administration of the state." He also understood the difference between the Spanish and the English colonies regarding
political experience and participation: "If we could at least have managed our
domestic affairs and our internal administration, we could have acquainted
ourselves with the processes and mechanics of public affairs." Had that
opportunity existed, he insisted, Latin Americans might have acquired "the
abilities and political virtues that distinguish our brothers of the north" and
thus been able to construct viable governmental institutions.[1]

These practical and ideological impediments to establishing stable and
effective political institutions were complicated by an even more profound

challenge: the creation of legitimate authority—authority accepted by citizens, or rule with the consent of the governed. The authority of Spanish and Portuguese kings had been legitimate—at least until the Enlightenment raised doubts among a few intellectuals about the divine rights of monarchs—even when some of the kings' personnel or policies were unpopular. Hence the refrain, "Long live the king, down with bad government." The kings' legitimacy did not automatically transfer to the new republican governments; legitimacy had to be earned. Creating legitimacy in the new republics following the evaporation of the traditional legitimacy of kings was an extremely difficult challenge—one that would take time to achieve.

As a result of these conditions, most Latin American countries experienced extreme political instability, bordering in some cases on anarchy, during the half century following independence. Between 1821 and 1845, Peru underwent twenty-four regime changes, an average of one per year; and by 1860 had had two rival presidents on more than one occasion, fought three foreign wars, and adopted ten constitutions. Mexico began its independent history as a monarchy that lasted less than a year, then had thirty different presidents and over seventy presidential administrations, averaging seven months in length, over the next fifty years. Chile adopted eight constitutions between 1812 and 1833 and suffered innumerable revolts and two civil wars by 1859. In 1819, newly independent Argentina broke into sixteen disunited, autonomous provinces that were not effectively reunited until 1852. Bolivia's Manuel Isidoro Belzú (1848–1855) may have set the record for surviving the most coup attempts against a sitting president: forty-two in seven years.

THE *CAUDILLOS*

During the decades of economic stagnation or contraction and governmental instability that followed independence, caudillos dominated the political life of most new Spanish American countries. There is no universally accepted definition of a caudillo; the closest appropriate English terms may be "warlord" or "strong man." Most caudillos shared several characteristics. They continued the colonial practice of authoritarian governance. They were charismatic, and many developed cults of personality that exalted them. Some caudillos identified with the common people, even if they hailed from a higher social class, and excelled at the manly virtues of fighting, riding, drinking, and carousing. Others effected aristocratic traits that elevated them above their countrymen.

Caudillos tolerated no political opposition, and either co-opted or persecuted potential rivals. When in power, they controlled or ignored their country's legislature and courts. Most caudillos in the early post-independence period came from a military background in the colonial militias or the independence wars. Others rose through the ranks of informal fighting units such as the *montoneros* of the Argentine *pampas* or the *llaneros* of the Venezuelan plains. With a few exceptions, caudillos did not represent ideologies or political principles; they served themselves and their men, and seized power for its own sake, to enrich themselves, and to reward their supporters.

Caudillos ruled in Argentina from 1820 to 1852. Formally known as the United Provinces of the Río de la Plata, Argentina in reality was disunited after the fifteen provinces of the interior rebelled against an 1819 draft constitution that centralized power in the capital, Buenos Aires. Underlying this rebellion, which led to the proliferation of caudillos, was the interior's opposition to the colonial pattern of centralized rule from the capital. Economic issues were also critical. The elites of Buenos Aires, Argentina's principal port, favored free trade, as they would control and profit from the flow of goods in and out of the country. Free trade, however, threatened the artisan producers of textiles, ironwork, and handicrafts in the interior, who advocated high tariffs for protection from cheaper, factory-produced imports.

Throughout the vast interior, a territory populated by a handful of people and millions of wild cattle, caudillos seized control of the provincial governments. Most were rough-hewn plainsmen, or *gauchos,* who though unlettered and unrefined, were intent on protecting their provinces and their personal interests. Their supporters were mainly other gauchos, skilled at riding, using *bolas* to fell the wild cattle of the pampas, and fighting. Domingo F. Sarmiento, a Buenos Aires intellectual and future president, penned a description of the gauchos and one of the caudillos of the interior, Facundo Quiroga.

> It is necessary to see their [the gauchos'] visages bristling with beards, their countenances as grave and serious as those of the Arabs of Asia, to appreciate the pitying scorn with which they look upon the sedentary denizen of the city, who may have read many books, but who cannot overthrow and slay a fierce bull, who could not provide himself with a horse from the pampas, who has never met a tiger alone, and received him with a dagger in one hand and a poncho rolled up in the other, to be thrust into the animal's mouth, while he transfixes his heart with his dagger. [p. 37] Facundo is a type of primitive barbarism. His rage was that of a wild beast. The locks of his crisp black hair, which fell in meshes over his brow and eyes, resembled the snakes of Medusa's head. Anger made his voice hoarse and turned his glances into dragons. Wanting ability to manage the machinery of civil government, he substituted terror for patriotism and self-sacrifice.[2]

Although a professed federalist, the caudillo governor of Buenos Aires province after 1829, Juan Manuel de Rosas, set out to unite the country under his rule. Following deaths and military defeats of the caudillos of the interior, he

Figure 1.1 Argentine gaucho as described by Domingo F. Sarmiento
Library of Congress

gained control of the entire country in 1838. Rosas was a large landowner who identified with his gaucho followers and exhibited the manly traits they respected. His armed gangs known as the *mazorca* (ear of corn) instilled fear and enforced his orders. People were required to wear the color red, at least a ribbon, or face the mazorca's wrath. Rosas developed a cult of personality that exalted him as the national leader and savior: His portrait was placed on church altars alongside that of Jesus Christ, implying super-human stature and powers. These methods served Rosas well until 1852, when he was defeated and exiled to England.

Mexico also had its share of caudillos, none more colorful than and few as durable as Antonio López de Santa Anna, known in the United States as the villain of the Alamo. He was so dominant that the period of his ascendancy, 1833 to 1855, is known as the "age of Santa Anna." Prior to the country's independence in 1821, Santa Anna, a creole—or person of Spanish lineage born in America—was an officer in the Spanish army in Mexico. He led the first two successful military coups in independent Mexico: the first in 1823 against Agustín Iturbide, the emperor he had helped install a few months earlier, and the second five years later to overturn the outcome of a presidential election. Santa Anna was elected president in 1833 as a liberal, then switched to the conservatives and led a coup against his former allies. He served as president a total of eleven times, usually abandoning the office after a short while to return to his hacienda in Veracruz. Santa Anna espoused no particular ideology or policy; his only principle was opportunism. During the age of Santa Anna, the presidency changed hands thirty-six times.

Rather than identify with the common folk, as Rosas did, Santa Anna developed a sophisticated style and created a cult of personality underpinned by polished rhetoric. He styled himself after Napoleon Bonaparte, with the front-combed hairdo and lavish dress uniform. After a few years, he upgraded his presidential title from "His Excellency" to the regal "His Most Serene Highness." But it was not only his title that befit a monarchy rather than a republic: His birthday was also celebrated as a national holiday; his portrait hung in public buildings throughout the country; and streets and plazas were renamed in his honor. Statues of Santa Anna proliferated around the capital, and wags noted that a finger on one of the larger ones pointed directly at the national treasury. A crowning moment in the construction of his cult of personality came in 1842, when he held a state funeral for the preserved leg he lost in battle during an 1838 French invasion known as the Pastry War.

Santa Anna abandoned and resumed the presidency at will. He was able to quickly raise an army or augment the standing army, whether to seize the presidential palace or to fight a foreign or domestic enemy. The Mexican army was a predatory body much more adept at pillaging and overthrowing governments than defending the national borders. Santa Anna led that army in the war of Texas secession (1835–1836), attaining infamy, from the U.S. standpoint, by his actions at the Alamo and his order to execute all prisoners following the battle of Goliad. He was captured and eventually released after signing treaties granting Texas independence. When the United States invaded in 1846, launching the U.S.-Mexican War, Santa Anna rose to the occasion but retreated rather than engage the enemy. President again after the onerous 1848 Treaty of Guadalupe Hidalgo took half of Mexico's territory, he sold the Gadsden Strip in today's southern Arizona and New Mexico to the United States for ten million dollars in 1854. His last presidency ended the following year.

In contrast to most of the new republics, Paraguay began independent life with remarkable political stability owing to José Gaspar Rodríguez de Francia, generally known as Francia, who governed as a dictator from 1814 to his death in 1840. Born into the elite, he studied theology and taught at the seminary in Asunción until expelled for espousing progressive ideas derived from the French Enlightenment, after which he studied law. He dominated the junta established during the independence movement and authored the country's first constitution, adopted in 1813 by a congress of over a thousand delegates elected by universal male suffrage. As a result of his ambition, forceful personality, and keen political instinct, the congress named him "supreme dictator" in 1814—hence his sobriquet *El Supremo*. He had "perpetual" added to his title two years later.

Francia pursued a nationalist economic policy that was unique in Latin America: He restricted international commerce and imposed virtual autarchy on his landlocked country. He made the national government a major economic force: The state built and ran textile and shipbuilding industries, confiscated around half the country's land from the large landowners and the Church and leased some of it to peasants, and operated numerous agricultural and cattle enterprises. These policies generally favored the humble over the elites. In addition to taking church lands, Francia closed Paraguay's only seminary where he had earlier taught, banned religious orders, and abolished the *fuero eclesiástico*, or independent church court where ecclesiastics were tried for civil as well as religious offenses. In response, Pope Pius VII excommunicated him.

Paraguay under Francia was a police state and El Supremo brooked no opposition. The massive congress that elected him perpetual dictator disappeared within a few years, and Francia appointed all civil and military officials. His secret police, called in the native Guaraní language *pyragües* ("hairy feet"), ruthlessly repressed potential opponents and dissenters. After the pyragües allegedly uncovered a plot to assassinate him, the dictator had some two hundred of Paraguay's elite executed. Despite his immense power, Francia lived modestly; he did not glorify his persona as did Santa Anna and Rosas and left his unspent salary to the national treasury upon his death.

Francia's authoritarian style was carried on by a father and son succession of dictators, Carlos Antonio López (1841–1862) and Francisco Solano López (1862–1870). The latter led Paraguay in 1864 into a war against three neighbors—Brazil, Argentina, and Uruguay—in the War of the Triple Alliance, or simply the Paraguayan War. Paraguay paid a huge price for its dictator's folly: Up to one third of its population, 38 percent of its territory, and the industry that Francia had built were lost. The war also ended the authoritarian stability that Francia had established: After only three rulers from independence to 1870, the country had thirty-two presidents between the war's end and 1932.

Authoritarian stability was eventually restored in the brutal thirty-five year dictatorship of Alfredo Stroessner (1954–1989).

INSTITUTIONS FOR ENABLING FUTURE POLITICAL DEMOCRATIZATION

Beneath the prevailing dystopian scenario of authoritarianism, instability, and caudillos were three institutions that, in the very long run, would serve to enable political democracy and eventually socioeconomic democracy: constitutions, national legislatures, and elections. All these institutions were alien to Latin America's colonial traditions, as Spanish and Portuguese kings had ruled by the grace of God, not the will of the people; were not constrained by constitutional norms; and did not hold elections. The fledgling independent states embraced constitutions, legislatures, and elections owing to the timing and circumstances of Latin America's independence.

At the time of the Latin American independence movements, written constitutions were new. The first of these was the U.S. Articles of Confederation (1777) and the second the U.S. Constitution (1787). Successive French revolutionary governments adopted three constitutions in the 1790s, followed by three more that anchored Napoleon's reign. Latin American leaders of course were familiar with the Spanish constitution of 1812, written by liberals during the absence of their king, Ferdinand VII, who was held captive by Napoleon. All of these constitutions limited the powers of the executive, whether presidents or kings. After drawn-out and bloody wars for independence against Ferdinand, who was restored to the throne in 1814, creoles increasingly viewed the king as a tyrant, making the limiting of executive power through a written constitution a popular idea. Even Brazil, which adopted monarchy rather that the republican form of government embraced by the Spanish American countries, adopted a constitution as early as 1824.[3]

The constitutions of the new republics established governments consisting of three separate powers: executive, legislative, and judicial. The second branch was new to Latin Americans: having lived under absolute monarchs, they had no experience with making laws beyond mundane municipal regulations. But the U.S., French, and Spanish constitutions had included legislative powers, and many creoles had been introduced to the making of policy decisions during the independence wars. Thus, every country, including monarchist Brazil, made provision for a national congress and, in the few countries that opted for a federal system, for state or provincial legislatures. These legislatures were often trampled upon, ignored, stacked with supporters of the executive, or disbanded, but the idea of citizen legislatures would persist and eventually provide the means for the expansion of citizen participation in governance—a crucial step toward democracy.

The Spanish American creole elites were introduced to elections even before independence. When Napoleon's troops invaded Spain and captured King Ferdinand VII in 1808, the resistance organized a series of loosely elected bodies to govern in the king's absence. The American colonies were invited to participate, on a limited basis, and between 1809 and 1812 conducted indirect elections three times to select their representatives to the Junta Central and two successive iterations of the ancient Spanish parliament, the *Cortes*. Beginning in 1809, administrative capitals throughout Spanish America elected juntas to run their affairs in the king's absence. With this background and the examples of the United States, Spain, and France, upon attaining independence the new republics codified the election of presidents and congresses.

These early elections were improvised. They lacked modern features such as registries, secret ballots, defined parties, and election authorities. They fell well short of the current minimal standard for democratic elections: free, fair, and open. They were often fraudulent and their outcomes frequently overturned by violence. Yet from the early nineteenth century, small numbers of Latin American men voted for presidents, members of congress, constitutions, and sometimes for local officials. In the few countries that embraced federalism, including Latin America's largest by area—Brazil, Argentina, and Mexico—they also elected state or provincial legislatures and governors. Even some dictators attempted to legitimize their rule through elections they tightly controlled. These hundreds of elections in nineteenth-century Latin America established the electoral process as the norm for selecting men, and eventually women, to govern.[4]

LATIN AMERICA AND THE GLOBAL ECONOMY

Latin America experienced a profound transformation between 1850 and 1900. In 1850 the colonial period lingered almost everywhere. The pace of life was slow in city and countryside. Goods were still transported by pack mule or oxcart, and the small volume of exports was loaded in primitive ports onto sailing ships. Even the capital cities were still small. By 1900, modernization had transformed the cities and extended into the countryside in select regions. Railroads had penetrated the hinterlands, replacing animal traction in the conveyance of foodstuffs to the cities and minerals, sugar, wheat, cattle, coffee, and other commodities for export to modernized ports that accommodated large steamships. Mechanized agriculture had appeared in some areas and refurbished or newly opened mines featured steam-driven machinery and giant ore crushers. Telegraph lines carried news instantly, and electricity and telephones occasionally reached beyond the cities. While profound, Latin America's transformation was also selective: Some regions were little changed during this half century, while in others there were few reminders by 1900 of the lingering colonial aura that was so evident in 1850.

The eventual achievement of stable, effective governance in most countries was driven by Latin America's integration into a new global economy that had begun to develop by mid-century. By the 1880s, globalization had impacted many of the world's countries and Europe's colonies, and the pace of the world market's expansion continued to accelerate until it was set back by World War I. After a few years of recovery, the Great Depression that began on Wall Street in October 1929 destroyed the economic ties that bound the world together and ended the first global economy (we now live in the second global economy).

The world economy grew out of the Industrial Revolution that began in the late 1700s, and by the mid nineteenth century, industrialization had advanced to the point that Britain, France, and a few other European countries had accumulated capital to export and required large and growing quantities of raw materials that they could not acquire domestically; the United States was not far behind. The industrial countries also needed markets abroad for their manufactured products. These dynamics drew the independent countries of Latin America and Europe's Asian, African, Australasian, and Caribbean colonies into a close economic relationship with the industrial countries based on the exchange of raw materials for manufactured goods.

Latin America had great potential for participation in the global economy: abundant mineral resources, plenty of land suited to agricultural production, and available labor in most locales. But unlike in their Asian, African, and Caribbean colonies, Europeans did not exercise direct control over Latin America—except for Spain in Cuba and Puerto Rico—and thus could not impose the order that capitalists sought to protect their investments. Experience in the early post-independence years, when British investments went sour from the political turmoil, predatory caudillos, and government defaults, had taught the capital-exporting countries that a modicum of stability was a precondition for investing.

By the middle years of the nineteenth century, some of the divisive issues that had stoked the early post-independence chaos had been partially or fully resolved. Chile ended nearly two decades of political disarray early, with the conservatives' decisive military victory over the liberals and the adoption of the very durable yet flexible 1833 constitution. With the defeat of the caudillo Rosas in 1852, Argentines put the country on the path to stability with the constitution of 1853 (still in force today, much amended). In Mexico, the issue of the power and prerogatives of the Roman Catholic Church, which viscerally

divided liberals and conservatives, was tentatively settled by the 1857 constitution's stripping of Church power and property. With the 1867 defeat of the
French Intervention, which had placed the French-backed emperor Maximilian
on an invented throne, Mexican liberals held decisive sway over very weakened conservatives. By 1854, the abolition of African slavery everywhere save
Brazil, Paraguay, and Spanish Cuba and Puerto Rico resolved another divisive
issue. In most countries, then, the decades after mid-century witnessed a cooling of political passions and turbulence. Liberals and conservatives could
agree in principle that the divisions and wars of the past had not served their
countries well, and some embraced the doctrine of positivism whose motto,
"order and progress," became a guiding principle for new leaders.

Foreign capitalists noticed the change. From initially small, tentative
investments, they gained confidence in the host countries and loosened their
purse strings. The industrializing European countries and the United States
invested their capital in railroads, mines, land, processing plants, ports, steam-
ship lines, and other facilities designed to extract raw materials or grow foodstuffs and transport them to market. They also invested in government bonds,
which were much less risky by the 1880s than they had been at the time of
independence, and in banks and utilities such as power plants, urban light-
ing, and streetcar companies. Most capital came initially from Great Britain.
The leader in the Industrial Revolution, Britain had funds to invest around
the globe: Its investment in Latin America grew nearly tenfold between 1870
and 1914, to some 3.6 billion U.S. dollars, accounting for around half of total
foreign investment in the region. Meanwhile, the United States became the
dominant foreign investor in the Caribbean Basin by the turn of the twentieth
century, having placed around a billion dollars in Mexico and hundreds of
millions in the Caribbean islands and Central America.

With capital and technology flowing in, Latin America was exporting on
an unprecedented scale by the 1880s. Mineral exports included silver, which
recovered from its post-independence decline, gold, nitrates for fertilizer and
gunpowder, copper for the nascent electric industry, tin, petroleum, and a
host of other minerals with specialized uses. Among the food staples destined
for a hungry Europe were wheat, barley, and other grains, beef, lamb, and
bananas—a newly introduced food which quickly gained favor in the United
States and Europe. With the rise of disposable income among the middle
and working classes in the industrializing countries, coffee, sugar, and cacao
(for chocolate), formerly destined for the wealthy, became items of mass
consumption. Other exports included rubber from the Amazon basin, wool,
cotton, quinine (for use against malaria), henequen from Mexico's Yucatán
peninsula, which supplied the demand for agricultural binding twine, and
other regionally important commodities. Of the main comestible agricultural
and animal-based exports, only cacao is native to the Americas.

Figure 1.2 Bustling Buenos Aires harbor during export boom, c. 1910
Library of Congress

THE OLIGARCHIES

As material life changed, so did political life. While British and other foreign investors reaped the benefits of Latin America's integration into the world economy, the transformation created the oligarchies that ruled following the era of caudillos. These oligarchies normally originated in rural land owner-ship, commerce, and mining dating from the colonial period. The export economies opened new paths to wealth, including banking, export-oriented agriculture, urban real estate and development, and light manufacturing for domestic consumption. The emerging oligarchies were invigorated and expanded by immigrant entrepreneurs who became rich and married into the prestigious colonial families. These hybrid oligarchies featured non-Hispanic surnames—Pellegrini and Drysdale in Argentina, Edwards and Subercaseaux in Chile, Gildermeister and D'Onofrio in Peru, Creel and Limantour in Mexico—alongside those of the native creole elites. Thus fortified, the oli-garchies normally coalesced in the national capitals where they built their mansions in Second Empire or Georgian style, educated their children in exclusive schools, and socialized together at select venues. Every country had one or more men's organizations, membership in which certified oligarchic status: the Club Nacional and the Club de la Unión in Lima, the Club de la

Unión in Santiago, the Jockey Club and the Sociedad Rural in Buenos Aires, and the Jockey Club in Mexico City.

Hand in hand with Latin America's economic transformation, major parts of Latin America experienced remarkable political change. In contrast to the instability of the early years, most countries achieved stable and effective governance. These governments were not political democracies; they were run by and for the elites, not the masses. While a few advocates of socioeconomic democracy appeared, such as the Chilean Democratic Party, founded in 1887, the Peruvian anarchist Manual González Prada and his National Union, founded 1891, and the Mexican anarchist Ricardo Flores Magón, whose Mexican Liberal Party was established in 1906, the oligarchic governments normally repressed or marginalized them. These stable governments came in two basic forms: long-term dictatorships and elected oligarchic regimes that had the trappings but not the substance of democracy, while some countries alternated between the two forms. Reflecting their citizens' expectations, some of the dictatorships held elections, which were rigged to ensure continuity in power.

In the unbridled enthusiasm that accompanied independence, some countries initially adopted universal male suffrage, but almost all later imposed property, income, and/or literacy requirements for voting. These restrictions were partially responsible for the low level of electoral participation, which rarely exceeded 2 percent of the national populations in the nineteenth century. Other factors impeded participation, even in Argentina where universal male suffrage was established by the 1853 constitution, or in Chile, where property requirements were ended in 1874. These factors included apathy, ignorance of the right to vote, obstacles to registering, scarcity of polling places, and cynicism about the prevailing practices of vote buying, landowners' harvesting their workers' votes, and government manipulation of electoral outcomes. Despite these limitations, elections became more meaningful in the later nineteenth century as, in contrast to the earlier period, their results were rarely undone by violence. Meanwhile, constitutions tended to become more durable and parliaments more institutionalized under the oligarchic regimes. These constitutions, legislatures, and elections would underpin future democratization.

The virtual disappearance of caudillo-style overthrows of governments and the growing institutional stability were results of the bounty produced by the export economies. As foreign trade ballooned, so did government revenues from import duties, export taxes, land sales, and mining and other concessions. This enhanced revenue allowed some governments to reduce or pay off their foreign debts, which in the past had sometimes led to foreign military intervention aimed at securing overdue debt payment. It also underwrote the creation of national armies and equipped them with materiel, including repeating rifles, Gatling guns, and artillery, that provincial caudillos could not afford. Latin American governments brought European training missions from Germany, Britain, and France and sent officers to European military academies for advanced study. By the early twentieth century, most countries had established their own military academies, based on European models, that trained young men for careers in professional armies and navies. Coupled with the telegraph, which instantly informed governments of actual or suspected rebellions, and railroads and improved roads that expedited the dispatch of troops to areas of concern, the professional armies discouraged uprisings or quashed them before they could spread and threaten to overthrow governments.

Following the professionalization of Latin America's armed forces, old-style, caudillo-led rebellions rarely succeeded. Thereafter, most success-ful rebellions originated within the armed forces themselves, and military coups became the standard non-electoral method of changing governments in the twentieth century. The main exceptions were the popular uprisings that precipitated Latin America's three social revolutions: the Mexican in 1910, the Bolivian in 1952, and the Cuban in 1959.

OLIGARCHIC GOVERNMENTS

Mexico offers the best example of a long-term dictatorship that ruled for the wealthy. After its rocky start as an independent country, Mexico underwent a remarkable transition that was synonymous with one man: Porfirio Díaz, a mestizo born in 1830 in the southern city of Oaxaca. He achieved national recognition for his central role in defeating an invading French army at Puebla on May 5, 1862, temporarily halting its advance on Mexico City—a rare victory of Mexican arms over a foreign adversary, celebrated more in the United States than in Mexico as the *cinco de mayo*. A liberal, Díaz ran unsuc-cessfully for president in 1871 and again the following year. When incumbent Sebastián Lerdo de Tejada announced for reelection in 1876, Díaz rebelled under the slogan "effective suffrage and no re-election." Once installed in the presidency, Díaz forgot his campaign promise and stayed in power, with one brief hiatus, through multiple reelections, lending his name to his thirty-four-and-a-half-year reign: the *Porfiriato*, 1876–1911.

Recognizing Mexico's potential in the emerging global economy, Díaz and his advisors focused on establishing the political stability that would give for-eigners the confidence to invest capital and technology to develop Mexico's exportable resources. Thus they set out to eliminate the sources of instability that had plagued the republic since its inception. Among the initiatives were the strengthening of a constabulary—the *rurales*—to suppress the endemic rural banditry and professionalization of the army to curtail its propensity to rebel. These measures, along with growing railroad and telegraph networks, allowed Díaz to discourage rebellions.

Knowing from Mexico's history that unpaid foreign debt offered a pretext for foreign military intervention, as had occurred several times since independence, Díaz paid as much and as quickly as possible to foreign creditors. Fortunately for him, the thorny issue of the status and power of the Catholic Church, which had incited constant conflict, had been tentatively resolved in the 1850s. Finally, Díaz co-opted the regional caudillos and powerful families by offering them participation in the political machine he was creating. If they delivered their states' votes to his reelections, they earned governorships and lucrative business contracts. If they refused to cooperate or challenged him, he responded with force. Díaz called this approach to politics his "patriarchal policy"; others called it *"pan o palo"* (bread or the club). By attacking the sources of instability, he created Mexico's first effective central government since independence. True to his promise of no reelection, Díaz stepped aside after his first term in favor of a place holder. But from 1884 on, he was regularly reelected along with a national Congress and state governors and legislatures in contests that he tightly controlled.

The Díaz regime perfectly illustrates the relationship between economic development and political stability that characterized much of Latin America during the era of the export economies. As signs of stability appeared, foreign capital began to flow into Mexico. The influx of capital enhanced governmental revenue and ensured adequate military budgets, strengthened the central government, and furthered continuity and stability. Encouraged by the emergence of stability and a government capable of controlling potential labor conflicts, European and U.S. capitalists invested more confidently in railroads, mining, petroleum, banking, and utilities, while domestic capital went into agriculture and manufacturing, including a steel mill that opened at Monterrey in 1900. Mexico's foreign trade grew by nearly ten times during Díaz's dictatorship, with each increase bringing more tariff revenue. In 1894, Mexico achieved a balanced budget for the first time in its history, and Mexican bonds were selling above par by 1900.

In September 1910, Porfirio Díaz presided over the centennial of Mexico's independence, which celebrated his remarkable achievements.[5] Most of the foreign dignitaries attending the glittering celebration were unaware of the other side of the Porfiriato—the usurpation of much of Mexico's communal village land, the strict prohibition of workers' unions and brutal repression of strikes, and what many saw as the giveaway of the county's natural resources to foreigners. This other side of the glowing economic statistics and political stability was the fuel that would soon ignite social revolution.

Figure 1.3 Porfirio Díaz, president/dictator of Mexico 1876–1911
Library of Congress

In contrast to the oligarchic dictatorships, Chile offers a good example of an elected oligarchic regime that featured the trappings but not the substance of political democracy. Chile's early post-independence period was as turbulent as that of any of the new republics—and more so than several. That changed with the conservatives' smashing 1830 military defeat of their rival liberals, which led to the development of one of the most stable governments in Latin America. The 1833 constitution, Chile's eighth in twenty-two years, was well adapted to the country's reality. It continued the colonial institution of a strong executive, centralized power in the capital, Santiago, and established very limited suffrage—a blueprint for uncontested upper-class rule. While the constitution provided the framework, a victorious war against the Peru-Bolivia Confederation (1836–1839) and modest economic growth contributed to Chile's early political stability.

More sustained economic development came after Chile defeated Peru and Bolivia in the War of the Pacific, 1879–1883. Chile annexed the two countries' nitrate-rich provinces, expanding its territory by a third and leaving Bolivia landlocked. For the next half-century, nitrate exports underpinned prosperity for British and Chilean mine owners and yielded abundant tax revenue that built, among other things, a national railroad network, a public education system, and a professional army and navy.

A power struggle between Congress and President José Manuel Balmaceda, elected in 1886, led to the first interruption of Chile's remarkable governmental continuity: After a standoff, Congressional forces rebelled and, supported by the navy, routed the president and his supporters and launched the "Parliamentary Republic," a period of Congressional authority over a series of weak presidents.

The Parliamentary Republic, 1891–1925, marked the zenith of Chile's oligarchy, which blended prestigious families of colonial origin and financially successful European immigrants. This oligarchy was diversified in its economic underpinnings: nitrates, banking, commerce, publishing, mining, and agriculture. Ownership of rural estates, the hallmark of oligarchic status, also anchored the oligarchy's political power. An 1891 law transferred control of the electoral machinery from the president to municipalities, which in rural areas were dominated by the large landowners; despite the continuing literacy requirement, this facilitated the estate owners' harvesting of their laborers' (*inquilinos'*) votes and thus secured the dominance of the historic Conservative and Liberal Parties in Congress. Following their rather meaningless congressional debates, the patricians adjourned to the Club de la Unión to consume luxury food and drink and make their deals.

At the onset of the twentieth century, the Chilean oligarchy was confident of its wealth, its power, and its future. A visiting U.S. academic, Paul Reinsch, was so impressed with this oligarchy that he described it in 1909 in the *American Political Science Review* as "an aristocracy of birth and wealth [that] . . . still has full and acknowledged control of the economic, political and social forces of the state in which they live."[6] Several other Latin American countries would have qualified for Reinsch's description. What he did not realize, and the Chilean oligarchy tried to ignore, was that elite power, as in Mexico, rested on a foundation far less solid than it appeared.

Peru's oligarchy failed to achieve the long-term stability found under different forms of government in Mexico and Chile. The country experienced periods of anarchy, dictatorship, and caudillo rule, beginning with an average of one regime change per year between 1821 and 1845. The Peruvian oligarchy developed early by virtue of a thirty-year boom beginning in 1840 in the exploitation of guano, nitrate-rich bird droppings found on the offshore Chincha Islands that were prized in Europe as fertilizer. The guano business enriched numerous families with ties to government, who later diversified into banking, commerce, publishing, and other activities generated by the export economy. By the 1870s the oligarchy had become a hybrid of

Figure 1.4 The Club de la Unión, where the Chilean oligarchy gathered
Library of Congress

prestigious colonial families intermarrying with entrepreneurial non-Hispanic immigrants in "gold and blood" alliances that formed the fabled "forty families."[7] Unlike in Chile, where land ownership conferred more prestige than wealth, a substantial part of the Peruvian oligarchy's fortune came from coastal plantations producing sugar and cotton for domestic consumption and export.

Following half a century of military ascendancy, the oligarchy founded the Civilista Party in 1871 with the goal of governing directly. Manuel Pardo y Lavalle, elected the following year, was the first Civilista president. He was succeeded by another Civilista, Mariano Ignacio Prado, but the War of the Pacific (1879–1883) interrupted his presidency and governmental stability. The conflict with Chile was a disaster for Peru: After winning a series of naval battles, Chilean troops occupied Lima and major parts of the country, forcing Peru to sign the 1883 Treaty of Ancón which surrendered the nitrate-rich province of Tarapacá to Chile and denied Peru a source of wealth that would enrich victorious Chile for the next half-century.

Instability returned with the war and continued until 1886, after which relative stability was restored. The Civilistas regained power in 1899 and held the presidency to 1919, with a three-year interruption, following which a new period of dictatorship began under Augusto C. Leguía (1919–1930). Thus up to the Great Depression, which destabilized much of Latin America, Peru failed to achieve the institutional stability that characterized Chile, Mexico, and other Latin American countries during the era of the export economies.

With a few exceptions, by the late nineteenth century Latin America's political systems had matured from the early post-independence period of chaos and caudillo rule. In most countries, the days of strong men overthrowing governments and running roughshod over congresses and courts were over. Enriched by the export economies, the elites ruled directly or through friendly dictators. This political maturation had produced nothing resembling real political democracy and certainly no socioeconomic democracy. But by the early twentieth century, building on the institutions of constitutions, legislatures, and elections, forces of change in a few countries would expand citizen participation and adopt policies designed to enhance the material welfare of the middle and working classes. In other words, Latin America would experience the emergence of both political and socioeconomic democratization.

SUGGESTIONS FOR FURTHER READING

Bethell, Leslie, ed. *The Independence of Latin America*. Cambridge, UK: Cambridge University Press, 1987.

―――――. *Spanish America after Independence, c. 1820–1870*. Cambridge, UK: Cambridge University Press, 1987.

Bulmer-Thomas, Victor. *The Economic History of Latin America since Independence*. Cambridge, UK: Cambridge University Press, 2003.

Burns, E. Bradford. *The Poverty of Progress: Latin America in the Nineteenth Century*. Berkeley: University of California Press, 1987.

Bushnell, David and Lester D. Langley, eds. *The Emergence of Latin America in the Nineteenth Century*. New York: Oxford University Press, 1994.

Collier, Simon. *Chile: The Making of a Republic, 1830–1865: Politics and Ideas*. Cambridge, UK: Cambridge University Press, 2003.

Cortés Conde, Roberto and Shane J. Hunt, eds. *The Latin American Economies: Growth and the Export Sector, 1880–1930*. New York: Holmes and Meier, 1985.

Drake, Paul W. *Between Anarchy and Tyranny: A History of Democracy in Latin America, 1800–2006*. Stanford: Stanford University Press, 2009.

Fowler, Will. *Santa Anna of Mexico*. Lincoln: University of Nebraska Press, 2009.

Gilbert, Dennis. *Oligarchy and the Old Regime in Latin America, 1880–1970*. Lanham, MD: Rowman & Littlefield, 2017.

Lynch, John. *Caudillos in Spanish America, 1800–1850*. Oxford, UK: Clarendon Press, 1992.

Nunn, Frederick M. *Yesterday's Soldiers: European Military Professionalism in South America, 1890–1940*. Lincoln: University of Nebraska Press, 1983.

Peloso, Vincent C. and Barbara A. Tenenbaum, eds. *Liberals, Politics, and Power: State Formation in Nineteenth-Century Latin America*. Athens: University of Georgia Press, 1996.

Stevens, Donald F. *Origins of Instability in Early Republican Mexico*. Durham: Duke University Press, 1991.

Topik, Steven and Allen Wells. *The Second Conquest of Latin America: Coffee, Henequen, and Oil During the Export Boom, 1850–1930*. Austin: Institute of Latin American Studies, University of Texas Press, 1998.

Tutino, John, ed. *New Countries: Capitalism, Revolution, and Nations in the Americas, 1750–1870*. Durham: Duke University Press, 2016.

Williams, John Hoyt. *The Rise and Fall of the Paraguayan Republic, 1800–1870*. Austin: Institute of Latin American Studies, University of Texas Press, 1979.

NOTES

1. Harold A. Bierck Jr., ed., *Selected Writings of Bolívar*, compiled by Vicente Lecuna, translated by Lewis Bertrand, Vol. 1 (New York: Colonial Press, 1951), 103–22.

2. Domingo F. Sarmiento, *Life in the Argentine Republic in the Days of the Tyrants, or, Civilization and Barbarism*, translator not listed (New York: Collier Books, 1961), 37, 80.

3. Mexico was the only country besides Brazil to have a monarchy. The 1822–1823 reign of Emperor Agustín I (Agustín Iturbide) lasted ten months.

4. Paul Drake emphasizes the importance of elections in the advancement of political democracy: Paul W. Drake, *Between Tyranny and Anarchy: A History of Democracy in Latin America, 1800–2006* (Stanford: Stanford University Press, 2009).

5. Like the United States, Mexico celebrates its independence on the date of the beginning of its independence movement, not of its culmination.

6. Paul S. Reinsch, "Parliamentary Government in Chile," *American Political Science Review* 3, no. 4 (1909): 508.

7. Dennis Gilbert, *The Oligarchy and the Old Regime in Latin America, 1880–1970* (Lanham, MD: Rowman & Littlefield, 2017) uses the term "gold and blood." Gilbert found that rather than the reputed forty families, only twenty-nine possessed true oligarchic credentials.

Chapter 2

Early Democratization, 1900–1930

The colonial social structure persisted well into the nineteenth century in most of Latin America. This consisted of a tiny, mostly white minority of elites, a poor mass of people of mixed race, and in most countries sizeable Indian populations, including majorities in the Andean region and Guatemala. Brazil, a few Spanish American republics, and much of the Caribbean were home to large numbers of African-descended peoples, many of them enslaved in Cuba and Brazil until 1886 and 1888, respectively. There was almost no middle class and no modern working class, or proletariat, of the type found in industrial societies.

By the turn of the twentieth century, this social order had evolved, particularly in the larger and more developed countries. The economic expansion and modernization generated by the export economies brought about the development of more articulated class distinctions. Economic development stimulated retail, wholesale, and import-export commerce and led to the growth of government bureaucracies and limited public education. Employment in these sectors, which required literacy and some education, yielded a white-collar work force. Clerks in commercial establishments and banks, accountants, bureaucrats, teachers, foremen, military officers, policemen, and small business owners came to constitute a fledgling middle class that developed a consciousness of its distinction from both the elites above and the masses beneath its status.

The building and operation of thousands of miles of railroads and work in mines, meat processing plants, flour mills, oil fields, construction, on the docks, on banana and sugar plantations, and in other new, mostly urban occupations produced another new social class: the proletariat. Facilitated by protective tariffs adopted in the 1880s and 1890s, the factories that grew up in the larger South American countries and Mexico to provide for local needs—food and tobacco processing establishments, textile mills, breweries, iron foundries, furniture factories, glass and cement works, and similar domestic-oriented industries—augmented the new working class.

Women were included in the emerging social groups. As the export econo-mies drove the growth of urban occupations, women gained employment in both the white and blue-collar sectors. By the turn of the twentieth century, women had become important components of the factory labor force, par-ticularly in the manufacture of tobacco products, textiles, and garments. By the 1910s women constituted over 70 percent of workers in São Paulo's booming textile factories and a quarter of Chile's and nearly 20 percent of Buenos Aires's factory workers. The advance of public education offered opportunities for women to enter the middle class. While reaching only a fraction of the Latin American population, public education through high school had been established in national and many state or provincial capitals, and females enrolled in increasing numbers; in 1873 nearly a third of Brazil's enrolled students were female. Education prepared women to fill white collar jobs as teachers, clerks in government and private sector offices, nurses, and salespersons in shops and the new department stores. Women constituted a majority of teachers in Argentina and Chile by the 1910s, but they were still disenfranchised and denied full citizenship.

By the turn of the twentieth century in Brazil, Argentina, Chile, Uruguay, Mexico, and a few other countries, the middle and working classes created by the export economies had begun to make their voices heard. In response, several countries enacted modest measures to ameliorate the worst work-ing conditions: requiring Sunday rest, regulating women's and children's working conditions, and implementing minimal workplace safety measures. But none extended rights to the unions that appeared wherever a signifi-cant working class developed. Among the first proto-unions to appear were mutual aid societies, which offered members little more than brotherhood and funeral expenses. European immigrants brought advanced ideas: anarchism, anarcho-syndicalism, and Marxism, and in some countries organized unions along those lines. While the more radical unions, which were illegal and per-secuted, ultimately aimed to abolish capitalism, they also sought to defend or enhance their members' wages and working conditions by the only means available to them—the strike.

Both foreign investors and national elites insisted that governments pro-hibit strikes. Thus strikes were perilous, as they were normally put down by force, often leading to massacres of great proportions. In Argentina, strikes roiled the country in 1905 and again in 1909, with numerous casualties. In Chile, crowds rallied by labor unions to protest an unpopular tariff on Argentine cattle overwhelmed the authorities and took over Santiago for two days in 1905 before troops arrived to restore order. Following a series of smaller but deadly strikes, Chilean nitrate workers struck in 1907 and gathered in the main plaza of the port city of Iquique, where soldiers fired on them, killing or wounding up to two thousand strikers. In Mexico, workers at

Figure 2.1 Women making tobacco products in Mexico City factory, 1903
Library of Congress

the U.S.-owned Cananea copper mine near the Sonora-Arizona border struck in June 1906; Arizona rangers and Mexican army troops ended the strike with at least twenty-three deaths. Six months later, a strike at a large cotton mill in Río Blanco, Veracruz state, was violently repressed, with numerous casualties. The great 1928 banana strike against United Fruit Company in Colombia, put down under heavy U.S. pressure by Colombian troops, was among the bloodiest anywhere.[1] The appearance of national labor federations in Argentina in 1905 and Chile in 1909 increased the concern of those countries' oligarchic governments.

Despite their growth and, by virtue of their literacy, their right to vote, middle class males by and large channeled their political participation through existing parties rather than by founding new parties to represent their interests. In addition to establishing unions, workers founded small and ineffectual anarchist or Marxist parties that were normally incapable of competing in electoral politics and were usually banned and persecuted. The main exceptions in both cases were Chile and Argentina.

In Chile, the Radical Party, established in 1863 to oppose the dominant conservatives, had become a vehicle of the middle classes and was well represented in Congress by 1900. The Democratic Party, dating from 1887, was the electoral voice of the working class. It stood for the "political, economic, and social liberation of the people [*pueblo*]" and elected its first representative to Congress in 1894.[2] Its left wing split off in 1912 as the Socialist Workers' Party, which subsequently became the Communist Party in 1922. In Argentina, the Unión Cívica Radical (Radical Party, UCR), founded in 1890, was associated with middle class interests and, following an electoral reform, became the most powerful party in the country. The Socialist Party, dating from the mid-1890s, advocated for workers' interests and gained its first congressional seat in 1904. Thus by the early twentieth century, both middle- and working-class interests in Argentina and Chile had obtained representation and growing political influence.

THE ECLIPSE OF OLIGARCHIC MONOPOLIES OF POWER: MEXICO, URUGUAY, ARGENTINA, AND CHILE

The openings to broader political participation occurred differently in each country. The most important variable was the attitude and response of the elites to the signs of growing opposition to their monopolies of power. In Mexico, the ruling elites did nothing to accommodate rising demands for change; rather, they continued to use the repression that had served them well for decades. As a result, the Díaz system was blown apart by a massive rebellion, and a new order emerged from the ruins. In Uruguay and Argentina, reformist factions of the oligarchies achieved power and enacted preemptive reforms within the framework of the existing political systems, facilitating relatively smooth transitions to expanded citizen participation while retaining significant power. In Chile, the oligarchy also split, but intransigents blocked the reforms pushed by the reformist faction as the depth and breadth of popular protest grew, stoked by the crisis accompanying World War I. Reform occurred only when the political framework that had supported Latin America's most durable civilian political system collapsed, miring the country in nearly a decade of institutional instability.

Mexico

Hailed for bringing economic development and political stability to the country, the Porfiriato also sowed the seeds of its destruction. Díaz's impressive record was achieved on the backs of Mexico's working class and its indigenous and mestizo villagers. As elsewhere in Latin America, the export economies created new kinds of manual work which, in turn, formed a substantial proletariat that was heavily exploited and denied the right to defend its interests by forming unions and striking. As their lands became valuable for market-oriented production, Mexico's *ejidos*—the communal landowning villages that practiced subsistence agriculture—came under attack from hacienda owners and entrepreneurs. With Díaz's support, they expropriated some or all the land of around five thousand villages, turning independent farmers into a rural proletariat.

U.S. investment in Mexico exceeded 1.5 billion dollars by 1910 and U.S. capital dominated important sectors of the economy. Whether entrepreneurs competing with better-capitalized U.S. companies or men working for U.S.-owned railroads, mines, or oil companies, the dominating U.S. presence made some Mexicans feel like aliens in their own country and generated a strong nationalist reaction. Hence the refrain: "Mexico is the mother of foreigners and the stepmother of Mexicans."

Despite widespread discontent shared by workers, displaced peasants, the middle classes, and those among the elites who neither enjoyed Díaz's favor nor shared the bounty of economic development, the regime faced only nominal opposition owing to Díaz's political astuteness and powers of repression. The only significant opposition party, the anarchist Mexican Liberal Party, became too extreme to be tolerated and was driven out of the country. However, the regime faced a series of challenges in 1906 and 1907: major labor unrest, drought that drove up food prices, and a bank panic. Despite these warning signs, the dictatorship took no steps to accommodate those affected by the recent developments.

In March 1908, Díaz shocked Mexicans by announcing that he would retire in 1910, at the end of his current term. Although he soon changed his mind, his announcement set off an unprecedented flurry of political activity. Díaz's opposition rallied behind Francisco Madero, the scion of an aristocratic family, whose education made him an advocate of democracy. A new party named for Díaz's original slogan, the Anti-Reelectionist party, nominated Madero as its presidential candidate. Alarmed, Díaz had the audacious Madero and hundreds of his supporters arrested before the June 21, 1910, election which, as always, the dictator won by an announced landslide.

Following the election, Madero escaped from jail in San Luis Potosí and crossed the border to San Antonio, Texas, where he issued the back-dated

Plan de San Luis Potosí. The plan declared Díaz's reelection illegal, named Madero provisional president, and called for political democracy: "In Mexico, as a democratic Republic, the public power can have no other origin nor other basis than the will of the people."[3] Madero called for a national uprising on Sunday, November 20, 1910, at 6 pm. What began as an insurrection to overthrow a government would become, after numerous twists and turns, Latin America's first social revolution.

When Madero crossed the border into Mexico on November 20, he was greeted by a handful of supporters rather than the hundreds he expected. But soon, thousands of Mexicans of all occupations and social classes, driven by pent-up grievances that had accumulated for years, took up arms. Led by such colorful characters as Pancho Villa and Emiliano Zapata, they defeated Díaz's army—half of whose ranks were "paper" soldiers—and drove the dictator into exile in May 1911. Madero was overwhelmingly elected president five months later.

Madero's administration was fraught with peril from its inception. An idealist who never wavered from his conviction that political democracy was a panacea for the country's ills and who believed in the rule of law, Madero was ill-suited to govern during turbulent times. With Díaz gone, so was the common enemy that had united very disparate interests and groups. Madero refused to take advantage of his great popularity to dissolve the national and state governments that Díaz had put in place and replace them with men loyal to him. He urged the rebels who had defeated Díaz to disarm but left the federal army with its Díaz-appointed commanders intact. Thus the old regime remained intact while Madero waited for regularly scheduled elections that he hoped would replace it.

Madero did not live to witness elections. He immediately faced rebellion from Díaz loyalists on the right and Emiliano Zapata, a fierce advocate for the immediate return of stolen ejido lands, on the left. After Madero fended off rebellions for fifteen months, two of Díaz's generals, Victoriano Huerta and the former dictator's nephew, Félix Díaz, murdered him on February 21, 1913, in a plot hatched in the U.S. embassy.

Madero's assassination plunged Mexico into civil war that brought chaos, huge loss of life, and immense material destruction. Huerta assumed the presidency, but Villa and Zapata, along with northerners Vestuniano Carranza and Álvaro Obregón, rebelled and eventually defeated Madero's assassin in July 1914. The victors then split: Zapata and Villa in a loose alliance fought against Carranza, the self-proclaimed "First Chief of the Constitutionalist Army," and his ally and principal military asset, Obregón. After Obregón decisively defeated Villa in April 1915, Carranza, a former governor under Díaz, emerged as the country's acknowledged leader and provisional

Figure 2.2 Pancho Villa and Emiliano Zapata taking turns in the presidential chair, 2014
Library of Congress

president. Both Villa and Zapata fought on, with little effect, until Zapata was assassinated in 1919 and Villa retired from the fray the following year.

Carranza decided to cap his success and assure his place in history by giving Mexico a new constitution, as liberal hero Benito Juárez had done in 1857. The document that he drew up closely paralleled the 1857 constitution but strengthened the powers of the executive; it did not address social or economic matters. The constitutional convention he had assembled, comprised exclusively of his supporters, surprisingly rejected his draft in December 1916. After two months of acrimonious but creative proceedings, it produced the world's most advanced constitution, a blueprint for revolution in Mexico.

How did Mexico pivot from an insurrection designed simply to replace dictatorship with democracy to adopting its 1917 constitution that committed the country to revolutionary change? There is no simple answer, but several factors were in play. The idea of radical change was not new in 1917. The Liberal Party, persecuted by Díaz, had developed a radical agenda during the dictatorship's last decade. More calls for radical change surfaced after 1910: Several leaders of the bands that fought against Díaz and continued fighting following Madero's assassination announced plans for workers' rights, agrarian reform, and recovery of Mexico's resources from the Yankees. None was more influential than Zapata's Plan de Ayala that called for restoration of stolen ejido lands and dismantling the dominant hacienda system. Moreover, Mexico by 1916 lay in ruins. Battles, wounds, epidemics, and starvation had killed between one and two million people since 1910. The economy was shattered: Mines, factories, and railroads had been destroyed and agricultural production disrupted. The country had been humiliated by U.S. military interventions in 1914 and 1916. And Venustiano Carranza, an old man who had been a state governor under Díaz, was in charge. The delegates at the constitutional convention, a majority of them relatively young men, had to wonder what purpose had been served by years of warfare and destruction and what could be done to prevent a recurrence.

The new constitution was a clear rejection of the Porfiriato. In addition to calling for political democracy, it laid the basis for socioeconomic democratization. Article 123 ordered the states to draw up labor legislation following guidelines that included a minimum wage, an eight-hour workday, legalization of unions and their right to strike, and equal wages for equal work. Article 27 subordinated private property rights to the public interest, as determined by the government, and incorporated Zapata's principles by recognizing only two legal types of agricultural holdings: the ejido, or traditional communal landowning village, and "small" property. It also challenged U.S. economic dominance by limiting foreign land ownership and claiming for the nation the sub-soil resources, including oil, that Díaz had sold. Article 3 required free public education for all. In sum, if implemented, the constitution would create a political and socioeconomic democracy in Mexico.

The constitution, however, was only paper. It rejected the past, both the recent Porfirian past and the more remote colonial past. It was a blueprint for the future, a set of ambitious revolutionary goals. Carranza's and succeeding governments through 1933 began implementing the constitution, but cautiously. They were concerned with rebuilding the shattered country and wary of offending the great power to the north, possibly leading to yet another military intervention to protect U.S. interests. But after nearly eighteen years, with a new generation in power, the revolution would commence in earnest (chapter 3).

Uruguay

In Uruguay, political and socioeconomic democratization went hand in hand. Uruguay's exports of wool, meat, and hides provided a modest prosperity, and protective tariffs beginning in the 1880s helped develop light industry in the capital, Montevideo. In the late nineteenth century, Uruguay's scant population was overwhelmed by European immigrants, who pushed the country's population to one million by 1900. Among this million were members of the new working and middle classes. Workers organized and struck on occasion, but the authorities broke the strikes and arrested their instigators.

After half a century of instability, civil wars, and caudillo rule, an oligarchy had emerged in Uruguay by the 1870s. Two parties, the more conservative, rural-based Blancos and the more progressive, urban-based Colorados (whites and reds, but not the red associated with communists) had developed; the Colorados monopolized the presidency.

José Batlle y Ordóñez was the country's dominant political figure from his first presidency (1903–1907), through his second (1911–1915), to his death in 1929. The son of President Lorenzo Batlle (1868–1872), he was a member of the elite and a journalist. He rose through the ranks of the Colorado Party, serving in both the Chamber of Deputies and the Senate until his election as president in 1903.

Reforms did not figure in Batlle's campaign platform, but after weathering a serious revolt by the Blancos—the War of 1904, in which thousands were killed or injured—he evolved into a champion of both political and socioeconomic democracy. He did not believe in the Marxist concept of the class struggle, but rather felt that an interventionist state should regulate class relations. The changes he wrought made Uruguay the most socially progressive country in Latin America, without the cataclysmic revolution that transformed Mexico after 1910. During his first term, he carried out several important reforms, including abolition of the death penalty, divorce by mutual consent, expansion of free public education, and a progressive labor bill. Although the Catholic Church was not powerful in Uruguay, Batlle pushed secularization of the state, going so far as to ban crucifixes in state-run hospitals and eliminate references to God in public oaths.

Following his first term he went to Europe, where he observed the continent's social and political struggles during a four-year sojourn. Elected to a second term, he returned home determined to make Uruguay a "model country." With Colorado control of Congress, he was able to implement systemic reforms. In the economic realm, he created a strong state sector by creating a government monopoly over power generation, nationalizing much of the banking and insurance sectors, and buying the British-owned railroads. He promoted national industries through tariff protection and controls over foreign-owned businesses. He raised taxes on the wealthy, lowered them on items of basic consumption, and established unemployment compensation. Batlle furthered public education by establishing free high schools in departmental (provincial) capitals throughout the country and opening the University of the Republic to women. He also laid the groundwork for several other programs enacted following the end of his second term, including

Figure 2.3 José Batlle y Ordóñez, architect of Uruguay's early democratization
Library of Congress

the eight-hour day, retirement pensions, and occupational safety standards. Together, Batlle's reforms created a modern welfare state.

Adopted following Batlle's second presidency, the 1918 constitution confirmed the autonomous state institutions that Batlle had established and formally separated church and state. In the political arena, it included universal male suffrage and the secret ballot. It also established a bold experiment meant to secure and fortify political democracy: the plural executive.

Although he had expanded the realm of presidential authority, Batlle feared the potential for abuse of executive power, or a regression to Uruguay's earlier period of authoritarianism. His idea for securing political democracy and preventing authoritarian presidencies was to adopt a version of the Swiss plural executive system. The new constitution incorporated Batlle's proposal, but not the pure system that he had advocated. Powers were divided between a president, who was responsible for foreign relations, national security, and defense, and a nine-person *colegiado* with responsibility for all other aspects of national life. This system lasted until 1933, when the presidential system was restored. Batlle would have been gratified had he been present at the adoption of the 1952 constitution, which established his version of a plural executive: a nine-person colegiado, called the *Consejo Nacional de Gobierno*. This radical experiment in political democracy lasted until, during a period of growing political strife and polarization, the 1967 constitution restored the presidential system.

Uruguay during Batlle y Ordóñez's lifetime and under his continuing influence set the standard for socioeconomic democracy in Latin America. While the plural executive that Batlle advocated ultimately did not last, Uruguay's political democracy did. It survived twelve years of authoritarianism and repression between 1973 and 1985 and recovered robustly (chapters 7 and 8).

Argentina

In Argentina, an oligarchy began to consolidate its power from the time of Bartolomé Mitre's presidency (1862–1868). It established and retained control through manipulation of the electoral machinery, fraud, violence, and the success it could claim: the spectacular economic development resulting from Argentina's burgeoning exports of meat and grains to Europe. The oligarchy coalesced around the National Autonomist Party (PAN), founded in 1874, which became the oligarchy's instrument of control; all presidents through 1916 came from its ranks.

The middle and working classes expanded as Argentina's export economy boomed. The Radical Party (UCR) represented the middle class as well as factions of the elite who broke from the PAN. The Radicals critiqued the PAN for its use of fraud and exclusion of most Argentines from political participation and promised political reform. Realizing that the PAN's tight control would guarantee its continued political dominance, the UCR, following its motto, "Relentless struggle," first tried rebellion to gain power, failing in three attempts between 1893 and 1905. Thereafter it turned to aggressive organizing, becoming a mass-based party that threatened the oligarchy's hold on power. Meanwhile, labor unions and strikes had proliferated in the late nineteenth and early twentieth centuries, posing another danger to elite interests.

As the UCR's campaign for honest elections and government gained traction, the PAN split into conservative and reformist wings. A PAN member of the Chamber of Deputies argued for preemptive reform: "For a generation both government and nation have lived in a constant state of having either to suppress rebellion or in fear that rebellion is about to break out."[4] He and other reformers were convinced that only by meeting the Radicals' challenge and enacting preemptive reform could the PAN sustain its electoral dominance.

The 1910 election of PAN reformist Roque Sáenz Peña as president led to an electoral reform, the 1912 Sáenz Peña law. The law established the secret ballot and compulsory voting while confirming universal male suffrage as established by the 1853 constitution. It also limited the majority party to two-thirds of the seats in the Chamber of Deputies. A companion law purged the electoral rolls of many years' accumulation of dead and invented voters, an important part of the PAN's electorate. The PAN gambled that Argentine citizens would reward it for reforming the corrupt electoral system by keeping it in power.

The PAN lost its gamble. In the 1912 election, the UCR won a third of the Chamber of Deputies seats and three governorships. It also set out to broaden its base in preparation for the 1916 presidential election, organizing at the local level and recruiting men who had not previously participated, including sons of the third of Argentina's population who were immigrants. The results were the election of Hipólito Yrigoyen, founder of the UCR, as president and control of the national Chamber of Deputies and several provinces. The PAN retained control of the national Senate, allowing it to block most of the modest reforms that the UCR proposed. An exception was the founding of the state petroleum company, *Yacimientos Petrolíferos Fiscales* (YPF).

The democratic political climate created by the Yrigoyen victory contributed to an important development in Latin America's progress toward democracy. While university students had been active in politics and some had formed organizations, the 1918 reform at the University of Córdoba, Argentina, was the catalyst for transforming universities around Latin America. At Córdoba, largely middle- and working-class students wrested control of the very traditional university from elite control. The students denounced universities in general as "the secular haven of the mediocre, the reward of the ignorant, a shelter for intellectual invalids. . . . The universities have therefore become faithful images of our decadent societies, and sad spectacles of senile immobility."[5] The reforms included modernization of the curriculum to make it more relevant to contemporary issues; creation of a new form of co-governance involving students, faculty, and alumni; and establishment of university autonomy. While normally continuing to rely on government funding, the principle of autonomy meant that governance could not be imposed from outside and, very importantly, that police and military were prohibited from entering university grounds and buildings. Although this autonomy was violated on occasion, it, along with the other reforms, gave university students the ability to be important drivers of democratization.

The Córdoba reform spread quickly through the state-run universities of Latin America, whose students tended to be of the middle and lower classes (youth of elite families gravitated to Catholic-run universities). Student federations were quickly formed in several countries and inserted themselves into national politics on the side of political and socioeconomic democracy. Among the more active was the Peruvian Student Federation (FEP), which resisted the dictatorship of Augusto C. Leguía (1919–1930). University of Chile students organized the Federation of Chilean Students (FECh) and engaged in national politics, including in the radical Workers' Assembly of National Nutrition (see below). The student federation of the University of Havana was notorious for its strident involvement in national politics; among its alumni was Fidel Castro. Overall, the rise of student federations within universities reformed in the Córdoba manner added an important protagonist in the struggle for democracy.

World War I disrupted the Argentine export economy and caused significant social strife, which culminated in 1919 in what Argentines call the *Semana Trágica* (tragic week). With Buenos Aires overrun by protesters and services disrupted by strikes, the Yrigoyen administration sent troops into the streets, killing or wounding hundreds of workers. Despite this black mark, the UCR's Marcelo T. de Alvear handily won the 1922 presidential election.

By this point the UCR had built a powerful political machine by dispensing favors and padding the rolls of the bureaucracy. The Alvear administration proved to be even less reformist than its predecessor. Despite the Radicals' lack of accomplishments, the 1928 election, which returned Yrigoyen to the presidency, demonstrated that the oligarchy was unable to recover the power it had wielded prior to 1916 by electoral means. Battered by the Great Depression and a loss of support, Yrigoyen's administration succumbed to a coup led by General José Felix Uriburu in September 1930, ending a period of democratization that expanded the electorate and ended oligarchic monopoly of political power but did not follow neighboring Uruguay down the path of socioeconomic democratization.

Chile

Described by Professor Reinsch in 1909 as having "full and acknowledged control of the economic, political, and social forces of the state in which they live," the Chilean elites nonetheless began to pay attention to social unrest, which they termed "the social question," early in the new century.[6] Despite the evidence, some denied the existence of a problem. Conservative Congressman Eulogio Díaz Sagredo, for example, opined: "In truth it cannot be said that the worker problem or question which is the cause of so much worry in Europe has developed here." In a book on the social question, Javier Díaz Lira laid the blame for the misery of the lower classes on "the enormous development of their vices." Conservative Congressman Juan Enrique Concha declared the answer to be "social stewardship": The wealthy should get to know the poor by visiting their workplaces and tenements to "make them see the absurdity of socialist utopias, and disabuse them of the false idea of economic equality by showing them there is a providential order which they must respect." He further argued that the social question was not an economic matter, but "fundamentally a psychological, moral, and religious question, whose solution will be found, the world willing, only in the teaching of Christ."[7] Congress appointed commissions to investigate the social question and university students produced theses on the issue, but those in power took no significant action to address what would soon become an urgent problem.

As in Uruguay and Argentina, the oligarchy split over how to deal with rising demands by the Radical and Democratic parties, labor unions, and university students for political and socioeconomic inclusion. In contrast to the other two South American countries, where the oligarchies' loss of monopolistic power transpired relatively smoothly, in Chile the transition brought a decade of institutional disruption. The timing of Chile's transition was determinant in the way it unfolded. Uruguay's and Argentina's reforms occurred before World War I; Chile's came after. While all of Latin America was affected by the wartime disruption of the world economy, Chile was unusually severely impacted as during the war German scientists successfully produced artificial nitrates, sending Chile's primary export of natural nitrates into a tailspin and putting some 50,000 nitrate laborers out of work.

Faced with the collapse of the nitrate sector, mass unemployment, and rampant inflation that further radicalized workers and the broader population, the oligarchic government offered no significant relief. Focusing on food price inflation as a rallying point, labor and student leaders in 1918 formed the Workers' Assembly of National Nutrition. The Assembly quickly spread beyond Santiago. In August 1919 it held rallies in twenty-three cities and towns throughout the country; 100,000 rallied in Santiago alone. The Workers' Assembly held a national convention the following March, at which point it began to broaden its program beyond food price controls. The convention adopted a fifty-point program of social and political demands that emphasized wages, working conditions, housing, electoral reform, and even called for a people's militia. This incipient revolutionary movement soon was eclipsed by the 1920 presidential election.

Against this backdrop of continuing economic crisis and political mobilization, the election split the oligarchy into two factions. Aristocrat Luis Barros Borgoño was the candidate of the more conservative National Union coalition, while the moderately progressive Liberal Alliance nominated Arturo Alessandri Palma, a veteran politician of upper middle-class background. Alessandri did not disguise his intentions, calling himself "a threat to those who resist all the just and necessary reforms."[8] The election results were so close that the Congress established a "tribunal of honor" to decide the winner; it selected Alessandri. Alessandri's narrow victory, however, did not resolve matters; intransigents still controlled Congress, blocking Alessandri's proposed social legislation while the protesters continued to demonstrate and strike. This standoff deepened the political turmoil that would destabilize Chile into the 1930s as the country adjusted to mass politics.

The impasse was resolved in September 1924 by military intervention—an anomaly in Chile. The military did not overthrow the president but forced Congress to enact Alessandri's agenda of labor laws, social security protections, and income tax while also enhancing military salaries and benefits. As the military encroached on his authority, Alessandri resigned later in the month but, with the officers unable to form a functional government, resumed his office in March 1925. He then oversaw a plebiscite that enacted a progressive constitution that strengthened presidential authority over the obstructionist Congress, subordinated private property rights to the public good, and established the state's commitment to social welfare for the working and middle classes. Under renewed military pressure, Alessandri resigned again in October 1925.

The mid-1920s saw a partial economic recovery from the deleterious effects of the war. Following a brief conservative presidency, the ambitious General Carlos Ibáñez del Campo seized power and had himself elected president in May 1927. Ibáñez was a progressive and an authoritarian. During his four-year rule, he dominated Congress and launched the developmentalist and social welfare state that lasted in Chile until 1973. He stacked Congress and repressed opposition but passed laws that implemented Alessandri's program and elements of the new constitution: a labor code, social security legislation, and even a modest agrarian reform. Under the severe impact of the Great Depression, Ibáñez resigned in July 1931, launching a brief period of even greater political turbulence. By this time, the oligarchy that had ruled

Chile for nearly a century had lost its monopoly of political power and control of the state.

OTHER DEVELOPMENTS AFFECTING DEMOCRACY

As democratization transformed the political systems of Uruguay, Mexico, Argentina, and Chile, developments external to Latin America began to affect the course of democracy throughout the region. The 1917 Bolshevik Revolution in Russia, which brought Vladimir Lenin and the Communist Party to power, had a long-term effect on Latin America. Seeking international support for their initially beleaguered government, the Russian communists in 1919 established the Communist International (Comintern) and began promoting the formation of communist parties around the world. Between 1919 and 1922, communist parties appeared in Mexico, Argentina, Brazil, and Chile, and by 1930 virtually every Latin American country had a communist party. Commonly, socialists and anarchists set their differences aside to form the communist parties, while in some cases, such as Chile and Uruguay, existing workers' parties changed names and joined the Comintern. In several countries, most notably in Central America, the parties were forced to operate clandestinely.

The communists soon gained footholds in the labor movements and formed the Latin American Trade Union Confederation (CSLA) in 1929. Buenos Aires hosted a Congress of Latin American Communist Parties the same year. While the communists embraced socioeconomic democracy and rejected political democracy as bourgeois, they eschewed insurrection, following Comintern dictates to focus on building their parties and penetrating the labor movements. The appearance of communist parties broadened the options open to Latin Americans for political involvement and created a new driver of socioeconomic democracy.

Another external development that influenced Latin America's socioeconomic democratization was the founding of the International Labor Organization (ILO). Against the backdrop of growing industrialization and labor militancy in Europe and beyond, the ILO was created by Section XIII of the 1919 Treaty of Versailles that ended World War I. Its mission was to establish international standards for working conditions and labor organization. While it lacked enforcement authority, by issuing conventions and recommendations on such matters as hours of work, child and women's labor, workmen's compensation, and sickness insurance for industrial and commercial workers, the ILO worked to shape labor regulation in the interest of social peace and harmony and of justice for workers. By 1928, almost all Latin American countries had become ILO members, and as such were influenced to some degree by the evolving body of international labor standards. Enactment of some national labor standards followed, and by the 1940s most countries had made at least token commitments to upholding some of the ILO-sponsored regulations.

A home-grown revolutionary party appeared shortly after the founding of Latin America's first communist parties. The Peruvian intellectual and radical Víctor Raúl Haya de la Torre, exiled by the dictator Augusto B. Leguía (1919–1930), found revolutionary Mexico a congenial host country. There he founded the American Popular Revolutionary Alliance (APRA) in 1924. As the name suggests, the party was to be pan–Latin American as well as revolutionary. Its platform consisted of five principal points: action of the Latin American countries against Yankee imperialism; political unity of Latin America; nationalization of land and industry; internationalization of the Panama Canal; and solidarity of all the oppressed people and classes of the world. Haya's ambitious plan for pan–Latin American revolution inspired militants in several countries, but the APRA developed into a major party only in Peru.

While the appearance of communist parties and the APRA expanded the options available to voters, the Latin American electorate, with a single exception, remained exclusively male through 1930; and given literacy requirements, only literate males were qualified in several countries. The prevailing patriarchal culture, inherited from the colonial period, was partially responsible for the retarded enfranchisement of women. Suffragist organizations dated only from the 1910s in a handful of countries. U.S. ratification of the nineteenth amendment in 1920 was a catalyst to more suffragist organizing, and in 1928 the Pan American Union established the Inter-American Commission of Women to gather data. But a decade passed before the Pan American Union resolved that women should have equal political rights with men. Only one country enfranchised women prior to 1930, but not as a result of women's advocacy. Ecuador granted women the vote in 1929 because conservatives believed they could count on them, considered obedient to the Catholic Church, to thwart rising demands for reform. Progressives elsewhere in Latin America also believed that women would be conservative voters and thus hesitated to push for their enfranchisement.

THE UNITED STATES AND LATIN AMERICAN DEMOCRACY

Even as oligarchies lost their monopolies of political power in a few countries, and as the founding of the ILO and communist parties foreshadowed more political and socioeconomic change, the United States was cementing

its economic dominance over the hemisphere—and with that, major political influence that would weigh heavily in the contest over democratization.
Indeed, the advances and setbacks of Latin America's democratic trajectory
cannot be understood without taking into account U.S. influence.

From early in its history, the United States aspired to exercise tutelage
over the Western Hemisphere. Even before the Latin American independence
movements had concluded, the young northern republic began to project its
influence southward by proclaiming the Monroe Doctrine. Concerned that
a group of European monarchies might aid Spain to recover its colonies,
President James Monroe announced in 1823: "The American continents, by
the free and independent condition which they have assumed and maintain,
are henceforth not to be considered as subjects for further colonization by
any European powers." He added, "the political system of the [European]
allied powers is essentially different . . . from that of America. . . . We shall
consider any attempt on their part to extend their system to any portion of
this hemisphere as dangerous to our peace and safety."[9] Their "system" was
monarchy; the new American countries, except for Brazil and briefly Mexico,
were republics. The United States lacked the military power to enforce the
Monroe Doctrine, but British naval power dissuaded the Europeans from
attempting to re-colonize and potentially close off British access to Latin
American markets. The Monroe Doctrine would endure as the cornerstone
of U.S. policy toward Latin America and undergo transformations to accommodate changing times.

While opposing European territorial acquisition, the United States early
on began its own territorial expansion into Latin America. The first major
act was the 1846–1848 U.S.-Mexican War which cost Mexico half its territory. The 1849 California gold rush turned U.S. attention to Central America.
Seeking an alternative to the arduous overland and Cape Horn routes to
California, U.S. interests considered a canal across the isthmus but settled on
a railroad across Panama, then a province of Colombia. However, the idea of
a canal persisted, eventually to materialize as the Panama Canal. Meanwhile
in 1870 an attempt to annex the Dominican Republic failed by only a few
votes in the U.S. Senate.

In the wake of the industrial boom that followed the Civil War, U.S.
manufacturers and financiers began to focus on the potentially lucrative
opportunities for trade and investment in Latin America, where British economic interests were dominant. At the behest of the U.S. government, the
United States and the Latin American countries founded the International
Union of American Republics and its Commercial Bureau of the American
Republics—forerunners of the Pan American Union and the OAS—in 1889.
The Bureau facilitated both U.S. trade and investment, which focused on
the proximate area, the Caribbean Basin, consisting of Mexico, Central

America, Haiti, the Dominican Republic, and the Spanish colonies of Cuba and Puerto Rico.

Events at the turn of the twentieth century cemented U.S. territorial and economic dominance in the Caribbean Basin. After intervening in 1898 in the second Cuban war of independence and defeating Spain, the United States acquired Puerto Rico, the Philippines, and Guam and established a protectorate over Cuba. The United States had annexed Hawaii on the eve of the 1898 war. The overnight creation of an overseas empire refocused attention on an isthmian canal and its commercial and military value in linking the far-flung U.S. possessions in the Caribbean and the Pacific Ocean. In 1903 President Theodore Roosevelt promoted a revolt in Panama, immediately recognized Panama's independence, and secured rights to build a canal, which opened in 1914.

By 1910 U.S. firms had invested over two billion dollars in the Caribbean Basin, and where the dollars went, the flag followed. In order to secure stable, pliant governments capable of protecting U.S. economic interests, Roosevelt and his successors exercised "Gunboat Diplomacy" justified by the Roosevelt Corollary to the Monroe Doctrine. Demonstrating the Doctrine's flexibility, Roosevelt declared, "Chronic wrongdoing, or an impotence which results in a general loosening of the ties of civilized society, . . . may require intervention by some civilized nation, and in the Western Hemisphere the adherence of the United States to the Monroe Doctrine may force the United States, however reluctantly, in flagrant cases of such wrongdoing or impotence, to the exercise of an international police power."[10] The United States, of course, would determine whether a country committed wrongdoing or was impotent and required intervention.

President William Howard Taft in 1912 added "Dollar Diplomacy" to the justifications for intervening and occupying. To end the European practice of occupying Caribbean Basin countries to collect unpaid debts, the U.S. banks would buy those debts and, in cases of default, the United States would assume the duty of occupying the countries' customs houses until the debts were repaid.

The United States dispatched troops to invade and occupy eight countries: Cuba, Haiti, the Dominican Republic, Guatemala, Honduras, Nicaragua, Panama, and Mexico. The occupation of Mexico's port of Veracruz in 1914, during the Mexican Revolution, was one of the briefest; the occupations of Nicaragua (1909–1933 with two brief intervals), Haiti (1915–1934) and the Dominican Republic (1916–1924) were the longest.

As democratization unfolded in the Southern Cone and Mexico after 1900, the Central American and the Hispanic Caribbean countries were subjected to the heavy hand of U.S. imperialism. With political and economic decisions affecting them being made in Washington rather than Tegucigalpa or Santo

Chapter 2

Figure 2.4 US Marines rounding up "bandits" during US occupation of Haiti
Getty Images/Bettmann/Contributor

Domingo, the Caribbean Basin countries lost the self-governance that they had exercised since their independence. Under these circumstances, democratization was impossible and the prospects for future democratization clouded. Only in 1933, after U.S. Marines failed to defeat the nationalist rebel Augusto C. Sandino in Nicaragua, did the United States, under President Franklin D. Roosevelt's Good Neighbor Policy, forswear military intervention and allow the return of self-governance in the region. By that time, Latin Americans had adopted a principle that they learned from bitter experience and from which they never wavered: non-intervention, aimed squarely at the United States.

Although Gunboat and Dollar Diplomacy did not extend beyond the Caribbean Basin, the U.S. sphere of influence did. Hard hit by World War I, Britain, the largest investor in South America, turned inward to rebuild domestically and outward to secure its vast global empire. Into this vacuum flowed U.S. investment, and by 1930 the United States had replaced the British as the primary investor in every country except Argentina. By that time the United States had a huge economic stake in virtually all of Latin America. As in the Caribbean Basin, the flag would follow the dollars into South America. In contrast to its behavior in the Caribbean Basin, the United States would not invade and occupy countries in South America; but through other means, it would play a decisive role in the contest between advocates and opponents of democracy.

The export economies created a new social structure in Latin America. In three countries where middle- and working-class pressure for reform was strongest by the early twentieth century—Uruguay, Argentina, and Chile—elected oligarchic regimes made the transition to an expanded electorate and, in two of them, instituted significant socioeconomic reforms. In Mexico, where a brittle and repressive dictatorship ruled, such a transition was impossible and the system imploded. Despite the success of middle- and working-class groups in breaking the oligarchies' monopoly of power, the traditional elites retained substantial influence and, by and large, opposed further democratization, thus drawing the battle lines of politics for nearly a century. Women and rural workers were still excluded almost everywhere. Meanwhile U.S. economic and political dominance spread from the Caribbean Basin to South America, so that by 1930, the United States had become the ultimate arbiter of democratization in all of Latin America.

SUGGESTIONS FOR FURTHER READING

Albert, Bill. *South America and the First World War: The Impact of the War on Brazil, Argentina, Peru, and Chile*. Cambridge, UK: Cambridge University Press, 1988.

Alexander, Robert J. *Arturo Alessandri: A Biography*. Ann Arbor: Published for Latin American Institute, Rutgers University, by University Microfilms International, 1977.

Blanchard. Peter. *The Origins of the Peruvian Labor Movement, 1883–1919*. Pittsburgh: University of Pittsburgh Press, 1982.

De Laforcade, Geoffrey and Kirwin Shaffer. *In Defiance of Boundaries: Anarchism in Latin American History*. Gainesville: University Press of Florida, 2015.

Drinot, Paulo and Alan Knight, eds. *The Great Depression in Latin America*. Durham: Duke University Press, 2014.

Gilderhus, Mark T., David C. LaFevor, and Michael J. LaRosa. *The Third Century: U.S.-Latin American Relations since 1889*. Second ed. Lanham, MD: Rowman & Littlefield, 2017.

Gobat, Michel. *Confronting the American Dream: Nicaragua under U.S. Imperial Rule*. Durham: Duke University Press, 2005.

Greenfield, Gerald Michael and Sheldon L. Moran, eds. *Latin American Labor Organizations*. New York: Greenwood Press, 1987.

Hart, John Mason. *Revolutionary Mexico: The Coming and Process of the Mexican Revolution*. Berkeley: University of California Press, 1987.

Knight, Alan. *The Mexican Revolution*. 2 vols. New York: Cambridge University Press, 1986.

O'Brien, Thomas F. *Century of U.S. Capitalism in Latin America*. Albuquerque: University of New Mexico Press, 1999.

Porter, Susie S. *Working Women in Mexico City: Public Discourses and Material Conditions, 1879–1931*. Tucson: University of Arizona Press, 2003.

Rock, David. *Politics in Argentina, 1890–1930: The Rise and Fall of Radicalism.* Cambridge, UK: Cambridge University Press, 1975.

Smale, Robert L. *"I Sweat the Flavor of Tin": Labor Activism in Early Twentieth-Century Bolivia.* Pittsburgh: University of Pittsburgh Press, 2010.

Tillman, Ellen D. *Dollar Diplomacy by Force: Nation-Building and Resistance in the Dominican Republic.* Chapel Hill: University of North Carolina Press, 2016.

Vanger, Milton I. *Uruguay's José Batlle y Ordóñez: The Determined Visionary, 1915–1917.* Boulder: Lynne Rienner, 2010.

Wolfe, Joel. *Working Women, Working Men: São Paulo and the Rise of Brazil's Industrial Working Class, 1900–1955.* Durham: Duke University Press, 1993.

NOTES

1. Gabriel García Márquez offers a fictionalized version of the strike in *One Hundred Years of Solitude*, tr. Gregory Rabassa (New York: Harper & Row, 1970).

2. Brian Loveman, *Chile: The Legacy of Hispanic Capitalism*, third ed. (New York: Oxford University Press, 2001), 163.

3. "Plan de San Luis Potosí" (accessed at staff.4j.lane/edu/~hamill/Americas/ayala/htm).

4. David Rock, "Radical Populism and the Conservative Elite, 1912–1930," in David Rock, ed., *Argentina in the Twentieth Century* (London: Duckworth, 1975), 73.

5. Luigi Einaudi, "University Autonomy and Academic Freedom in Latin America," *Law and Contemporary Problems* 28, no. 3 (1963): 637.

6. Paul S. Reinsch, "Parliamentary Government in Chile," *American Political Science Review* 3, no. 4 (1909): 508.

7. James Oliver Morris, *Elites, Intellectuals, and Consensus: A Study of the Social Question and the Industrial Relations System in Chile* (Ithaca: New York State School of Industrial and Labor Relations, Cornell University, 1966), in order: 177, 129–30, 126, 123.

8. Loveman, *Chile*, 179.

9. Monroe Doctrine, 1823 (accessed at www.ourdocuments.gov).

10. Roosevelt Corollary, 1904 (accessed at www.ourdocuments.gov).

Chapter 3

Advances and Setbacks for Democracy, 1930–1948

The two decades following the successful challenges to oligarchic monopolies of power in Mexico, Uruguay, Argentina, and Chile brought mixed results for the advancement of democracy. The Great Depression severely damaged the export economies that underpinned Latin America's prosperity. It also created grave economic, social, and political challenges to sitting governments and gave rise to military coups in half of the twenty Latin American countries. Several countries, all of them in the Caribbean basin and all previously or currently occupied by U.S. troops, fell under long-term military dictatorships that prevented reform. Others, whether established by coup or by election, took steps toward democratization—political, socioeconomic, or both—between 1930 and 1948. Some of these advances were ephemeral, others lasting.

DEVELOPMENTS IN THE EARLY DEMOCRATIZING COUNTRIES

Mexico's commitment to political and socioeconomic democracy, set forth in its revolutionary 1917 constitution, remained largely unrealized through 1930. Elections resulted in preordained winners, and while beginnings were made in the agrarian and labor reforms promised in the constitution, both slowed down in the late 1920s under the influence of President Plutarco Elías Calles. This would change with the 1934 election of Lázaro Cárdenas, whose populist government is examined below.

Between 1930 and 1948, the political and socioeconomic reforms enacted in Uruguay during Batlle y Ordóñez's ascendancy suffered some setbacks. The plural collegiate executive system established in 1918 survived the early Depression years, and women achieved the vote in 1932. Then in 1933, conservative Colorado President Gabriel Terra (1931–1938) dissolved the collegiate executive, claiming it was inefficient, and established an authoritarian regime. His 1934 constitution strengthened presidential powers but fell short of creating an outright dictatorship. In concert with the conservative Blanco Party, he repressed the labor movement and blocked further reform. Terra's handpicked successor, his brother-in-law General Alfredo Baldomir (1938–1942), eliminated some authoritarian provisions of the 1934 constitution and relaxed the repression. By 1947, the Batlle wing of the Colorado Party regained power, and Batlle y Ordóñez's nephew, Luis Batlle Berres, president from 1947 to 1951, stabilized the political system and resumed the path of socioeconomic reform launched by his uncle.

The 1912 Sáenz-Peña Law ended the oligarchy's monopoly of power in Argentina, and the first presidential election featuring compulsory male citizen voting and a secret ballot, held in 1916, brought the middle class–oriented UCR to power under Hipólito Yrigoyen. The following fourteen years of Radical government brought a modicum of reform and a modest expansion of the electorate, but women remained excluded. In 1930, General José Félix Uruburu overthrew the second Irigoyen administration and launched what Argentines call the "infamous decade," 1930–1943. This long decade was characterized by alternating military and civilian rule, repression, extensive corruption, and sympathy, especially within the military, for the rising fascists of Europe. A military coup in 1943 overthrew a civilian government and paved the way for Juan Domingo Perón's populist government (1946–1955, see below). Military thirst for power and distrust of civilian rule became engrained during the infamous decade, to the point that after 1951, no civilian administration was able to finish its term of office until the 1990s.[1] Thus ended Argentina's promising start toward political democratization.

The Great Depression's impact on Chile was especially severe. The fragile democratic breakthrough of 1924–1925 under military pressure launched nearly a decade of institutional rupture in the country that heretofore had been the most stable of the elected oligarchic regimes. The democratic opening was set back by President Carlos Ibáñez del Campo, a military man and political independent, who governed in an increasingly authoritarian fashion from 1927 until he resigned under pressure in 1931. The following seventeen months saw a variety of brief military, civilian, and mixed short-term regimes, including a hundred-day "Socialist Republic" that decreed several popular measures, including price controls on basic foods, but could not survive the economic and social crisis created by the Depression. Eventually power devolved to the president of the Supreme Court, who called for presidential and congressional elections.

Arturo Alessandri, the protagonist of the 1925 democratic breakthrough, was elected in October 1932 to a six-year term, by the end of which political democracy had been consolidated. In 1938, Chile elected Latin America's only Popular Front government, comprised of the Communist, Socialist, and middle-class Radical parties. The Radical party held the presidency for the next fourteen years, heading various coalitions. Paralleling the forging of political democracy was the deepening of socioeconomic democracy as the functions and coverage of the 1924 labor and social security laws and Ministry of Social Welfare, established in 1927, were expanded. Yet only a fraction of the urban population benefited, while the rural landless continued to be marginalized. As of 1948, Chile had not enacted women's suffrage at the national level, illiterates were disenfranchised, and the percentage of the national population who voted remained low.

LONG-TERM CONSERVATIVE MILITARY DICTATORSHIPS

The Great Depression devastated the Central American export economies and stoked social and political tensions. The most dramatic case of the sociopolitical fallout of the Great Depression occurred in El Salvador, where the price of coffee, the country's principal export, collapsed, throwing thousands of poor rural Salvadorans out of work. Led by the head of the country's small Communist Party, Farabundo Martí, these rural workers organized to demand relief. Government troops confronted the workers in January 1932 and killed between 10,000 and 30,000 persons in what is known as *La Matanza* (the slaughter)—the worst massacre in modern Latin American history.

Against the backdrop of the Great Depression, long-term conservative military dictators took power in the majority of Central American countries: Jorge Ubico in Guatemala (1931–1944); Maximiliano Hernández Martínez in El Salvador (1931–1944); Tiburcio Carías Andino in Honduras (1933–1949); and the most durable of all, Anastasio Somoza García in Nicaragua (1936–1956), whose two sons extended family rule until 1979. In all four countries, the drivers of democratization—progressive parties, labor unions, and organized university students—were weak and closely controlled by the regimes. The U.S press dubbed this group the "dictators' league"; however, beneath the regimes' similarities, the rivalries and hostilities that had characterized the region since independence prevented meaningful cooperation across borders.

Despite their entrenched power, three of these dictators were eventually forced from office by popular pressure. In El Salvador, after quashing a military revolt in April 1944, General Hernández Martínez faced urban unrest led by students and blue-collar workers. The army's support of the president began to waver and the U.S. embassy, seeking an orderly transition that would prevent democratic and potentially radical groups from seizing power, persuaded Hernández Martínez to leave the country. Before civilians could consolidate power, the military reasserted itself, overthrew the civilian junta, and continued the country's pattern of military dictatorship.

General Jorge Ubico was elected president of Guatemala in February 1931 and moved expeditiously to establish a dictatorship. Within three years he had crushed the communists, other leftists, labor unions, and unfriendly media. He abolished debt slavery for the rural, heavily indigenous population but replaced it with a notorious vagrancy law that required individuals to work a certain number of days per year and prove it by carrying a certificate signed by landowners, primarily coffee planters. He also used forced labor for his large-scale public works projects. University students unsuccessfully launched opposition to Ubico in 1941, but by 1943 were joined by some military officers and other urban elements. Ubico tried appeasing the growing opposition by enacting a minimum wage law in 1943 and raising the salaries of government employees. These gestures failed to deter the pro-democracy movement which launched a series of strikes that drove the dictator to resign in June 1944, to be replaced by a democratically elected government (chapter 4).

Influenced by the fall of dictators in neighboring Guatemala and El Salvador, students and other urban groups in Honduras began protesting in the mid-1940s, backed by women agitating for the release of political prisoners. The Carías dictatorship held on, but Carías declined to run for reelection in 1948, installing a handpicked successor, Juan Manuel Gálvez Durón. Gálvez continued some of Carías's policies through the end of his term in 1954 but reduced repression and enacted minor labor and tax reforms.

After some twenty-four years of U.S. military occupation of Nicaragua, the Yankees faced a rebellion, led by dissident Liberal Augusto César Sandino, which they failed to defeat. Before withdrawing in 1933, the United States created a National Guard as a "non-political" constabulary to replace the highly politicized Nicaraguan army and named the English-speaking, affable Anastasio Somoza García as its commander. By the beginning of 1937, Somoza had assassinated potential rival Sandino, purged the National Guard's officer corps of Conservatives, replaced them with fellow Liberals, and assumed the presidency. Somoza ruled as a dictator until his 1956 assassination; he was succeeded by two sons, Luis Somoza Debayle (1956–1963) and Anastasio "Tachito" Somoza Debayle (1967–1972 and 1974–1979). During the forty-three years of family rule, the Somozas occasionally installed trusted lieutenants as president but no one other than a Somoza ever commanded the National Guard, their personal armed force. The Somozas enjoyed unwavering U.S. support, regardless of the repression they used to maintain control. The Somozas used their power to accumulate great personal wealth; when he was overthrown in 1979 by Sandinista revolutionaries, Tachito reputedly owned a quarter of the Nicaraguan economy.

Along with most of Central America, the Dominican Republic also endured a long-term conservative military dictatorship. A 1930 coup opened the way for thirty-one years of Rafael Trujillo's heavy-handed rule. Trujillo had served in the National Guard that the United States created in 1924 before withdrawing from its long-term occupation, and quickly rose to command the force. As with the Somozas, Trujillo's dictatorship was based on his control of the National Guard and the support of successive U.S. governments. Whether serving as president (1930–1938 and 1942–1952) or pulling his puppets' strings, Trujillo ruled with an iron fist: He brutally repressed his enemies and massacred thousands of immigrant Haitian workers in 1937. He created a cult of personality that reinforced his power: He promoted himself to generalísimo, gave himself grandiose titles, had streets and plazas named in his honor, and even renamed the Western Hemisphere's oldest European city, Santo Domingo, as Ciudad Trujillo. He fended off several exile invasions led by a loose grouping of pro-democracy groups collectively known as the Caribbean Legion. His long reign ended with his assassination in 1961.

POPULISM

While the Great Depression propelled several countries into long-term military or military-backed dictatorships, it sent others in a different direction. Just as the development of the global economy in the nineteenth century created Latin America's export economies, the collapse of that global economy led to a loss of faith in free trade and nineteenth-century liberal economics and brought about a new economic order in Latin America's larger and more developed countries. To counter the effects of the Great Depression that crippled Latin America's exports and the ability to import manufactured goods, governments adopted import-substitution industrialization, a policy of state-sponsored industrialization. Abandoning the prevailing laissez-faire liberal economic model, in countries with sufficiently large markets, governments became directly involved in the economy. They erected high tariff barriers to protect nascent manufacturing industries and further promoted industrialization through subsidies, building infrastructure, and direct investment. This state-led industrialization in turn fostered rapid growth of the urban working classes that had begun to appear during the era of the export economies.

Labor organizing began in the late nineteenth century, and early mutual aid societies gave way to politicized unions run by socialists and anarchists. By wielding the weapon of the strike, these unions began to exercise a modicum of political influence in the more developed countries in the early twentieth century. Even before the advent of state-promoted industrialization, a few organizations appeared that enhanced the political power of unions: national workers' federations or confederations. With the burst of industrialization following the Great Depression, federations and confederations spread and acquired additional influence. Some were controlled by progressive governments; others were independent actors. In either case, they became important drivers of democracy, particularly socioeconomic democracy.

The Great Depression, industrialization, and the creation of powerful labor movements created a new political model: populism. Populism involved alliances between the growing ranks of industrial labor and the new industrialists, sometimes with middle class support, and the partial exclusion of the agrarian and mining interests that had been the backbone of the export economies. Labor backing of populist regimes was premised on state support of unions and the delivery of better wages and living standards. Private-sector industrialists supported leaders who provided conditions necessary for the growth of manufacturing. Powerful, usually authoritarian presidents kept the alliance intact and repressed opponents, both left and right. In some cases, the national armed forces constituted integral parts of the populist coalitions. These regimes, some influenced by European fascism, normally sacrificed political democracy to their agenda of promoting socioeconomic democracy. They embraced economic nationalism and state ownership of resources, such as railroads, ports, minerals, oil, and urban utilities that had been developed by foreign investors during the period of the export economies. Despite these commonalities, each populist regime developed its own characteristics.

Getúlio Vargas of Brazil headed Latin America's first populist regime (1930–1945). After coming to power through a military coup, Vargas adopted policies to promote economic development and favor the growing urban labor force while shifting power from the oligarchic state political machines that dominated the country during the First Republic (1889–1930) to the national government. Reflecting the influence of Italian fascism, his 1934 constitution included a corporatist arrangement for electing some members of the Chamber of Deputies by trade unions and professional associations. The constitution contained provisions for socioeconomic democracy focusing on labor, including a national minimum wage, eight-hour workday, paid vacations, and other benefits to be enforced by a labor court. Finally, it confirmed voting rights for literate women that Vargas had granted by fiat in 1932.

In November 1937, Vargas seized emergency powers under the pretext of facing a fictitious communist-engineered coup. The same day he promulgated a new constitution creating the *Estado Nôvo*, or New State, which granted him dictatorial powers. It dissolved political parties and empowered him to appoint state and municipal authorities, overriding Brazil's federalism.

Figure 3.1 Getúlio Vargas, populist dictator of Brazil, 1930–1945
Getty Images/Hulton Archive/Stringer

Individual liberties were suspended under a permanent state of emergency. Article 180 gave Vargas the power to legislate by decree-law until a congress should meet, which never happened. Vargas issued over 8,000 decree-laws between 1937 and 1945. His measures of economic nationalism included construction of the state-owned Volta Redonda steel mill and the nationalization of the power and telephone services. Vargas continued to shower benefits on the workers he organized into unions. Without participating directly in governance, the military propped up the Vargas regime until the winds of democracy generated by the Allied victory over fascism in World War II made his fascist-tinged authoritarian regime untenable. Vargas was elected to a new term in 1950, but he faced continuing opposition and was overthrown in 1954, leading to his suicide.

President Lázaro Cárdenas of Mexico (1934–1940) was a different kind of populist. Like his contemporary Vargas, he promoted socioeconomic democracy and economic nationalism, but rather than perpetuate the authoritarianism that still prevailed in post-revolutionary Mexico, he sought to instill political democracy in a peculiarly Mexican way. Cárdenas was elected president at a propitious time for implementing the reforms mandated by the revolutionary 1917 constitution. Mexico was in the depths of the Great

Depression: With production down and unemployment soaring, the dire situation called for bold solutions.

A priority for Cárdenas was implementing the constitution's Article 123 on labor relations. To accomplish that, he supported a new, progressive national union, the Mexican Confederation of Labor (CTM). The 1931 national labor code required government-appointed arbitrators to resolve strikes that could not be settled amicably. Using this tool, Cárdenas encouraged strikes and the government-appointed arbitrators normally sided with workers, resulting in real advances in wages and working conditions. Cárdenas also used article 27 to accelerate agrarian reform. The six presidents in office from 1917 to 1934 had distributed some 26 million acres to individuals and ejidos, or collective villages; Cárdenas distributed nearly 50 million acres, primarily to ejidos, and established a credit bank that made loans to over 3,500 ejidos during his term. In addition to distributing land to traditional ejidos, he formed larger ejidos that practiced market-oriented collective agriculture. By 1940 around a third of Mexico's heavily rural population had received land. The landless rural population fell from 68 percent in 1930 to 36 percent in 1940; millions of *campesinos* had been liberated from the exploitation and degradation of life as hacienda laborers. As a result of Cárdenas's action, agrarian reform became an article of faith among Latin America's reformers and revolutionaries, from Cuba to Chile.

Until Cárdenas's presidency, the constitution's promise of political democracy had remained illusory. The presidents had been the victorious revolutionary generals, accustomed to command. Authoritarianism was entrenched at the national level and in numerous states where generals ruled like old-fashioned caudillos. As president, Cárdenas was also head of the National Revolutionary Party (PNR) which had been cobbled together by the generals in 1929, and he used that as an instrument to promote his vision of democracy.

His strategy was a corporatist scheme to counter the generals' power by bringing broad sectors of the population into a mass-based party, which he renamed the Party of the Mexican Revolution (PRM). The PRM's statement of purpose was "the preparation of the people for the establishment of a workers' democracy as a step toward socialism."[2] He divided the party into four sectors with ostensibly equal power: the military; the "popular," which included bureaucrats, white collar workers, and business interests; the CTM representing labor; and the National Peasant Confederation (CNC) which he established in 1935 to organize the beneficiaries of agrarian reform. Cárdenas's vision was that rather than competing in the political arena as separate parties, the sectors would bargain within the PRM on issues such as government policies and candidates for office.

This restructured party was renamed the Institutional Revolutionary Party (PRI) in 1946. Although the PRI eventually became the lynchpin of an undemocratic political system, in the 1930s Cárdenas's corporatist arrangement brought millions of Mexicans into the political system through their associations—and for the first time in Mexico's history made politics accessible to ordinary men. Women waited until 1953 to exercise the franchise.

In 1934 Cárdenas launched a six-year plan centered on an enhanced role of the state in the economy, including recovering the country's natural resources that Porfirio Díaz had granted to foreign interests. Cárdenas's administration expropriated numerous foreign, largely U.S.-owned enterprises through application of the labor code, and foreign holdings were also taken in the course of redistributing land. But since the 1917 Constitution's promulgation, the major issue involving foreign economic holdings had been oil. Development of oil fields along the Gulf of Mexico by U.S. and British companies had made Mexico a major producer and exporter of petroleum. Article 27 of the constitution negated private ownership of sub-soil resources that Díaz had sold, including oil, and the threat of expropriation caused concern abroad, especially in the United States, which exerted intense pressure to prevent it.

Figure 3.2 Lázaro Cárdenas, populist president of Mexico, 1934–1940
Library of Congress

Rather than invoke Article 27, Cárdenas took advantage of a 1936 oil workers' union strike to recover Mexico's oil. The strike went to arbitration, which favored the union; the companies made a counteroffer along with a demand that the government not intervene again in their business. Insulted by their arrogance, Cárdenas expropriated the companies on March 18, 1938, and created a government monopoly, Petróleos Mexicanos (PEMEX), over the production and distribution of oil and gasoline. PEMEX became a primary symbol of Mexican economic nationalism and March 18 was designated the Day of National Economic Independence.

Juan Domingo Perón presided over a different variant of populism in Argentina from 1946 to 1955. Thirteen years after ending Argentina's fledgling democracy, the military seized power again in 1943. Perón, who had achieved influence in the tight-knit group that engineered the coup, was rewarded with a seemingly unimportant position as head of the Department of Labor and Social Security. Aware of the untapped potential of the working class that had expanded with Argentina's industrialization, Perón used his position to promote unionization, support strikes, and deliver benefits to the workers. Having firmed up his power within the military and developed a loyal and growing labor movement, Perón handily won the 1946 presidential election.

Peron's populism combined socioeconomic democratization, economic nationalism, and authoritarianism. As president, Perón continued to cultivate labor. During his nine years in power, the number of unionized workers, all affiliated with the General Confederation of Workers (CGT) grew from some 500,000 to 2.5 million. With arbitration resolving most strikes in favor of workers and Perón's establishment of the mandatory Christmas bonus of a month's pay—the *aguinaldo*—workers' real wages rose approximately one third between 1945 and 1949.

Perón's economic nationalism was designed to take control of the economy from foreign, primarily British ownership and to enhance Argentina's international power and prestige. Perón launched a five-year plan for rapid economic development in 1947, the same year that he paid off Argentina's entire foreign debt and declared the country's economic independence. Reaping huge profits from the sale of Argentine cereals and meat in war-ravaged Europe, the government purchased the British-owned railroads, French-owned port facilities, and U.S.-owned utilities in 1948, creating a large public sector in the economy.

Perón's regime became increasingly authoritarian over time. His congressional majority facilitated the enactment of legislation enhancing his powers. In 1947 he founded his own party, the *Partido Justicialista* (untranslatable), which has been a reliable driver of socioeconomic democracy and remains the country's largest party today. Particularly in his later years, Perón came to rely on extralegal enforcers to silence dissent and dissuade overt opposition.

His wife, Evita Perón, a former radio actress, was essential to the regime. She was charismatic and developed an almost magical bond with the common people, the *descamisados* (shirtless ones). Her Evita Perón Foundation delivered goods to workers and their families. In these ways, she kept the masses loyal to her husband and his policies. She also founded the Feminist Peronist Party, whose efforts in favor of women's suffrage bore fruit in 1947, significantly expanding political inclusion. A grateful Congress designated her "spiritual chief of the nation."

Forbidden by the constitution from succeeding himself in the presidency, Perón had the pliant congress amend the charter to allow reelection and to insert a bill of social rights. His 1951 reelection marked the pinnacle of Peronism. By that time, prices for Argentina's exports had fallen, cutting into workers' gains. Perón and his regime suffered a huge blow when Evita died of cancer in 1952 at age thirty-three, after which her followers launched a campaign to have the Pope canonize her. Further economic decline, conflict with the Catholic Church, and disquiet within the military took their toll. In September 1955 the military forced his resignation and he left for exile in Spain. He left behind a deeply divided country. Juan and Evita Perón were gone, but their influence lived on.

Figure 3.3 Evita and Juan Perón greet a crowd from presidential palace balcony, 1950
AP Images

OTHER APPROACHES TO DEMOCRATIZATION

In addition to the populist regimes that appeared in the larger countries, several other governments that pursued democratization came to power in the 1930s and 1940s. Some were led by military men who chose radically different paths than their Central American counterparts, becoming proponents of socioeconomic democracy. These reformist regimes reflect a diversity of political views within Latin America's military institutions that would become increasingly rare after the onset of the Cold War and especially after the Cuban Revolution. As with Vargas and Perón, these regimes tended to subordinate political to socioeconomic democracy and some were influenced by European fascism. These reformist governments arose in smaller, less developed countries that lacked the powerful, unionized working classes that underpinned populism in Brazil, Argentina, and Mexico. Thus they were vulnerable to the machinations of the elites whose interests they targeted for reform and, therefore, were usually short-lived. As a result, they were often unable to advance their progressive programs to implementation.

The Chaco War (1932–1935) between Bolivia and Paraguay for control of territory in the Chaco region disputed by the two countries provided the backdrop to the rise of military-led reformist governments in both countries. While the war's repercussions were far greater in Bolivia, which lost a war its people expected to win and ruthlessly used the majority indigenous population as cannon fodder, victorious Paraguay also experienced political consequences from the conflict. The elite-controlled Liberal Party, which had ruled since 1904, led the country during the war. The "February Revolution" arose out of frustration on the part of thousands of conscripts demobilized at war's end without pensions or other benefits, officers dissatisfied with the conduct of the war, students, and peasants weary of vassalage to large landowners. Backed by this disparate and inchoate coalition, Colonel Rafael Franco led a coup on February 17, 1936, that toppled President Eusebio Ayala.

The *Febreristas* had no coherent ideology: Influenced by European fascism, they were nationalistic, authoritarian, and reformist. Franco abolished all political parties. His pro-fascist minister of the interior drafted a law to establish a corporatist state, which Franco quashed in the face of stiff opposition. A May 1936 decree-law ordered the nationalization and distribution of five million acres of land, of which the regime managed to distribute half a million acres to ten thousand peasant families. A Ministry of Labor was established in June 1936 and the country's first labor code called for the eight-hour working day, the right to organize unions and strike, and paid vacations. In a concession to the indigenous and mestizo majority, the government made Guaraní an official language on par with Spanish.

Conservative military officers ended the Febrerista regime by coup in August 1937. During its eighteen months, the revolution upended oligarchic rule and carried out previously unthinkable reforms, but the regime was unable to consolidate a base of support capable of defending it. The brief Febrerista interlude was followed by a series of dictatorships that reversed most of the reformers' accomplishments.

Since the turn of the twentieth century, Bolivia had been ruled by a tight-knit oligarchy known as *La Rosca* (loosely, the ring or clique), that had coalesced around the country's large landowners and the owners of the mines that produced much of the world's supply of tin. Having provoked the war by attacking Paraguayan outposts in the Chaco, President Daniel Salamanca ordered mass conscription of over 250,000 men, mostly untrained Indians, of whom nearly a quarter were killed. In addition to initiating the political awakening of the repressed indigenous majority, Bolivia's loss to Paraguay engendered bitter disillusionment among the country's small urban middle class and military officers. This "Chaco Generation" began to challenge the long-standing rule of the corrupt oligarchy.

Two officers of the Chaco generation, Colonels David Toro and Germán Busch, instituted "military socialism" in an attempt to reform and modernize Bolivia. They overthrew President José Luis Tejada in May 1936 and Toro assumed the presidency. Influenced by European fascism like many contemporaries, Toro announced the establishment of "syndicates" that all Bolivians would be required to join—foreshadowing a corporatist state that did not materialize. Toro created a labor department and extended legal recognition to the Bolivian Workers' Union Confederation. Consistent with the view that Indians should be acculturated into the hispanicized culture of the elites and middle class, he ordered the creation of schools for Indians on haciendas and mining camps. He also nationalized Standard Oil of New Jersey, which held concessions in the Chaco and which many Bolivians held largely responsible for Bolivia's defeat. Toro's decree of March 13, 1937 preceded Cárdenas's oil nationalization by a year.

Germán Busch overthrew his former ally Toro in July 1937. Elected president in May 1938, he oversaw a convention that produced a new constitution that reflected the tenets of "military socialism." It subordinated private property to the common good; mandated government intervention in economic and social matters; legalized indigenous communities (*ayllus*); instituted a labor code; and called for free primary and secondary education. It did not extend the franchise to the illiterate indigenous majority or to women. In a challenge to the tin barons' immense power, he decreed that foreign exchange earnings be deposited in the Central Bank and taxed, provoking a failed rebellion financed by the mine owners. Met with increasing resistance from the tin magnates and hacienda owners, Busch was unable to implement most of his policies. Frustrated, he committed suicide in August 1939, after which the oligarchy regained power and stifled reform.

Reform resumed following the "December Revolution" of 1943, led by an uneasy coalition of the secret military lodge Cause of the Fatherland (RADEPA) that had formed during the Chaco War and the reformist Nationalist Revolutionary Movement (MNR). The new president, Gualberto Villarroel, a veteran of the Chaco War, resumed the labor-oriented reforms of the military socialists. He also directed attention to the rural indigenous majority. In an unprecedented initiative, in May 1945 he convened a National Indigenous Congress in which Indian grievances, including the usurpation of much of their communal land, were aired. The oligarchy's resistance to reform, U.S. political and economic intervention, and disunity within the RADEPA-MNR coalition rendered the government vulnerable; it fell in July 1946, and a mob killed Villarroel and hung his body from a lamppost.

The Bolivian reformers of the 1930s and 1940s implemented significant reforms for labor. They also raised tantalizing but unfulfilled prospects of salvation for the country's subaltern indigenous majority. Nonetheless, the Chaco War, the military socialism of Toro and Busch, and the actions of the Villarroel government planted the seeds of change that would culminate in Latin America's second social revolution when the forces of reform regained control in 1952.

Cuba also followed the path of democratization beginning in 1940, under the guiding hand of a military man, Fulgencio Batista. The island's belated independence from Spain in 1898 did not amount to real independence: Following the U.S. intervention in Cuba's second war of independence, Cuba became a protectorate under the Platt Amendment, which was incorporated into Cuba's 1901 constitution. This granted the United States "the right to intervene for the preservation of Cuban independence [and] the maintenance of a government adequate for the protection of life, property, and individual liberty."[3] The U.S. government, of course, would determine when intervention was necessary, and it liberally interpreted its responsibility through both military means and political pressure until the Platt Amendment was abrogated in 1934. However, powerful U.S. influence over Cuba continued until ended by Fidel Castro.

Gerardo Machado, a long-serving repressive and corrupt dictator, was overthrown in 1933. Batista seized power later that year as head of the "sergeants' revolt," promoted himself to colonel and head of the army, and as the country's de facto leader, installed and controlled a series of presidents. In 1940, during the presidency of Federico Laredo Brú whom Batista had placed in office, Cuba adopted a new, radical constitution. One of Latin America's most progressive, the 1940 constitution reaffirmed political democracy, invoked nationalism, and called for measures to promote socioeconomic democracy. It subordinated private property rights to the public interest; banned very large landholdings (*latifundia*); and restricted foreign ownership of land. Its provisions for labor included the right to a job; union prerogatives; a minimum wage; an eight-hour day; and pensions and vacations.

Batista was elected to a four-year term as president in 1940 and was followed by two civilians belonging to the reform-minded Auténtico Party. While this appeared to be a promising pivot toward political democracy, Batista's successors proved inept at corralling the violence and corruption embedded in the political system. Moreover, most of the socioeconomic provisions of the 1940 constitution remained dead letters whose implementation was impeded by conservative interests and the still-dominant U.S. power over the island. But the progressive 1940 constitution provided Fidel Castro his platform during his struggle to overthrow Batista, who returned to power in 1952 via a military coup.

Civilians were the prime movers in other democratic movements. In Guatemala, opposition to dictator Jorge Ubico began to surface in 1942, and two years later a loose coalition of students, intellectuals, military men, and workers took to the streets and forced Ubico, who was suffering health problems, to resign in July 1944. A military junta oversaw elections, won by philosophy professor Juan José Arévalo, who took office in March 1945 for a six-year term. A new constitution, adopted later that year, provided for a labor code, social security system, enhanced funding for education, and other policies to benefit the urban working and middle classes; it made voting by secret ballot optional for literate women and allowed illiterates to vote, but in public. Although Article 91 of the constitution prohibited latifundia, Arévalo left essentially untouched the oppressive land tenure system and rural serfdom that afflicted the majority Indian population, as well as the vast holdings of the United Fruit Company (UFCO) in the tropical lowlands where the company grew and exported bananas. He attempted to enforce the new labor code for UFCO workers but faced strong opposition from the company and the U.S. embassy. Arévalo's successor, Colonel Jacobo Árbenz, would apply the constitution's agrarian reform provisions to UFCO and, to his and Guatemala's misfortune, learned the limits of reform in a small country during the Cold War (chapter 4).

Venezuela's political history from independence to the 1940s was a parade of military dictators, including Juan Vicente Gómez, who ruled with an iron fist from 1908 to his death in 1935—the period during which Venezuela became the world's largest exporter of petroleum. He was succeeded by two more military dictators, the second of whom, General Isaías Medina Angarita, was forced to make some concessions to a rising democratic opposition, including legalization of a dynamic new party, Democratic Action (AD), and token reforms. These measures did not satisfy AD and a group of younger military officers, the Patriotic Military Union, who together overthrew the Medina government in October 1945 and launched what is known as the *Trienio*, a three-year regime that pursued both political and socioeconomic democracy.

A civilian-military junta led by AD founder Rómulo Betancourt enacted a new, more nationalistic petroleum law and instituted the direct election of presidents. AD won a majority in a constitutional convention, which produced a very progressive constitution in 1947. It mandated labor rights, social security, and free and obligatory primary education; it also enfranchised women. Like other progressive constitutions of the time, it called for agrarian reform: Article 69 required the state to "transform the national agrarian structure" to accomplish "the social and economic emancipation of the peasant (campesino) population."[4] Novelist Rómulo Gallegos, the AD nominee, won the 1948 presidential election to become the first democratically elected president in Venezuela's history. Supported by a cooperative Congress, Gallegos enacted a higher tax on the foreign-owned oil companies and an agrarian reform law that allowed expropriation with compensation. Before these reforms could bear fruit, however, Gallegos was overthrown in a November 1948 military coup, which ended Venezuela's first period of democracy.

Costa Rica, meanwhile, experienced a sharp shift in national politics beginning in 1940. Dominated by the large coffee planters of the Central Valley, the *cafetaleros*, the country achieved political stability relatively early. Important turning points included marginalizing the military from politics during the presidency of Tomás Guardia Gutiérrez (1870–1882) and the 1889 election, in which the incumbent party lost and eventually surrendered power to the opposition party—a maturity not reached in most of Latin America until decades later. Early and continuous investment in public education created one of Latin America's most literate societies. The remaining illiterates were enfranchised in 1913, and the secret ballot was adopted in 1925. The last military coup occurred in 1917 during the crisis provoked by World War I. By 1930, Costa Rica had laid the groundwork for political democracy.

Costa Rica had made a modest beginning on social reform prior to 1930, but the 1940s witnessed a burst of socioeconomic legislation. As earlier in Uruguay, Argentina, and Chile, a conservative party representing the interests of the elites split, and the reformist wing of the National Republican Party came to power in 1940 with Rafael Ángel Calderón Guardia as president. In alliance with the country's relatively powerful Communist Party, Calderón enacted sweeping socioeconomic policies including a social security system with national health insurance, a labor code guaranteeing the right to organize and strike, a minimum wage, and a modest land reform. While these measures elicited strong opposition from conservative forces, Calderón succeeded in having his chosen successor, Teodoro Picado Michalski, elected president in 1944.

Picado's term was less innovative and contentious than Calderón's, but tensions arose with Calderón's announcement of his candidacy for the February 1948 presidential election. In a disputed outcome, the more conservative Otilio Ulate Blanco was certified by the electoral board, but Congress, where Calderón's party had a majority, declared the election null and void. This opened the way for the brief but bloody civil war of March 12–April 24, 1948, Costa Rica's most serious episode of political violence in the twentieth century, which left between two and four thousand people dead and thousands exiled. The war began as a rebellion led by the charismatic José Figueres Ferrer, aided by communist volunteers, and ended with the defeat of the small national army. Figueres took the title of "President of the Founding Committee of the Second Republic," a junta of the civil war victors, and engineered further reforms that cemented Costa Rica's democracy (chapter 4).

PREEMPTIVE REFORMS

In response to the economic deprivation and social tensions created by the Great Depression, the decade of the 1930s witnessed the enactment of social programs and legislation under reformist regimes, as described above. Some elite-dominated governments established similar although more modest programs in order to undercut the appeal of more radical agendas. In

Figure 3.4 Irregular fighters in 1948 Costa Rica civil war
Getty Images/Bettmann/Contributor

Peru, for example, the various military and civilian administrations of the 1930s, despite their conservative orientation, implemented make-work projects, worker housing, new labor legislation, a social insurance system for blue-collar workers, and state-run diners.

In Colombia, a General Labor Office had been established in 1923, and the decade of the 1930s spurred more workers' gains under elite governments. A 1931 law granted the right to form unions; 1936 laws created a Department of Labor and a Social Protection Savings Bank; and in 1938, the Ministry of Labor, Hygiene, and Social Protection was established. Peru and Colombia are examples of modest but institutionalized socioeconomic democratization during the 1930s designed to preempt rising pressure for reform in countries where oligarchies continued to exercise control.

THWARTED DEMOCRATIC MOVEMENTS

In Peru, the APRA, founded in 1924 as a mass-based revolutionary party, posed a serious threat to the oligarchy that still ruled Peru either directly or through friendly dictators. Banned and exiled during the Leguía dictatorship (1919–1930), Víctor Raúl Haya de la Torre returned to Peru and declared his candidacy for the 1931 presidential election on a reformist, nationalist platform that included controlling foreign capital, redistribution of income and wealth, and agrarian reform. He lost the election to Colonel Luis Sánchez Cerro by a margin of 51 to 35 percent, an outcome that many observers attributed to fraud.

The following year, a violent incident effectively eliminated the APRA as a driver of democracy in Peru. In the northern city of Trujillo, an uprising of APRA militants resulted in a bloody conflict with the national army, with atrocities on both sides, including executions of military men. This provided the pretext for outlawing and persecuting the APRA, marginalizing the party and its founder and leader, Haya de la Torre, from national politics except for a brief period of legalization in the 1940s. Repressing the APRA allowed the oligarchy to extend its control of Peru for over three decades.

In Colombia, the potential for democratization was lost in 1948 with the assassination of Jorge Eliécer Gaitán. In the 1930s and 1940s, the country was still controlled by an oligarchy represented by the Liberal and Conservative parties. By 1946 the Liberals had split into two factions, leading to the Conservatives' victory in that year's presidential election. Gaitán, leader of the Liberals' progressive wing, a former education and labor minister and mayor of Bogotá, had been one of the party's two presidential candidates in 1946. His reform proposals included reducing income inequality, extending educational opportunity, land redistribution, and other progressive initiatives.

His popularity was such that many assumed he would be elected president in 1950—a scenario that would have put a proponent of both political and socioeconomic democracy in power. His March 1948 assassination in Bogotá led to large-scale riots with thousands of deaths and ended the prospect of a reformist presidency. The *Bogotazo*, as the urban violence was named, intensified existing Liberal–Conservative rural strife and launched the period known as *La Violencia* that ended only in the 1960s after causing some two hundred thousand deaths. Rather than move toward democratization, Colombia remained mired in political stalemate for decades.

WOMEN'S SUFFRAGE

Between 1930 and 1948, the long and gradual process of building political inclusion advanced significantly through the incorporation of women. With the enfranchisement of Argentine women in 1947, half of Latin America's countries had adopted women's suffrage. These countries accounted for well over half of the region's women.

In enfranchising women, Latin America lagged behind most of Western Europe, the United States, and Canada, all of which had done so around the time of World War I (1914–1918). The continuation of colonial patriarchal culture into the twentieth century was largely responsible for the delay. As noted, progressives' fear that the alleged power of the Catholic Church over women would slow democratic progress was another factor.

The suffrage movements that eventually appeared were influenced by both domestic and external developments. Women established feminist organizations in several countries in the early twentieth century, and the First International Feminist Congress was held in Buenos Aires in 1910 with participants from Peru, Uruguay, and Chile. Suffrage was not the most important concern of these early feminist organizations: Those run by upper- and middle-class women focused on women's education, child welfare, and public morality while working-class feminists prioritized labor issues. The economic disruptions caused by World War I, which led to unprecedented popular mobilizations in several countries, influenced some women toward political involvement.

External developments also pushed Latin American women toward suffrage advocacy. U.S. ratification of the nineteenth amendment to its constitution in 1920 brought attention to the issue. In 1928, the Pan American Union established the Inter-American Commission of Women to gather data on women's suffrage. A decade later, after four countries had incorporated women into their electorates, the Pan American Union concluded that women should have equal political rights with men.

Suffrage was enacted in different ways. Progressive Uruguay enacted a suffrage law in 1932. In Brazil, as noted, Getulio Vargas granted women the vote by decree in 1932, then formalized their voting rights in his 1934 constitution. In 1935, Chilean women gained the right to vote in municipal elections, but not in national elections until 1949. Cuban women mounted a long struggle which resulted in enfranchisement first by decree in 1936, then by the 1940 constitution. Evita Perón created a women's political party that convinced her husband, President Juan Perón, to have the Argentine Congress enfranchise women in 1947. By these and other routes, the majority of Latin American women became eligible to vote and hold office, but in some countries, only if they were literate.

1948: A DEMOCRATIC MOMENT

Latin America was not immune to the worldwide vogue of political democracy that followed the victory of the democratic Allies over the Axis Powers in World War II. During 1948, the number of dictatorships fell to its lowest

Table 3.1 Chronology of Women's Suffrage in Latin America*

Country	Year
Ecuador	1929
Brazil	1932
Uruguay	1932
Cuba	1934
El Salvador	1939
Dominican Republic	1942
Guatemala	1945
Panama	1946
Venezuela	1947
Argentina	1947
Costa Rica	1949
Chile	1949
Haiti	1950
Bolivia	1952
Mexico	1953
Colombia	1954
Honduras	1955
Nicaragua	1955
Peru	1955
Paraguay	1961

Source: compiled by the author

* Qualified to vote in national elections, but the literacy requirement in several countries excluded many women from voting.

level since the spate of military coups provoked by the fallout of the Great Depression, and one of the lowest since independence. Beginning on June 3, 1948, with the end of the Mirínigo dictatorship in Paraguay, only Nicaragua, El Salvador, Honduras, and the Dominican Republic remained outright dictatorships. Even coup-prone Paraguay, Haiti, Bolivia, and Ecuador had elected governments. Some of these elected governments were grounded in free elections, while others resulted from tainted or restricted elections, but all were free of military control.

In the early democratizing countries, political democracy took root in Uruguay and Chile, Mexico democratized in the 1930s under Lázaro Cárdenas, and the military snuffed out Argentina's fledgling political democracy in 1930. The Great Depression precipitated numerous military coups, several of which led to long-term conservative military dictatorships. On the positive side, women's enfranchisement furthered political inclusion. Socioeconomic democratization advanced in the countries with populist regimes and in several smaller countries, but with few exceptions, gains such as labor laws, social security, and expanded educational opportunities did not reach beyond urban areas. With the prevalence of elected governments during five months in 1948 and the socioeconomic advances made since 1930, many Latin Americans had experienced democracy, however briefly, in one or both its forms by the late 1940s.

SUGGESTIONS FOR FURTHER READING

Alexander, Robert J., ed. *Aprismo: The Ideas and Doctrines of Víctor Raúl Haya de la Torre*. Kent, OH: Kent State University Press, 1973.

Becker, Marjorie. *Setting the Virgin on Fire: Lázaro Cárdenas, Michoacán Peasants, and the Redemption of the Mexican Revolution*. Berkeley: University of California Press, 1995.

Bell, John Patrick. *Crisis in Costa Rica: The 1948 Revolution*. Austin: University of Texas Press, 1971.

Bergquist, Charles W. *Labor in Latin America: Comparative Essays on Chile, Argentina, Venezuela, and Colombia*. Stanford: Stanford University Press, 1986.

Costa Pinto, António. *Latin American Dictatorships in the Era of Fascism: The Corporatist Wave*. London: Routledge/Taylor and Francis Group, 2019.

Crassweller, Robert D. *Perón and the Enigmas of Argentina*. New York: W. W. Norton, 1987.

———. *Trujillo: The Life and Times of a Caribbean Dictator*. New York: Macmillan, 1966.

Fraser, Nicholas and Marysa Navarro. *Eva Perón*. Second ed. New York: W. W. Norton, 1996.

French, John D. and Daniel James, eds. *The Gendered Worlds of Latin American Women Workers: From Household and Factory to the Union Hall and Ballot Box.* Durham: Duke University Press, 1997.

Guy, Donna J. *Women Building the Welfare State: Reforming Charity and Creating Rights in Argentina, 1880–1955.* Durham: Duke University Press, 2009.

Hahner, June E. *Emancipating the Female Sex: The Struggle for Women's Rights in Brazil, 1850–1940.* Durham: Duke University Press, 1990.

Hentschke, Jens R., ed. *Vargas and Brazil: New Perspectives.* New York: Palgrave Macmillan, 2006.

Millett, Richard. *Guardians of the Dynasty: A History of the U.S.-Created Guardia Nacional de Nicaragua and the Somoza Family.* Maryknoll, NY: Orbis Books, 1977.

Nallim, Jorge A. *Transformations and Crisis of Liberalism in Argentina, 1930–1955.* Pittsburgh: University of Pittsburgh Press, 2012.

Tamarin, David. *The Argentine Labor Movement, 1930–1945: A Study in the Origins of Peronism.* Albuquerque: University of New Mexico Press, 1985.

NOTES

1. President Raúl Alfronín (1983–1989) resigned before finishing his constitutional term primarily due to economic problems, not military pressure.

2. Susan Kaufman Purcell, *The Mexican Profit-Sharing Decision: Politics in the Authoritarian Regime* (Berkeley: University of California Press, 1975), 34.

3. Platt Amendment, 1901 (accessed at https://ourdocuments.gov/doc.php?flash =false&docs=55).

4. Constitutión de los Estados Unidos de Venezuela, 1947 (author's translation).

Chapter 4

Democracy in the Shadow of the Cold War, 1948–1958

The 1948–1958 decade was a period of both gains and losses in Latin America's movement toward democracy. Events unfolded in the shadow of the Cold War, which reached Latin America almost as soon as it originated in the post–World War II U.S.–Soviet Union confrontation. The five-month moment of democratic ascendancy in 1948 ended with military coups in Peru and Venezuela that overthrew elected governments and established dictatorships. More dictatorships followed in the next eight years. Meanwhile the well-established dictatorships in Nicaragua and the Dominican Republic continued with little challenge and military men continued to rule El Salvador. Guatemala's tradition of military governance resumed in 1954 after ten years of political and socioeconomic democratization.

This dystopian picture was partially offset by positive developments elsewhere. Chile and Uruguay continued on their democratic paths, both political and socioeconomic. Costa Rica cemented its political and socioeconomic democracy with its 1949 constitution and the abolition of its army. Bolivia experienced Latin America's second social revolution in 1952–1953. Between 1948 and 1958, eight more countries expanded political participation by enacting women's suffrage; Paraguay, the last holdout, finally enfranchised women in 1961. Illiterates were enfranchised in Bolivia and Venezuela, further reducing political exclusion. By the end of this period, driven largely by the growth of organized labor, several countries had enhanced their labor legislation and social security systems by increasing funding and creating cabinet-level ministries of labor and social welfare. However, except for the beneficiaries of agrarian reform in Mexico and Bolivia, the rural masses and the urban poor surviving in the informal economy continued to be marginalized.

LATIN AMERICA IN THE EARLY COLD WAR

The 1948–1958 decade in Latin America coincided with the beginnings of the Cold War. Following the end of World War II, the wartime cooperation of the Western allies and the Soviet Union collapsed, replaced by a bitter rivalry. The Soviets occupied the Eastern European countries they had liberated from the Nazis as well as a major part of Germany, including half of Berlin, building what Winston Churchill called an "Iron Curtain" across Europe. While there was no viable way to roll back these Soviet conquests, President Harry Truman determined to prevent further Soviet expansion. To that end, in March 1947 he announced the "Truman Doctrine," which was designed to "support free peoples who are resisting attempted subjugation by armed minorities or by outside pressures."[1] Although originally directed at Greece and Turkey, where communist insurgencies threatened pro-Western governments, the Truman Doctrine was applied globally throughout the 1948–1958 period and afterward. This policy was accompanied by financial and military aid in pursuit of the "containment" of Soviet ambitions for bringing new countries into its sphere.

While Latin America was distant from the center of conflict, the United States nonetheless acted preemptively to protect its hegemony over the hemisphere and keep the communists at bay. Adopted in September 1947, the Inter-American Treaty of Reciprocal Assistance, or the Rio de Janeiro Treaty, established a framework for collective hemispheric security against military aggression by the Soviet Union, based on the principle that an attack on one country was an attack on all. Given Latin America's remoteness from the actual and anticipated theaters of war, the region was of relatively little importance to U.S. global military strategy. Thus U.S. military aid consisted primarily of maintaining small missions in each country, providing military equipment, and training Latin American officers at service schools in the United States and at the School of the Americas in the Panama Canal Zone, which became known as the "school of assassins" for the number of its graduates who carried out coups and repression in their countries.

The founding of the OAS in 1948 to replace the Pan American Union was another step in fighting communism. All the Latin American countries, as well as the United States, had joined the United Nations (UN) at the time of its founding in October 1945. Also joining were the USSR and the communist-controlled countries of Eastern Europe. The UN's broad mandate to promote peace and resolve disputes among member countries potentially opened the door to Soviet influence in the Western Hemisphere. It was convenient, from the U.S. standpoint, to have a self-contained Western Hemisphere organization that would assume many of the UN's functions without the communist countries' intrusion. Taking advantage of the UN charter's chapter VIII, articles 52–54, which provide for the creation of affiliated regional organizations, the United States and like-minded Latin American countries formed the OAS, in part to keep communist influence out of the hemisphere. As the OAS was based in Washington, D.C., and financed predominantly by the United States, Washington enjoyed disproportionate influence within the new hemispheric organization. Although its charter makes no reference to communism, only six years after its creation the OAS formally adopted anti-communism as a core principle (see below).

U.S. Cold War policy went beyond boosting hemispheric military capability and founding the OAS: It also targeted Latin America's communists. Communist prestige had risen during World War II as a result of the Soviet Union's heroic defeat of the Nazi invasion of its territory and its overall importance to the Allied victory. Latin American communist parties gained acceptance and influence and their membership swelled from some 100,000 to nearly 400,000 during the war and immediate postwar years. Their representation in national congresses grew in countries where they could legally hold office. Under heavy U.S. pressure, eight countries outlawed their communist parties by the end of 1948 and in some cases, exiled their leaders; Chilean Nobel Laureate poet and communist Pablo Neruda was one of the more notable exiles.[2] Communists were removed from public office, many of their newspapers and supportive radio stations were closed, and membership in communist parties fell by half. Of the fifteen countries that had established diplomatic relations with the Soviet Union, twelve broke them off by the mid-1950s. Communists parties continued to exist clandestinely in several countries, and in some, including Cuba under Fulgencio Batista, they collaborated with dictators in exchange for permission to continue operating.

The United States also targeted communist and leftist-led labor unions. National federations and confederations had begun forming pan–Latin American labor organizations as early as 1918. As the Cold War began, the most powerful of these was the Latin American Confederation of Workers (CTAL), which had been founded in 1938 and soon came under communist control. With the collaboration of the American Federation of Labor (AFL), the U.S. government funded the Inter-American Confederation of Workers (CIT) in 1948 to compete with the CTAL and began introducing labor attachés in U.S. embassies. The AFL and the U.S. State Department replaced the CIT in 1951 with the Inter-American Regional Organization of Workers (ORIT), which gathered more unions and confederations under its banner and soon outpaced its communist-backed rival.

The Rio de Janeiro Treaty, the founding of the OAS, and the suppression of communist parties and labor organizations were not the only steps in the U.S. Cold War crusade against communism in Latin America. Driven largely by events external to the hemisphere, including the 1948–1949 Berlin blockade and airlift, the 1949 communist takeover of China, and the USSR's development of an atomic bomb the same year, anti-communism became a major focus of U.S. politics. The domestic anti-communist movement that culminated in McCarthyism focused not on Soviet military power but on perceived communist subversion within U.S. institutions. The alarm over suspected subversion carried over to Latin American policy. George Kennan, the architect of Containment, commented in relation to Latin America: "It is better to have a strong regime in power than a liberal one if it is indulgent and relaxed and penetrated by Communists."[3] In other words, in the case of real or suspected communist covert activity, the United States should support dictators over democrats. The proliferation of dictators that began in 1948 occurred with U.S. support.

The early Cold War period also produced a new lever of U.S. control over Latin America with the discovery of "underdevelopment" and the political risks it posed for U.S. interests. Underdevelopment became an issue as a result of the demise of western empires in Asia and Africa. The United States freed the Philippines in 1946, followed by British liberation of India a year later. Decolonization continued in Asia and reached Africa in the 1950s. Under colonial rule, the poverty, exploitation, and marginalization of impe- rial subjects had been the business of the colonial masters and their subjects. But the communists' promises of salvation through revolution and the Soviet Union's geopolitical designs on the former colonies made underdevelopment the business of the United States, the most powerful capitalist country.

Decolonization and the discovery of underdevelopment drove an impor- tant change in U.S. foreign policy. The fourth point of President Truman's January 1949 inaugural speech called for a program of international techni- cal assistance to underdeveloped countries. Termed the Point Four program, this first U.S. effort to ameliorate social and economic conditions in the underdeveloped world made international development a permanent and important part of U.S. foreign policy. The program was not wholly, or even primarily, benevolent. Its purposes were to create markets for U.S. produc- ers by promoting development and hence purchasing power, and to thwart the expansion of communism; in the words of State Department official Capus Waynick, "Point Four is the long-range answer to communism."[4] While initially directed primarily at South and Southeast Asia, where the communist threat in the underdeveloped world was greatest, Point Four set the precedent for the flow of U.S. developmental aid to Latin America. Both developmental and military aid would increase dramatically in the wake of Fidel Castro's accession to power in Cuba in 1959, and President Kennedy in 1961 created the U.S. Agency for International Development (USAID) to concentrate development aid in a single, well-funded agency. The granting or withholding of both streams of aid became a powerful weapon of persuasion in the U.S. war against communism and the left in general. The flow of aid further enhanced U.S. power within the OAS.

A PARADE OF DICTATORS

Between 1948 and 1956, eight countries fell under military or military-backed dictatorships. The abrupt U.S.-led change in the hemispheric political climate from the post–World War II enthusiasm for democracy to the Cold War embrace of anti-communism laid the groundwork for this anti-democratic trend. By burnishing their anti-communist credentials—even where no threat existed—these dictatorships normally earned solid U.S. support. In contrast to several dictators of the 1930s and 1940s, most of the new dictators were conservative or reactionary on socioeconomic issues, in keeping with the times and U.S. expectations. Thus in the countries where advances for the middle and working classes had been realized, the dictators normally froze or rolled them back. Within this generalized shift toward authoritarianism, the circumstances of the rise of dictators varied from country to country.

The leader of the parade of dictators was General Manuel Odría, commander of the Peruvian army and the latest in a succession of Peruvian dictators. Following an APRA-led uprising in Lima's port of Callao that involved lower-level military officers—an unacceptable breach of military discipline—Odría overthrew the beleaguered elected government of José Luis Bustamante y Rivero on October 29, 1948. For his first two years, Odría ruled with the title of provisional president. Seeking to legitimize his regime through election, as most dictators did, he ran unopposed in the 1950 presidential election. Regardless of title, he ruled as a dictator, suspending constitutional guarantees and harshly persecuting the APRA whose leader, Haya de la Torre, took asylum for five years in the Colombian embassy in Lima. Odría pursued economic development by enticing foreign investment in mining and petroleum and undertaking numerous public works projects. In a faint imitation of Evita Perón, Odría's wife, María Delgado de Odría, oversaw charitable projects focusing on the population of Lima's burgeoning slums. Facing growing opposition, Odría chose not to run for reelection, turning the government over to the elected conservative Manuel Prado in 1956. Not yet finished with politics, Odría ran unsuccessfully for president in 1962 under the banner of his eponymous party, the Odriísta National Union.

The fragile Venezuelan democracy led by President Rómulo Gallegos of the Democratic Action Party (AD) fell to a military coup led by General Marcos Pérez Jiménez less than a month after Odría seized power in Peru. Earlier, Pérez Jiménez led the group of progressive officers who seized power along with AD in 1945, launching Venezuelas's first experiment with democracy. By 1948 he had had enough of democracy and led the coup that terminated it. He dominated the ruling junta for the next four years, dissolving AD and reversing most of its democratic measures. The governing junta called elections in 1952, but when an opposition candidate appeared to be winning, Pérez Jiménez canceled the election. A constituent assembly under his control wrote a new constitution in 1953 and named him president. He repressed democratic parties and labor unions, censored the press, and closed the Central University of Caracas to quell student activism while creating employment through public works projects, which created much opportunity for graft. President Dwight D. Eisenhower awarded him the presidential Legion of Merit in recognition of his strong anti-communism. Rebuked in 1957 by the Archbishop of Caracas for his harsh repression, Pérez Jiménez was removed and exiled in January 1959 by more progressive officers. This opened the way for the AD government of Rómulo Betancourt (1959–1964), which launched four decades of democratic civilian governance.

Cuba's democratizing trend ended abruptly in 1952 after a dozen years. Strongman and former president Fulgencio Batista, a candidate in the June 1952 presidential election, trailed in the polls; rather than lose the election, with the support of army colleagues he overthrew the democratically elected government of Carlos Prío Socarrás on March 10. Many Cubans viewed Batista's seizure of power as an illegitimate act of naked self-interest and resisted him from the outset. University students and political party operatives published manifestos, held street demonstrations, and carried out strikes and sabotage. In order to hold on to power, Batista instituted a regime of repression—states of siege, censorship, university closings, arbitrary arrests, assassinations—all of which broadened the opposition. Disaffected military officers attempted coups, exile groups carried out invasions, labor unions struck, and by 1957 almost all of civil society had turned against him. But supported by Washington throughout most of his tenure, Batista hung on until a young lawyer named Fidel Castro finally ousted him on January 1, 1959.

The next military coup occurred in a country that had relatively little experience with dictatorship. But Colombia was hardly a democracy: It had been dominated for a century by the Liberal and Conservative parties, both instruments of oligarchic control. Colombia had been wracked by violence in the nineteenth century, in the War of the Thousand Days (1899–1902), and more recently by *La Violencia* unleashed by the assassination of José Eliécer Gaitán and the *Bogotazo* of 1948 (chapter 3). Five years into La Violencia, in June 1953, General Gustavo Rojas Pinilla seized power by coup at a time when both parties were discredited, promising to end the bloody conflict. His initial success through offering amnesty and aid to those who accepted it made him popular, and his public works projects and his wife's social welfare

Figure 4.1 Fulgencio Batista, Cuban president 1940–1944 and dictator, 1952–1959
Library of Congress

outreach engendered some popular support. But within a year, as the reforms fizzled and the violence resumed, his early support faded, and he turned to repression to cement his hold on power.

Rojas Pinilla dictated a new constitution that created a legislature in which one fourth of the members were his appointees. This legislature duly elected him president through 1962. These actions united the erstwhile rival Liberal and Conservative parties in opposition to the dictator. In June 1956 they forged an unprecedented arrangement: a National Front that called for parity in Congress and alternation between the two parties in the presidency. A groundswell of opposition forced Rojas Pinilla's resignation in May 1957, five years short of his designated term in office. The National Front took power in 1958 and governed until 1974. Several Marxist guerrilla fronts formed during the National Front's virtual monopoly of power, some of which continue to fight today.

Paraguay's first dictator, José Gaspar Rodríguez de Francia (Francia), established a draconian political stability that lasted to the end of the Paraguayan War in 1870 (chapter 1). Then the country had forty-six presidents in the next eighty-four years, who served an average of less than twenty-two months.

The pattern of extreme instability changed dramatically following a May 1954 coup that led to the third most durable dictatorship in twentieth century Latin America, exceeded only by Fidel Castro in Cuba and the Somoza family in Nicaragua. A career military man, General Alfredo Stroessner earned two medals during the Chaco War, made his way up the army's ranks, and became army commander in 1951. Following a staged presidential election, he set out to neutralize or eliminate potential opponents, purging fellow officers in 1955 and again in 1959. Stroessner excelled at political maneuvering and alliance-building. Melding the military with the historic Colorado Party, he created a vast support and patronage machine while wielding an efficient apparatus of repression. As was common among fellow dictators, he played the anti-communist card to receive U.S. diplomatic and economic support. Later in his career he joined the South American anti-leftist alliance, Plan Condor (chapter 7). Upon his 1989 overthrow by fellow officers, Stroessner left behind a trove of Condor-related documents known as the Archive of Terror.

In Argentina, the military's September 1955 coup that drove Perón into exile launched nearly two decades of political instability. Rather than a single dictator, Argentina experienced short-lived military regimes along with a few weak civilian governments. Underlying the instability was a division within the military: While united in resolve to marginalize the Peronists, the military establishment was divided between "liberals" who favored civilian rule without Peronists and hard-liners who advocated direct military governance. Between 1955 and 1966, the country had three civilian and three military governments. Then the hard-line nationalists won control of the military and installed General Juan Carlos Onganía, whose severe repression of all opposition foreshadowed the state terrorist regime that took power a decade later. Following Onganía's overthrow in 1970, four brief military regimes held power until, facing the reality that the Peronists constituted a majority of the population and would continue their tenacious resistance to the military's de-Peronization project, the generals conceded defeat and allowed Juan Domingo Perón to return in 1973 from his exile in Spain. As the two decades following his overthrow demonstrated, one of Perón's legacies was a deeply divided, virtually ungovernable country.

The Duvalier dictatorship in Haiti originated in a military-supervised election that installed a dynasty that would rule for nearly three decades: the father and son regime of François (Papa Doc) Duvalier (1957–1971) and Jean-Claude (Baby Doc) Duvalier (1971–1986), which brought oppressive stability to a notoriously politically unstable country. Francois Duvalier was the fifth black leader to follow a succession of mulatto presidents initially installed by the United States during its occupation of the country (1915–1934). This racial divide was a key to Duvalier's success in cementing his

Figure 4.2 François (Papa Doc) Duvalier, dictator of Haiti, 1957–1971

rule. Mulattos, or mixed-race people, were a small minority in the country but constituted the social and political elite. Embracing black nationalism, Duvalier, a physician, connected with the majority of Haitians who were rural, impoverished, and marginalized. He supported the native voodoo, a key element of Haitian popular culture. Shortly after his election, Duvalier began to gather all power into his hands by muzzling the press, neutralizing the army, killing or exiling his enemies, and turning his enforcers, the *Tonton Macoutes* ("bogeymen" in the Creole dialect) against any real or suspected opposition. Thousands of Haitians were killed and thousands more emigrated during Papa Doc's reign. He courted U.S. support by declaring his anti-communism. Despite his support among the black masses, he adopted no significant socioeconomic reforms to remedy their lamentable condition. Duvalier dictated three constitutions during his fourteen-year tenure, each one further enhancing his power; the last one made him president for life and authorized him to select his successor. His choice was none other than his son Jean-Claude, who ruled with continued violence and repression until being overthrown in a popular uprising in 1986.

GUATEMALA 1954: DEMOCRACY DERAILED

Guatemala became the first test case of U.S. resolve to keep communist influence out of the Western Hemisphere, by force if necessary. It also reflected the marked tendency of U.S. foreign policy makers to conflate communists with progressives, as occurred in the United States during the McCarthy period. This lack of discernment led to the demise of numerous non-communist, reformist governments in Latin America and beyond during the Cold War.

General Jorge Ubico, who took power in 1931 and established a dictator-ship, was driven from office in 1944. His successor was Juan José Arévalo, a progressive who enacted labor and social reforms, including a social security program. Colonel Jacobo Árbenz, a leftist committed to deeper reform, was elected president in 1950. Whereas Arévalo's reforms had focused on the urban working and middle classes, Árbenz looked beyond the cities to back-ward and impoverished rural Guatemala. Although not a communist himself, Árbenz was on good terms with the Guatemalan Communist Party and appointed a few of its members and allies to positions in his administration.

Árbenz's 1952 agrarian reform law was relatively moderate; it called for the expropriation of unused portions of large landholdings. 1.5 million acres were distributed to approximately one hundred thousand families within eigh-teen months, although the transfer of titles to the recipients lagged. Árbenz himself lost some 1,700 acres of land, acquired through his marriage, to the agrarian reform.

As throughout Central America and beyond, the United Fruit Company (UFCO) had acquired huge tracts of land in the lowlands, much of which it kept in reserve for future cultivation. Thus UFCO became a primary tar-get of the agrarian reform. The agrarian law authorized compensation for expropriated land in twenty-five-year bonds at 3 percent interest, based on its value as declared for tax purposes. As UFCO undervalued its lands to pay minimal taxes, the government calculated the value of its expropriated land at $628,000 while the company, backed by the U.S. State Department, demanded $15.9 million. The fact that Secretary of State John Foster Dulles and his brother, CIA director Allen Dulles, were closely associated with the law firm that represented the company played a role in the dispute's outcome. A separate concern of U.S. officials was that the Guatemalan agrarian reform could destabilize neighboring countries where UFCO was a major presence and the land tenure pattern was similar to Guatemala's.

With his communist connection and his agrarian reform, Árbenz violated the two cardinal rules of behavior that the United States established for Latin American countries during the Cold War: He expropriated U.S.-owned property without meeting the so-called Hull Doctrine of "prompt, adequate, and effective" compensation, as determined by the U.S. government; and he appeared to be, in the lexicon of the time, "soft on communism."

Consequently, the U.S. government began to prepare for action against Árbenz. A major magazine announced, "The battle of the Western Hemisphere has begun."[5] U.S. ambassador to Guatemala John Peurifoy, who constantly conspired to undermine Árbenz, declared: "We cannot permit a Soviet repub-lic to be established between Texas and the Panama Canal."[6] By the end of 1953, Congress, the Eisenhower administration, and public opinion had solidified in resolve to terminate Árbenz and his suspect regime.

At the March 1954 Inter-American Conference in Caracas, Secretary Dulles strong-armed the Latin American foreign ministers to adopt a Cold War corollary to the Monroe Doctrine. In 1823, President James Monroe declared the institution of monarchy incompatible with the predominantly republican Western Hemisphere; the updated version, the Declaration of Caracas, held that "the domination or control of the political institutions of any American state by the international communist movement . . . would constitute a threat to the sovereignty and political independence of the American states, endangering the peace of America."[7] The Latin American ministers, committed to the principle of non-intervention, insisted on an amendment that required, in the case of an alleged communist threat, a meeting of consultation of OAS foreign ministers "to consider the adoption of appropriate action in accordance with existing treaties."[8] Despite this apparent constraint on unilateral action, by substituting communism for monarchy as the enemy, the Caracas revision of the Monroe Doctrine nullified the Good Neighbor Policy and would serve as justification for the overthrow of Árbenz and for dozens of overt and covert U.S. interventions throughout the hemisphere. Ironically, the preamble to the Caracas Declaration reiterated the OAS's commitment to political and socioeconomic democracy, both of which the United States was preparing to extinguish in Guatemala.

Faced with rising internal opposition, the threat of U.S. military action, and a U.S. boycott of arms to Guatemala, Árbenz ordered a shipment of arms from communist Czechoslovakia, which arrived at Puerto Barrios in May 1954. To the Eisenhower administration, this confirmed Árbenz's communist credentials and required his immediate removal. The United States brushed off the requirement, to which it had just agreed, of a meeting of consultation with Latin America's foreign ministers. The U.S. Central Intelligence Agency (CIA) launched an intense propaganda and psychological warfare campaign in Guatemala while training and equipping an invasion force in neighboring Honduras. When the small force entered Guatemala on June 18, 1954, the army refused to engage it. Árbenz resigned, correctly blaming UFCO and the United States for his ouster. The overthrow of Árbenz and the extinction of the Guatemalan revolution satisfied President Eisenhower that "Latin America was free, for the time being at least, of any fixed outposts of Communism."[9] The leader of the invasion—Colonel Carlos Castillo Armas—took power, annulled Árbenz's reforms, and joined the parade of dictators of the Cold War era.

The resumption of U.S. military interventionism, only two decades after President Franklin D. Roosevelt had forsworn it in his Good Neighbor Policy, heralded a prolonged period of U.S. military and political intervention in the name of anti-communism.

76

Chapter 4

AGAINST THE CURRENT:
DEMOCRATIZATION IN COSTA RICA

Following Costa Rica's brief but bloody 1948 civil war, the head of the victorious rebellion, José Figueres Ferrer, established the Founding Committee of the Second Republic over which he presided. During its eighteen months (May 1948–November 1949), this junta took important initiatives that defined the country's future. On December 1, 1948, Figueres and the junta abolished the country's small, recently defeated army: in a ceremony at the Bellavista Barracks, Figueres symbolically eliminated the army by breaking a wall with a mallet. A small internal security force replaced the military.

As one of its final acts, the junta oversaw the adoption of a new constitution in November 1949. This constitution included the usual statement on civil liberties and incorporated many of the social guarantees implemented in the previous years. The constitution nationalized the banking system and made the state responsible for the general welfare, including an equitable distribution of wealth through a social security system. A labor court would enforce workers' rights: the right to organize and strike, a minimum wage, eight-hour day, forty-eight-hour week, overtime pay, and annual paid vacations. The constitution continued the long-standing policy of free and compulsory education while guaranteeing its funding at a minimum of 6 percent of gross domestic product.

The constitution also consolidated the country's political democracy, in part, by enacting women's suffrage. Another critical piece of this democratic consolidation was the creation of the Supreme Electoral Tribunal, an independent body of three voting members and six alternates, all appointed by a two-thirds vote of the Supreme Court. Through its rigor and transparency, this tribunal has anchored free and fair elections that set Costa Rica apart from most Latin American countries. Even during the major Central American crisis of the 1970s and 1980s, Costa Rica remained on the democratic path due in no small part to the legitimacy of its electoral system.

A DEMOCRATIZING REVOLUTION IN BOLIVIA

In 1952–1953, Bolivia experienced Latin America's second social revolution. The Bolivian Revolution was one of the most powerful blows for democracy in Latin American history. The political and socioeconomic democracy implanted by the revolution was far from perfect, but it supplanted an elite-controlled political system and a retrograde, rigidly hierarchical, highly exploitive social structure that rested on the marginalization of the country's indigenous majority.

Following the disastrous Chaco War, the "military socialism" of Toro and Busch in the 1930s first challenged the Bolivian oligarchy, "*La Rosca*," comprised of the tin magnates and large landowners. This initial attempt at reform focused on labor and the small urban middle class, while instituting a degree of fiscal control over the largest tin mining companies, owned by the three "tin barons"—the Aramayo, Hochschild, and Patiño families. The second period of reform, the 1943–1946 presidency of Gualberto Villarroel backed by the progressive military organization RADEPA and the MNR political party, built on the Toro and Busch initiatives and pushed the boundaries of reform beyond the tin mines and urban dwellers. The 1945 Indigenous Conference, Villarroel's decree abolishing personal service on haciendas, and the push for Indian schooling extended into the countryside where the majority of the landless indigenous population lived and worked on backward, semi-feudal haciendas in sub-human conditions (chapter 3).

Following violent protests that unseated and killed Villarroel in 1946, the Rosca regained control and reversed Villarroel's modest rural reforms. Meanwhile, the middle-class based MNR continued to proselytize among the tin miners and the urban population and launched failed insurrections in 1947 and 1949. Its appeal grew to the point that its candidate, Víctor Paz Estenssoro, overwhelmingly won the May 1951 presidential election, receiving 54,000 votes to the second-place finisher's 40,000. The election was quickly annulled, a military junta took power, Paz Estenssoro was exiled, and the MNR was repressed. However, Paz conspired with other MNR leaders to mount an insurrection, which occurred on April 9, 1952, in the major cities. The fighting in La Paz and the tin-mining center of Oruro was fierce; the rebels in the capital were reinforced by defecting army units and police and by civilians armed with weapons from captured arsenals. On the uprising's third day, armed tin miners arriving from the altiplano shifted the balance to the MNR-led insurrectionists and the junta surrendered.

As in the Mexican Revolution and the 1948 Costa Rican civil war, a popular uprising had defeated the national army. Following the 1911 overthrow of long-term dictator Porfirio Díaz, his successor Francisco Madero left the army intact with Díaz appointees in charge and paid the price (chapter 2). In Costa Rica, the army was abolished. One of the most critical decisions facing the victorious MNR was what to do with the defeated army. On this issue as on many others, there was disagreement within the MNR hierarchy. The left, led by miners' union leader Juan Lechín, favored abolition, leaving power to newly formed armed militias of miners and peasants. Paz Estenssoro, the centrist in the party, and the more conservative leaders feared the power of

Figure 4.3 Víctor Paz Estenssoro sworn in as president of Bolivia following MNR insurrection, 1952
Getty Images/Bettmann/Contributor

the miners' and peasants' militias to force a more radical revolution than they favored—a potential revolution from below that they could not control. The result was a compromise: army ranks were reduced from 20,000 to 5,000, the budget was drastically cut, and conservative officers were purged.

The successful insurrection morphed into a revolution in three primary steps. In July 1952, the government established universal suffrage by decree. Women and illiterates—together the great majority of the country's population—gained the vote. Voting age was twenty-one or eighteen for married individuals. In contrast to the long struggles for women's suffrage in most countries and the longer wait for illiterates to be enfranchised in some, every Bolivian adult qualified overnight to vote. The contrast with the pre-revolutionary literate male electorate was glaring: 4.4 percent of the population voted in the 1951 election while in the next presidential election in 1956, 30.5 percent of the total population voted.

The second step in revolutionizing Bolivia was the nationalization of the three mining companies that collectively owned most of the mines and dominated tin production. The tin barons were replaced by the government-owned Bolivian Mining Corporation (COMIBOL). As some U.S. stockholders were affected by the nationalization, the Bolivian government was immediately faced with the U.S. demand for "prompt, adequate, and effective" compensation. After years of wrangling, a settlement was reached. In the spirit of revolution and in recognition of the power of miners union leader Juan Lechín, from early in the revolution the union attained co-management of COMIBOL. This resulted in improved working conditions but also the addition of thousands of employees, many of them above-ground bureaucrats. As tin prices fell following the Korean War and the quality of ore declined, COMIBOL became an economic liability to the revolution. Yet nationalization of the country's primary export and foreign exchange earner was essential to wresting control from *la Rosca*, attaining national sovereignty, and delivering justice to the long-exploited mining labor force.

As with the Mexican Revolution, at the heart of the Bolivian Revolution was agrarian reform. The vast majority of the country's population was rural, indigenous, and landless. As occurred wherever indigenous peoples held land in pre-Spanish conquest communal villages—particularly Mexico, Guatemala, Ecuador, Peru, and Bolivia—governments enacted laws in the late nineteenth century to break up communal landholdings in keeping with the liberal doctrine of land privatization; the result was appropriation of most Indian land by the elites.

The assault on Indian communal lands—the *ayllus*—began early in Bolivia. Laws enacted in the 1860s ordered the sale of all communal lands, with a meaningless gesture allowing the impoverished communities to purchase their own lands. An 1874 law went further, abolishing the ayllu altogether and allowing impecunious individual Indians to buy private plots. Further laws in the 1880s continued to dismantle the ayllus. As in other countries with communal landholding villages, illiterate, non-Spanish-speaking Indians found it very difficult to defend their land against *hacendados* and lawyers. According to an 1846 census, 63 percent of Indians lived on ayllus; in 1900, after their numbers had grown by around 50 percent, only 27 percent of the larger Indian population clung to their communal lands. In the indigenous Andean tradition of rebellion against oppression, many Indians defended their land by force, successfully in some areas.

Despite Indian resistance, confiscation of their land accelerated. In the early twentieth century, the growth of the new tin export economy created large mining camps, spurred urban growth, increased demand for food, and elevated rural land values. In 1880, haciendas occupied one-third of the land on the altiplano, home of the densest indigenous population; by the 1920s, haciendas held two-thirds of the altiplano. By 1950, landlords held most of the power in the countryside where living and working conditions on the large estates were extremely exploitive, even serf-like. Tenants' duties normally included unremunerated personal service to the landlords beyond normal agricultural and pastoral requirements.

The post–Chaco War awakening of the indigenous majority had been contained by the last oligarchic government (1946–1952), but with the urban insurrection and the fall of la Rosca, Indians took matters into their own hands in large areas of the countryside. They revived *sindicatos* (unions) formed following the Chaco War and established new ones. They invaded haciendas and drove owners and administrators out, sometimes violently, and claimed the land as their own. The MNR had not intended for a revolution to spread through rural Bolivia, in part over concern about the potential disruption of urban food supplies. But faced with a fait accompli—an agrarian revolution from below—the government eventually opted for an agrarian reform decree to both legitimize and contain the disintegration of the traditional order in the countryside.

The August 2, 1953, agrarian reform decree was a compromise. It subjected large unproductive holdings to expropriation, while allowing productive large units, or "agricultural enterprises," to exist. The cumbersome and legalistic expropriation process afforded large landowners the means to defend their holdings or at least to postpone their demise. For the reformed sector, it allowed both communal and individual property. It reaffirmed the unenforced Villarroel decree abolishing the traditional uncompensated personal service to which hacendados subjected the Indians and fostered the creation of sindicatos. In practice, the MNR majority supported private holdings over the traditional subsistence ayllu, with a vision of transforming the Indian majority into small farmers producing for the market and acculturated into the world of capitalism and private property. The term *indio* disappeared from the official lexicon, replaced by *campesino* (peasant, a racially neutral term). By 1955, around half of Bolivia's rural population were de facto landowners, although most lacked titles. The result in the highlands was a patchwork of traditional ayllus, small farmers, and large estates—not a complete agrarian transformation. Meanwhile, huge landholdings thrived in the eastern lowlands where the indigenous population was sparse.

The more conservative Hernán Siles Zuazo succeeded Paz Estenssoro as president in 1956. Cognizant of the fate of Guatemala's democracy, during his presidency (1956–1960) Siles cultivated good relations with the United States by playing the anti-communist card and smoothing relations over the tin expropriation; in return, U.S. aid propped up his administration by subsidizing up to a third of his budget. President Siles also rebuilt the decimated armed forces as a counterweight to the powerful peasant and miner militias by increasing its personnel and budget and welcoming U.S. advisors. After 1960, when Paz Estenssoro assumed his second term (1960–1964), thinly veiled policy disagreements and power rivalries began to undermine the MNR. In 1961, Paz Estenssoro oversaw enactment of a new constitution that gave the revolution's three primary reforms—universal suffrage, state ownership of tin, and agrarian reform—constitutional standing.

The MNR continued to unravel. Leftist miners' union leader Juan Lechín, who had presidential ambitions, broke with the MNR in 1964 when Paz Estenssoro, having amended the constitution to allow for consecutive presidential terms, announced his candidacy. With the MNR in collapse, Paz turned to the resuscitated military for support, choosing General René Barrientos as his running mate. Shortly after the 1964 election, Barrientos overthrew Paz Estenssoro, launching an eighteen-year succession of military dictatorships that interrupted Bolivia's new political democracy but preserved COMIBOL and slowed but did not extinguish the revolution's agrarian reform program.

Latin America's second social revolution had much in common with its first, the Mexican Revolution. Both differed markedly from the twentieth century's benchmark revolutions: the Russian, Chinese, and Cuban. Neither Mexico nor Bolivia replaced capitalism with socialism but did significantly alter property rights and capital-labor relations. Neither completely eliminated the upper class but reduced its influence and opened the way for other social groups to advance. Unlike the Mexican prior to Cárdenas's democratizing measures in the 1930s, the Bolivian Revolution immediately established a political democracy that opened the political arena to the previously marginalized Indian majority. The Bolivian National Revolution went into eclipse in 1964, to be resurrected in 2006 by Bolivian's first indigenous president, Evo Morales.

The beginning of the Cold War had a major impact on Latin America. Almost overnight, the pro-democratic sentiment generated by the Allied victory in World War II gave way to a widespread skepticism, even hostility toward political democracy. Led by the United States, which made anti-communism the leading edge of its foreign policy, many Latin American countries followed suit, adopting an anti-communist posture normally rewarded with U.S. political and financial support. Dictatorships proliferated. There were only two bright spots for democracy: Costa Rica, where a new constitution and abolition of the national army consolidated a political and socioeconomic democracy that has persisted to the present; and Bolivia, where a revolution ended an exploitive oligarchic regime and gave the majority indigenous population a voice and a stake in the new society.

SUGGESTIONS FOR FURTHER READING

Abbott, Elizabeth. *Haiti: The Duvaliers and Their Legacy.* New York: McGraw-Hill, 1988.

Alexander, Robert J. *The Bolivian National Revolution.* Reprint. Westport, CT: Greenwood Press, 1974.

Ameringer, Charles D. *The Cuban Democratic Experience: The Auténtico Years, 1944–1952*. Gainesville: University of Florida Press, 2000.
———. *Don Pepe: A Political Biography of José Figueres of Costa Rica*. Albuquerque: University of New Mexico Press, 1978.
Bell, John Patrick. *Crisis in Costa Rica: The 1948 Revolution*. Austin: University of Texas Press, 1971.
Brands, Hal. *Latin America's Cold War*. Cambridge: Harvard University Press, 2010.
Child, John. *Unequal Alliance: The Inter-American Military System, 1938–1978*. Boulder: Westview Press, 1980.
Gleijeses, Piero. *Shattered Hopes: The Guatemalan Revolution and the United States*. Princeton: Princeton University Press, 1991.
Immerman, Richard H. *The CIA in Guatemala: The Foreign Policy of Intervention*. Austin: University of Texas Press, 1982.
Klein, Herbert S. *Parties and Political Change in Bolivia, 1880–1952*. Cambridge, UK: Cambridge University Press, 1969.
Kohl, James. *Indigenous Struggle and the Bolivian National Revolution: Land and Liberty!* New York: Routledge, 2021.
Lewis, Paul H. *Authoritarian Regimes in Latin America: Dictators, Despots, and Tyrants*. Lanham, MD: Rowman & Littlefield, 2006.
———. *Paraguay under Stroessner*. Chapel Hill: University of North Carolina Press, 1980.
Rabe, Stephen G. *The Killing Zone: The United States Wages Cold War in Latin America*. New York: Oxford University Press, 2011.
Schneider, Ronald M. *Latin American Political History: Patterns and Personalities*. Boulder: Westview Press, 2007.
Soliz, Carmen. *Fields of Revolution: Agrarian Reform and Rural State Formation in Bolivia, 1935–1964*. Pittsburgh: University of Pittsburgh Press, 2021.

NOTES

1. Truman Doctrine, 1947 (accessed at history.state.gov/milestones/1945–1952/Truman-doctrine).
2. See the Italian film *Il Postino*, directed by Michael Radford (1994).
3. Peter H. Smith, *Talons of the Eagle: Dynamics of U.S.-Latin American Relations* (New York: Oxford University Press, 1996), 126.
4. Quoted in Stephen Macekura, "The Point Four Program and U.S. International Development Policy," *Political Science Quarterly* 128, no. 1 (2013): 147.
5. Peter H. Smith, *Talons of the Eagle: Latin America, the United States, and the World*, fourth ed. (New York: Oxford University Press, 2013), 152.
6. Piero Gleijeses, *Shattered Hope: The Guatemalan Revolution and the United States, 1944–1954* (Princeton: Princeton University Press, 1991), 257.
7. Declaration of Caracas, March 28, 1954 (accessed at Avalon.law.yale.edu/20th_century/intam11.asp).

8. Gleijeses, *Shattered Hope*, 274.

9. Joseph Smith, *The United States and Latin America: A History of American Diplomacy, 1776–2000* (New York: Routledge, 2005), 122.

Chapter 5

The Cuban Revolution and Democracy, 1959–1970

Latin America evinced a marked tendency toward socioeconomic democracy beginning early in the twentieth century. The Uruguayan welfare state, the Mexican Revolution, and the reformist regimes of the 1930s and 1940s were early manifestations of socioeconomic democratization. The Árbenz government in Guatemala and the Bolivian Revolution were more recent instances. Several constitutions of the period, including those of Cuba, Venezuela, Guatemala, and Costa Rica, further attest to Latin America's proclivity for socioeconomic reform. The OAS charter and American Declaration of 1948 formalized the Latin American countries,' and the United States,' commitment to socioeconomic democracy. Yet the pall of the Cold War and the U.S. government's conflation of reformism and communism, clearly demonstrated in the fate of the Árbenz regime, appeared to eliminate the possibility of new governments committed to socioeconomic democracy taking root in the hemisphere. But to near universal surprise and the dismay of Washington and Latin America's elites and military establishments, such a regime appeared in 1959 in a country that, as much as any, was under the close control of the hegemonic power of the United States.

AN INSURRECTION THAT CHANGED LATIN AMERICA

A young lawyer named Fidel Castro was among the many Cubans who actively resisted the dictatorship of Fulgencio Batista, who seized power by military coup in March 1952. Castro was a veteran of the rough-and-tumble politics of the University of Havana students' federation. He rose to prominence through a bold and foolhardy action: an attack, with some 165 followers, on Cuba's second largest military installation, the Moncada Barracks in the island's second city, Santiago. His anti-Batista movement, the 26th of July

Movement (M-26–7), took its name from the date of the attack, July 26, 1953. The maximalist idea underlying the attack was that capturing the barracks would expose the regime's weakness and shock Cubans into a mass uprising that would drive Batista from power. Following the deaths of many comrades and his own capture, Castro was sentenced to fifteen years in prison. In May 1955 he benefited from a general amnesty and went to Mexico to prepare for his next action. Among those recruited to his cause in Mexico was the Argentine medical doctor Ernesto "Che" Guevara.

Fidel Castro is known for his successful guerrilla war, but that was not his preferred method of overthrowing Batista. In November 1956 he launched a second maximalist attack: a maritime invasion from Mexico with eighty-two men, designed to coordinate with an uprising in Santiago led by his M-26–7 followers. Due to faulty execution, the plan failed and the insurrection collapsed. Castro and some fifteen survivors took refuge in the nearby Sierra Maestra, Cuba's highest mountain range, where he launched his fabled guerrilla war out of necessity, not of choice.

With the aid of peasants living in the Sierra Maestra and a trickle of new recruits, Castro and his handful of men were able to establish a "liberated zone"—an area securely under their control—within a few months. Meanwhile, Batista was focused on the continuing urban resistance, whose

Figure 5.1 Fidel Castro and rebels in the Sierra Maestra, June 1957
Getty Images/Bettmann/Contributor

persistence and potency forced the dictator to use all his powers of repression in the cities—leaving Castro virtually unmolested in his mountain redoubt with his gradually expanding guerrilla force. Only after subduing the urban resistance in early 1958, eliminating in the process several of Castro's potential rivals for power, did Batista turn his full attention to Castro and his guerrillas. Trained for conventional, not guerrilla warfare, the army found its vehicles and heavy weaponry virtually useless in the rugged mountain and jungle terrain and withdrew in August. With the momentum gained by turning back the army, Castro's force grew and expanded beyond the Sierra Maestra. On December 31, 1958, a spinoff guerrilla band led by Che Guevara defeated the army in Santa Clara, a crucial city on the Havana to Santiago highway and railroad. At the news, Fulgencio Batista abandoned his New Year's Eve party and flew to the Dominican Republic and the embrace of fellow dictator Rafael Trujillo. His ranks swollen by last-minute recruits, Fidel Castro rolled into Havana ten days later, ready to change Latin American history.

POLITICAL DEMOCRACY IN THE NEW CUBA

When Batista fled, he left a power vacuum that only one person could fill. With his charisma, immense popularity, and the prestige gained by unseating the dictator, Fidel Castro was that person. By dissolving the defeated national army and replacing it with his rebel army, Castro ensured his grip on political power. With his control consolidated, Castro could have led Cuba in any of several directions. He chose political authoritarianism and socioeconomic democratization.

During his insurrection, Fidel Castro repeatedly proclaimed his allegiance to the M-26–7 program, which consisted of ten points that addressed the Cuban reality that he aspired to change: national sovereignty; economic independence; work for all; social justice; education; political democracy; civil authority; religious freedom; public morality; and constructive friendship with all countries. His July 1957 Sierra Maestra Manifesto emphasized the importance of political democracy: We want "free elections, a democratic regime, a constitutional government."[1] After his victory, he initially seemed inclined to honor his commitment to political democracy. Manuel Urrutia, a respected jurist, was the consensus choice of anti-Batista groups to become acting president following Batista's ouster. Urrutia selected a moderate cabinet, balanced between establishment figures and Castro supporters. The United States recognized the Urrutia government a week after Batista's flight, maintaining correct if not cordial relations.

As commander of the Rebel Armed Forces, Castro exercised the real power in the new regime, but he soon moved to institutionalize his de facto control.

On February 16, 1959, Castro had President Urrutia appoint him prime minister, formalizing his authority. As calls grew for the promised elections, Castro wavered on his commitment to political democracy, declaring on April 9, "revolution first, elections later."[2]

To Castro, as to most of the reformers of the 1930s and 1940s, enactment of far-reaching socioeconomic democratic measures appeared incompatible with political democracy. Castro recognized from Cuba's experience the constraints that constitutional democracies placed on radical change, which included the power of the United States to thwart reform and the role of money in the electoral and legislative processes. As he explained nearly half a century later, "If you're not radical you can't do anything . . . you hold twenty elections, and nothing happens."[3] From the postponement of elections, it was a short path to the permanent abandonment of the promised political democracy, which Castro came to characterize as "the dictatorship of the capitalists."[4]

Castro's authoritarian approach to governance was sealed by his phased establishment of a communist dictatorship. The Partido Socialista Popular (PSP), Cuba's communist party, had joined the anti-Batista movement late—in February 1958. Earlier, it had denounced Castro as a "bourgeois adventurer." Yet shortly after coming to power, Castro pursued a working relationship with the PSP, whose organization and control of important segments of the labor movement offered Castro some structure for his evolving regime. In July 1959 he removed Urrutia and installed a communist, Osvaldo Dorticós, as president while retaining the real power for himself. In July 1961 he merged his M-26–7 with the PSP and a smaller revolutionary party to form the Integrated Revolutionary Organizations (ORI). On December 2, 1961, Castro declared in a long speech: "I am a Marxist-Leninist and I will be a Marxist-Leninist until the last day of my life."[5] In 1965 he completed the Castro-communist merger by forming the Communist Party of Cuba (PCC).

The fact that he led the country into a communist dictatorship had and continues to have profound implications for Cubans, for U.S.-Cuban relations, and for Latin America. His reasons for embracing communism have been the subject of intense speculation: Was he a communist all along, without revealing it to avoid alerting the Cuban elites and the U.S. government? Did U.S. pressure, including the April 1961 Bay of Pigs invasion, drive him into an alliance with the Soviet Union, the only power potentially capable of protecting him from the United States in the bipolar world of the early 1960s? Was a formal conversion to communism the price of Soviet economic and military aid? Or did Castro become a Marxist-Leninist of his own volition? If the latter, were there practical considerations for Castro's conversion?

The "communist all along" thesis was comforting to anti-Castro Cubans who felt betrayed by Castro, but scholars have debunked it. There is no doubt that U.S. pressure played a role in Castro's alliance with the USSR, and that the Soviets expected ideological purity in exchange for their dangerous game of confronting the United States in its backyard, including the installation of missiles that led to the 1962 Cuban missile crisis. In a 1989 interview, Castro claimed to have become a communist on his own, deciding that capitalism was inappropriate for Cuba and Latin America: "I have had a very interesting and very effective schooling. This is simply . . . the process which, from my first questionings until the present moment, made me into a Marxist revolutionary."[6]

Castro's decision to establish a communist state may appear extreme from today's perspective, but it was not unreasonable at a time when communism was attractive to many in the developing world because it promised to solve problems of underdevelopment and social injustice. A significant portion of the world lived under communist rule at the time: the Soviet Union, several Eastern European countries, China, North Korea, and North Vietnam, while other countries enjoyed close relations with the communist regimes. As recently as 1956, Soviet premier Nikita Khrushchev had boasted to Western leaders, "History is on our side. We will bury you."[7] Thus choosing the communist path was not an irrational decision.

The establishment of Communist Party governance in Cuba was unique in the annals of communism. In Russia, China, Vietnam, and North Korea, communists seized power and established communist states. The USSR imposed communism on the Romanov Empire it essentially inherited and, following World War II, on Eastern Europe. In contrast to these scenarios, Castro seized power and then used the communists for his own ends. From the beginning, Castro and his trusted Sierra Maestra veterans, rather than PSP militants, held the important positions of power. His undisputed leadership was formalized in 1976 when a new constitution established a Soviet-replica communist state, which drew heavily on the Soviet Union's 1936 constitution, complete with an elected National Assembly of People's Power and a Council of State. Establishment of this formal governing apparatus did not alter the power structure on the island. Castro assumed the titles of president of the republic and head of the Communist Party and his brother Raúl was commander of the Rebel Armed Forces. Veterans of the Sierra Maestra held most of the other important posts. Cuba was both a communist and a personal dictatorship.

The 1976 constitution codified the authoritarian order that had taken root within months of Fidel Castro's rise to power. It labeled the Communist Party "the highest leading force of society and of the state, which organizes and guides the common effort toward the goals of the construction of socialism and the progress toward a communist society." It closely circumscribed the Western-style civil and political liberties inherent in political democracies. Freedom of speech and press, for example, were recognized "in keeping with the objectives of socialist society." And no right enumerated in the constitution could be exercised "against the existence and objectives of the socialist state nor against the decision of the Cuban people to construct socialism and communism."[8] The absence of political democracy, of course, was not a new experience for Cubans. The first three decades following independence from Spain were marked by close supervision from Washington, including several military interventions. Dictatorship or military oversight of civilian governments continued until 1940, when a dozen years of elected governments ensued—a brief interregnum insufficient to consolidate a strong democratic culture on the island. Yet the new politically undemocratic order established by Castro was different: It has lasted over six decades and socialized three generations of Cubans into the culture of authoritarian rule.

SOCIOECONOMIC DEMOCRACY IN THE NEW CUBA

Of the ten points of the M-26–7's program, three addressed socioeconomic democracy: work for all, education, and the very elastic term "social justice." During his struggle against Batista, Castro promised to implement the progressive 1940 constitution, which called for political democracy and extensive rights for labor. It also banned *latifundia* but left definition and implementation to governments which, given the power of U.S. and Cuban large landowners, failed to act on that constitutional mandate. Since the constitution banned latifundia, it implicitly called for agrarian reform.

Castro launched his socioeconomic revolution by reforming the agricultural sector, which provided the bulk of Cuba's foreign exchange in the form of sugar exports and employed a third of the island's labor force. This was the first step in the government's incremental appropriation of private property and businesses, a process that in less than a decade replaced Cuba's capitalist economy with a socialist, or state-owned economy. This transformation eventually made nearly every Cuban worker a state employee subject to wages and benefits set by a government committed to an egalitarian society.

Cuba's May 1959 agrarian reform was aimed at the largest landholdings, mostly sugar and cattle enterprises, many of which were U.S.-owned. The law established the maximum legal holding at 995 acres, with exceptions for unusually efficient units. It also abolished renting and sharecropping and restricted foreign ownership of agricultural land. The expropriated land passed into different types of holdings. Nearly 100,000 renters and sharecroppers of expropriated land received 67 acres and were allowed to purchase up to 99 acres more where the land was available; large sugar and cattle holdings worked by wage labor became cooperatives or state farms rather than being broken into inefficient small parcels; and unutilized land became state property. Owners of expropriated properties were offered compensation in twenty-year government bonds bearing 4.5 percent interest, based on declared value as reflected in the tax rolls. As owners typically undervalued their land for tax purposes, compensation would have been well below market value—leading the U.S. government to demand the familiar "prompt, adequate, and effective compensation" for its citizens.

In addition to the agrarian reform program, other developments furthered the expansion of state ownership of the Cuban economy. A major impetus to the growth of the state sector was the confiscation of all properties of "enemies" of the regime and of exiles. Shortly after taking power, Castro created the Ministry for the Recovery of Stolen Property to seize the assets of Batista and his collaborators, other "counterrevolutionaries," and after 1960, of all exiles. Castro initially established a policy of easy emigration that removed real and potential enemies as well as promoting the transfer of major economic assets to the state. The earliest exiles were Batista collaborators and supporters, but the flow of exiles swelled with Cubans' deepening realization of Castro's revolutionary intentions. In the early years the upper and middle classes predominated in the exodus which by 1974 reached some 600,000, or nearly a tenth of Cuba's 1958 population. As a result, the state inherited a significant share of Cuban-owned businesses, bank accounts, real estate, and rural land through the phenomenon of mass exile.

More growth of the state sector resulted from conflict with the United States. The 1959 agrarian reform drove a wedge between the two governments, as the boldness of the measure surprised Washington, and the State Department deemed payment for confiscated U.S.-owned land insufficient. Castro's coziness with the communists and his calls for revolution in Latin America also worried the U.S. government. Soviet Deputy Prime Minister Anastas Mikoyan's February 1960 visit to Cuba to sign a major trade and loan agreement further strained relations. The following month, President Eisenhower called for the CIA to clandestinely prepare an invasion force of Cuban exiles—a plan that soon became an open secret and would culminate in the failed April 1961 Bay of Pigs invasion.

All-out economic warfare began in April 1960, when the first Soviet-supplied oil arrived in Cuba. Prompted by Washington, the U.S.-owned refineries refused to process the crude; in response, Castro expropriated the refineries. When Washington retaliated by canceling Cuba's sugar quota, an annually adjusted allocation of a share of the U.S. market that was critical to the Cuban economy, Castro expropriated all U.S. holdings on the island. U.S.-owned agricultural land had already been affected, but the extent of U.S. investment was such—over a billion dollars—that the expropriations transferred major portions of the public utilities, banking, transportation, communications, sugar refining, and insurance sectors to the Cuban state.

As expropriation of the private economy proceeded at breakneck speed, Castro faced the anomaly of having a large remaining capitalist presence in agriculture. By 1961, implementation of the agrarian reform law had created a mixed agricultural economy of small and medium private holdings of 165 acres or less, larger private properties, cooperatives, and state farms. With the adoption of socialism as the revolution's goal, further measures to reduce the capitalist sector in agriculture were required. By 1962 the cooperatives were converted to state farms and a second agrarian reform law of October 1963 abolished holdings of over 165 acres. This resulted in the expropriation of some 10,000 properties which were incorporated into the state farm sector, which by 1965 encompassed approximately 60 percent of Cuba's agricultural surface and reached 79 percent by 1977 through purchase and additional expropriations.

Despite the successive agrarian reform laws, a substantial private farm sector of some 250,000 holdings averaging 32 acres remained. Rather than expropriate this reduced private sector, which produced primarily for the domestic foodstuffs market, Castro established an agency for its regulation. The National Association of Small Farmers (ANAP) organized a large majority of the smallholders into production cooperatives. Farmers were required to sell their produce at fixed prices to the state and were prohibited from selling land except to the state. These limitations blurred the distinction between peasant farmers and workers on state farms.

Following the confiscation of all U.S. holdings, Castro accelerated the expropriation of the remaining Cuban- and foreign-owned large enterprises. By 1964 the only remaining significant private activities outside of agriculture were retail business and services. In one blow, the 1968 "revolutionary offensive" expropriated the 56,000 remaining private businesses throughout the country: Restaurants, mechanic shops, laundries, and beauty parlors overnight became part of the state-owned economy. After the elimination of small business, the only remaining vestiges of the capitalist economy were the small farmers, whose economic rights were severely restricted. With the "revolutionary offensive," Castro completed the transition from a capitalist to a socialist economy and did so much more rapidly than had occurred in the Soviet Union or communist China.

After the transition, every working Cuban received wages or other income set by the government. In 1968 all unskilled and most skilled workers earned between 96 and 250 pesos monthly, with most salaries above that level reserved for ranking government functionaries. The minimum retirement pension was 60 pesos per month.[9] On one hand, this wage scale revealed pragmatic concessions to important government leaders, certain professionals, and skilled workers who were essential to the regime's functioning, as a means of dissuading them from emigrating. On the other hand, the great compaction of wage and wealth differences after the revolution took power reflects Castro's commitment to the principle of egalitarianism.

Two other elements of government policy furthered Cuba's socioeconomic democratization. First, full-time, year-round work was guaranteed. To underscore the significance of guaranteed jobs, even at the wage of a cane cutter, one need only compare the new order with the 1950s, when Cuba had approximately 10 percent year-round unemployment and most workers in the sugar sector found work for less than half the year. For those impoverished Cubans, 96 pesos per month, paid year-round, was a monumental gain. The second policy that raised living standards for the less well paid was the provision of free social services. Castro redirected much of the national budget toward establishing cradle-to-grave social welfare: free health care and education, adequate housing, subsidized transportation, vacations, and protection in old age. These policies were later incorporated into the 1976 constitution as fundamental rights.[10]

While the socioeconomic revolution proceeded, the Cuban economy faltered due to the U.S. trade embargo that began in 1960 and continues today; the disruption inherent in the transition from capitalism to socialism; and management miscues. Shortages of basic goods required the establishment of rationing in 1962. Yet with full-time, year-round employment at fixed wages and the host of social services available to all, life improved in terms of health, housing, education, and economic security; a majority of Cubans were materially better off after a few years of revolution than they had been under the old order. As the redistribution of resources threatened them, many of the upper class and substantial numbers of the middle class opted for exile over a reduced standard of living and the loss of social status. The socioeconomic revolution took from the rich and comfortable and gave to the poor and needy. It was this redistribution of societal goods, despite Cuba's lackluster economic performance, that gave the Cuban Revolution its enormous appeal to broad segments of the Latin American population.

THE CUBAN REVOLUTION: A THREAT TO LATIN AMERICAN POLITICAL DEMOCRACY

From the moment of his victory, Fidel Castro became a hero to many Latin Americans. His charisma and the prestige he won by defeating the Cuban national army with a small guerrilla force were partly responsible for his popularity throughout Latin America. Having the flamboyant and charismatic Che Guevara at his side reinforced Castro's appeal. The agrarian reform, widely publicized in the region, awoke landless peasants to their desire for land. The style of the revolution, the can-do approach taken by officials in the Sierra Maestra uniform—olive drab, boots, and beards—was a refreshing change from the normal suit-and-tie officials who made excuses rather than taking action. Typical of this attitude was the unprecedented 1961 literacy campaign that sent over 250,000 volunteers to the remotest corners of the island to teach the illiterate quarter of the Cuban population to read and write. When Castro defeated the April 1961 U.S.-orchestrated Bay of Pig invasion, he was hailed as the liberator of Latin America, a new Bolívar. These and other developments gave the Cuban Revolution immense appeal to millions of Latin Americans, above all the poor, the rural landless, youth, students, and those on the political left. And from the moment of his victory, Castro set out to export his revolution throughout Latin America.

Veteran *New York Times* journalist Herbert Matthews, an astute observer of Castro and Latin America, wrote in 1961: "Something new, exciting, dangerous, and infectious has come into the Western Hemisphere with the Cuban Revolution."[11] That something was *fidelismo*. In essence, fidelismo was the attitude that revolution should be pursued immediately and by all means possible—no excuses. Castro told Latin Americans, "the duty of every revolutionary is to make the revolution," and he meant *now*—not some distant future when all the conditions for revolution were in place, as posited by the orthodox communists.[12] He threatened to "convert the *Cordillera* of the Andes to the Sierra Maestra of the Hemisphere."[13] Che Guevara further

Figure 5.2 Fidel Castro and Che Guevara share a moment in Havana, 1959
Getty Images/GerardSIOEN/Contributor

stoked unrest throughout Latin America. His 1960 book, *Guerrilla Warfare*, made him the authority on unconventional warfare and seduced many into believing that they could easily replicate Castro's feat in their own countries. But above all it was the example of the Cuban Revolution—the guerrilla insurrection, the dramatic socioeconomic democratization, and the successful defiance of the Yankee—that mobilized people for change and destabilized Latin America like never before.

The Cuban-inspired mobilization took several forms: pro-Castro street demonstrations; increased strikes; revolutionary propaganda; peasant occupations of haciendas; exile-led invasions of Caribbean-area dictatorships; the formation of fidelista groups and parties; and a leftward shift of the political agenda. Guerrilla warfare broke out in the early 1960s in Peru, Venezuela, Guatemala, and Venezuela. Walls throughout Latin America sprouted the slogan "Cuba sí, yanqui no." Nothing like the breadth and intensity of the agitation inspired by the Cuban Revolution had occurred before in Latin America, and governments struggled to contain the mobilizations.

Adding to the momentum for change was the Alliance for Progress. Having failed to eliminate Castro and his revolution by various assassination attempts and the failed Bay of Pigs invasion, the Kennedy administration turned to promoting socioeconomic as well as political democratization in order to counter the appeal of the Cuban Revolution and stem the rising tide of revolution in Latin America. The Alliance, launched in August 1961, was to be "a vast effort to bring a better life to all the peoples of the continent" through political democracy, economic development, and social reform, backed by U.S. funding.[14] The Alliance urged governments to eliminate adult illiteracy, as done in Cuba's literacy campaign, increase taxes on the wealthy, extend public health measures, and build low-cost worker housing. Having witnessed the mass appeal of Castro's agrarian reform, Kennedy emphasized the "effective transformation . . . of unjust structures and systems of land tenure"—a measure the United States had opposed in both Guatemala and Cuba.[15] The Alliance's call for agrarian reform made the issue respectable—not just a communist plot. While the Alliance turned out to be more rhetoric than action, this highly publicized promise of reform reinforced Castro's call for revolution and further stoked the widespread clamor for change.

Fidel Castro came to power during a propitious time for propagating revolution in Latin America. The advent of the cheap transistor radio and the new medium of television facilitated the dissemination of his message and enabled it to reach the millions of illiterate Latin Americans. The demise of several dictatorships in the mid-to-late 1950s and early 1960s led to Latin America's most politically democratic period to date. This created a climate in which media censorship was relaxed in most of the region and the ability to demonstrate, strike, and organize new political groups, including pro-Castro organizations, was optimal. This resurgence of civilian governance allowed fidelismo to gain a foothold, at least until military coups quashed it, as happened within a few years in several countries: Guatemala, Ecuador, the Dominican Republic, and Honduras in 1963, and Brazil the following year.

BRAZIL, 1964

Fidelista mobilization was largely responsible for Latin America's largest and most populous country falling under military rule. Brazil had little experience with political democracy, having transitioned in 1930 from civilian oligarchic to authoritarian populist rule under Getúlio Vargas. The fifteen years following the Estado Nôvo's end in 1945 introduced limited political democratization, but the impact of the Cuban Revolution destabilized the emerging pattern of regular elections and civilian governance.

Brazil in the early 1960s exhibited the typical manifestations of fidelismo: growth in the number of strikes, increased political agitation, the appearance of pro-Castro political groups, and the rise of a radical organization of mostly illiterate landless peasants in the backward northeast, the *ligas camponesas* (peasant leagues) led by Francisco Julião. The growth and militance of the peasant leagues greatly concerned the political establishment and the armed forces, as the Brazilian political system rested on the exclusion of the rural poor and of the growing numbers of illiterates concentrated in urban *favelas* (slums). By the early 1960s, agrarian reform and enfranchisement of illiterates had become salient political issues. President João Goulart favored both.

Vice President Goulart ascended to the presidency in August 1961 when President Jânio Quadros unexpectedly resigned seven months into his term. Alarmed by Goulart's pro-labor stance and association with the late Getúlio Vargas, elements of the military opposed his inauguration until presidential powers were significantly reduced. This did not deter Goulart from advocating reform, particularly agrarian reform. After a January 1963 plebiscite restored the president's full constitutional powers, he introduced bills to institute agrarian reform and enfranchise illiterates, both rejected by a Congress where conservative interests were over-represented. This rejection normally would have killed both issues, but Brazil was not experiencing normal times and Goulart was not a normal president. At a huge rally in March 1964, he announced a renewed push for agrarian reform and the enfranchisement of illiterates. A president stridently aligned with the forces of revolution pushed the military toward a breaking point.

Facing potential Cuban-style revolution in such a crucial country, the CIA had carried out a covert campaign since 1962: first a failed attempt to moderate Goulart, then to prepare the ground for his overthrow. Meanwhile on the diplomatic front, Assistant Secretary of State for Latin America Thomas Mann authored the eponymous doctrine that annulled a central tenet of the late President Kennedy's Alliance for Progress. No longer would diplomatic recognition be based on a government's origin—election or military coup—but on its merits. In the Cold War in the Western Hemisphere, merit meant anti-communism.

Goulart's pardon of some two thousand enlisted military men punished by their superiors for holding an illegal political meeting was the final provocation needed for action. Encouraged by the announcement of the Mann Doctrine and the presence of a U.S. naval carrier task force offshore, the military removed Goulart on March 31, 1964. The military junta immediately broke diplomatic relations with Cuba, and the U.S. aid pipeline resumed its interrupted flow. U.S. ambassador to Brazil Lincoln Gordon declared the coup "the single most decisive victory for freedom in the mid-twentieth century."[16] The Brazilian people would enjoy the benefits of "freedom" under the military boot for the next twenty-one years, with both political and socio-economic democracy suspended and the drivers of democracy marginalized.

THE DOMINICAN REPUBLIC, 1965

The following year, President Lyndon Johnson unsubtly demonstrated the U.S. government's resolve to contain the impact of the Cuban Revolution and to privilege repression over the political democracy promoted by the Alliance for Progress. In April 1965, Johnson ordered U.S. troops to the Dominican Republic to shore up the conservative government of Donald Reid Cabral against a rebellion by supporters of former President Juan Bosch—the first president elected following the 1961 assassination of dictator Rafael Trujillo.

Facing the challenge of building a democracy in the absence of democratic tradition or culture, Bosch set out to implement reforms in the mold of the Alliance for Progress. A new constitution adopted in April 1963 articulated Bosch's vision for the Dominican Republic. The document affirmed political democracy while breaking new ground in socioeconomic democracy: It subordinated private property to the "progress and well-being of the conglomerate," legalized unions and the right to strike; promised extensive labor and social security legislation; established profit sharing; prohibited latifundia; called for agrarian reform; established free and secular state-run education; legalized divorce and all religions; and, in respect to the armed forces, still staffed by Trujillo loyalists, declared them "obedient, apolitical, and non-deliberative."[17] It went beyond Alliance for Progress norms by prohibiting foreigners from owning rural land.

These and other Bosch policies engendered resistance from both Dominican and U.S. economic interests, the Dominican military, the Catholic Church, and U.S. ambassador John Bartlow Martin, who accused Bosch of being soft on "Castro/Communists [*sic*]."[18] When faced with a choice between Bosch's project of building a democratic society on the ruins of Trujillo's three decades of dictatorship, or the short-term security of a military-backed government certain to protect U.S. interests and suppress suspected pro-Castro elements, President Kennedy vacillated. After cutting aid and discouraging Bosch's reform agenda, Kennedy stood by when the military overthrew the popular president in September 1963.

The developments that led to U.S. military intervention began on April 24, 1965, when a group of officers rebelled to restore Bosch to the presidency. Fighting spread to the civilian population and after four days the rebels appeared to be winning. At this point, Johnson ordered the landing of troops under the pretext of assuring the safety of U.S. nationals. Conflating reformers and communists, as was normal during the Cold War, Johnson changed his tune a few days later, declaring that the invasion had been intended to prevent "the establishment of another Communist government in the Western Hemisphere."[19] Subsequent U.S. Congressional hearings established that the allegations of major communist participation in the rebellion and the likelihood of communist control of a restored Bosch government were inconsistent with the facts.

Figure 5.3 US troops in the Dominican Republic during the 1965 invasion
Getty Images/HultonDeutsch/Contributor

After the invasion, the Johnson administration pressured the OAS into an ex post facto endorsement of the intervention and cajoled Brazil, Paraguay, Nicaragua, Honduras, El Salvador, and Costa Rica to send token contingents to join the 22,000 U.S. soldiers in a "collective" OAS peace-keeping exercise.[20] U.S. troops were withdrawn after restoring order and arranging for a caretaker government and subsequent elections. The Dominican intervention signaled clearly that when challenged by a situation that potentially threatened U.S. geopolitical and economic interests, repression would prevail over reform, leaving the Alliance for Progress a dead letter.

EXCEPTIONS TO THE TREND: VENEZUELA AND CHILE

Within the dystopian scenario of democratic demise resulting from the fallout of the Cuban Revolution, two countries stand out for advancing democracy in the 1960s. Venezuela, a country with almost no democratic experience, became a stable political and socioeconomic democracy despite strong challenges from both right and left, the latter inspired and materially supported by Cuba. Chile, a country that had consolidated political democracy by the 1940s, was also challenged by fidelismo, but rather than undermine Chilean democracy, the fallout of the Cuban Revolution deepened it.

Venezuelan dictator Marcos Pérez Jiménez was overthrown by progressive officers in January 1958. The junta that replaced him oversaw elections in December 1958, won by Democratic Action's (AD) founder Rómulo Betancourt. He assumed the presidency in February 1959, just six weeks after Fidel Castro took power in Cuba. Betancourt presided over a prosperous country by virtue of its petroleum exports and invested those resources in reforms. Working and middle classes benefited from programs of housing, education, health care, and jobs created by infrastructure development. A new 1961 constitution conferred labor rights and called for the establishment of a social security system. It declared: "The system of latifundia is contrary to the social interest" and reiterated the 1947 constitution's call for agrarian reform.[21] Owing to Venezuela's oil wealth, the government was able to offer expropriated landowners satisfactory compensation and thus avoid creating powerful enemies. Credit and technical aid accompanied land distribution, and between 150,000 and 200,000 families benefited from the agrarian reform.

Betancourt's greatest challenge was to overcome Venezuela's history of virtually uninterrupted authoritarian rule. This was no easy task. From the outset, he faced violence from both right and left. Seeing in the stridently democratic Betancourt a threat to his regime, Dominican dictator Rafael Trujillo mounted an assassination attempt in June 1960 that nearly succeeded, leaving Betancourt seriously wounded. Anticipating trouble from elements of the army, Betancourt invested in materiel to modernize the force. When army rebellions broke out in regional headquarters, the central command held firm. Violence from the left may also have contributed to the army command's acquiescence in the novelty of civilian rule by giving it the mission of fighting a protracted guerrilla war.

Betancourt and Fidel Castro initially got along, in part owing to their mutual enmity toward Trujillo. They soon parted ways as their two models of democratization proved incompatible. After their falling out, Castro actively supported Betancourt's overthrow in a concerted effort to derail the leading reformist alternative of the early 1960s to his style of revolution. By 1961, guerrillas were active in nine of Venezuela's twenty-five states. In an unusual development for Latin America's communists, the Venezuelan Communist Party joined the guerrillas in 1962. Peasant support of the government resulting from the agrarian reform stymied the rural guerrillas, while urban insurgents initially appeared threatening. An umbrella group, the Armed Forces of National Liberation (FALN), united the various armed groups and vowed to disrupt the scheduled 1963 elections. Despite threats and actions, over 90 percent of registered voters turned out in a defeat for the guerrillas. Thereafter guerrilla action declined until finally ending in 1969.

Betancourt's signal achievement was to implant political democracy in a country without democratic roots. The 1961 constitution confirmed the enfranchisement of all adults and attempted to broaden the electorate by making voting obligatory. But surviving all attempts to unseat him and passing the baton to his AD successor, Raúl Leoni, was even more important. Five years later, Rafael Caldera of the Social Christian Party (COPEI) was elected, marking another milestone in democratization. The fledgling two-party political democracy endured into the 1990s.

While the Cuban Revolution threatened but failed to derail Venezuela's nascent democracy, it contributed significantly to deepening Chile's socioeconomic democracy. Electoral reforms in 1958 had fortified the existing political democracy by making voting obligatory and, more importantly, by introducing the Australian (secret) ballot. These measures began to erode rural landowners' control of their workers' votes, the arrangement upon which the power of the traditional Liberal and Conservative parties had rested.

Fidelismo had its normal manifestations in Chile: increased agitation and strikes, worker and student mobilization, formation of fidelista groups, and rural unrest. Responding to the growing pressure for land redistribution, the conservative government of Jorge Alessandri (1958–1964) implemented a preemptive agrarian reform in 1962 that did little to dampen the growing peasant demand for land. Given the long-established subordination of the armed forces to civilian authority, the political effervescence of the 1960s would be resolved within the political system, not by military intervention.

As the 1964 presidential election approached, the right-wing Liberal and Conservative parties saw their power erode to the point that they decided against fielding a candidate for fear of opening the way for Socialist Salvador Allende, then running for a third time. Faced with a choice between two advocates of socioeconomic democracy, they reluctantly backed Eduardo Frei of the new, reformist Christian Democratic Party (PDC) as the lesser of evils. Reflecting the radicalization of Chilean politics in a few short years, the 1964 election offered voters a choice of revolutions: Allende's politically democratic socialist revolution and what Frei called his "revolution in liberty." With covert U.S. financial support, supposedly unknown by the candidate, Frei won handily with 55.6 percent of the vote.

Frei's platform promised radical change, but less radical than Allende's. The "revolution in liberty" called for an agrarian reform that would create 100,000 new landowners; legalizing unionization and establishing a minimum wage for agricultural workers; "Chileanization," or government co-ownership of the U.S. copper companies that supplied most of Chile's export revenue; profit sharing in industry; major investment in housing and education; and *Promoción Popular* (people's development), a plan to provide organization and political access for the underrepresented segments of society—peasants, urban slum dwellers, and women.

Eduardo Frei left office in 1970 with an impressive record of democratization. Rural workers were empowered by Frei's unionization and minimum wage laws while Promoción Popular raised political awareness and participation for the poor. A 1970 constitutional reform expanded the electorate by enfranchising illiterates and lowering the voting age from twenty-one to eighteen. The Chilean state acquired 51 percent ownership of the U.S. copper companies and an option to purchase the rest. Frei made significant progress in education and housing. His agrarian reform delivered titles to only a third of the promised 100,000 beneficiaries but expropriated enough land to create thousands more small landowners.

While Frei's reforms were unprecedented, they were unsuccessful in satisfying the demands for change generated largely by the Cuban Revolution and pushed by the left parties, unions, and student activists. The verdict of the 1970 presidential election was that Frei was too moderate for the times of growing radicalization and mobilization. Chileans elected a socialist, Dr. Salvador Allende, to lead a process of further socioeconomic democratization.

Fidel Castro's first decade in power was a difficult period for Latin American democracy. In Cuba, the possibility of rooting a political democracy was sacrificed to the construction of a model socioeconomic democracy. Throughout the region, elected governments fell to military coups if they were not sufficiently anti-fidelista. But it was also a difficult time for Castro's project of exporting revolution throughout Latin America. Despite the enormous appeal of the Cuban Revolution and Castro's active support of revolution, none of the guerrilla movements launched in several countries succeeded in replicating Castro's feat, and only Venezuela and Chile furthered democratization. Apart from Cuba's thorough socioeconomic democratization, setbacks clearly outweighed successes for democracy in the decade following Fidel Castro's accession to power.

SUGGESTIONS FOR FURTHER READING

Alexander, Robert J. *Rómulo Betancourt and the Transformation of Venezuela.* New Brunswick: Transaction Books, 1982.

Anderson, Jon Lee. *Che Guevara: A Revolutionary Life.* Second ed. New York: Grove Press, 2010.

Argote-Freyre, Frank. *Fulgencio Batista.* New Brunswick: Rutgers University Press, 2006.

Balfour, Sebastian. *Castro.* Third ed. Harlow, England: Pearson Longman, 2009.

Blight, James A. and Peter Kornbluh. *Politics of Illusion: The Bay of Pigs Reexamined.* Boulder: Lynne Rienner, 1998.

Bustamante, Michael J. and Jennifer L. Lambe, eds. *The Revolution from Within: Cuba, 1959–1980.* Durham: Duke University Press, 2019.

Castro, Fidel. *Revolutionary Struggle, 1947–1958.* Ed. Rolando Bonachea and Nelson P. Valdés. Cambridge: MIT Press, 1972.

Castro, Fidel and Ignacio Ramonet. *Fidel Castro: My Life, A Spoken Autobiography.* Trans. Andrew Hurley. New York: Scribner, 2008.

Chomsky, Aviva. *A History of the Cuban Revolution.* Second ed. Hoboken: John Wiley and Sons, 2015.

Domínguez, Jorge I. *To Make the World Safe for Revolution: Cuba's Foreign Policy.* Cambridge: Harvard University Press, 1989.

Fleet, Michael. *The Rise and Fall of Chilean Christian Democracy.* Princeton: Princeton University Press, 1985.

Guevara, Ernesto (Che). *Guerrilla Warfare.* Brian Loveman and Thomas M. Davies Jr., eds. Third ed. Wilmington: SR Books, 1997.

———. *Reminiscences of the Cuban Revolutionary War.* Trans. Victoria Ortiz. New York: Monthly Review Press, 1968.

Horowitz, Louis and Jaime Suchlicki, eds. *Cuban Communism.* Eleventh ed. New Brunswick: Transaction Publishers, 2003.

Kruijt, Dirk, Rey Tristán, and Alberto Martín Álvarez, eds. *Latin American Guerrilla Movements: Origins, Evolution, Outcomes.* New York: Routledge, 2020.

Lowenthal, Abraham F. *The Dominican Intervention.* Reprint. Baltimore: Johns Hopkins University Press, 1995.

Parker, Phyllis R. *Brazil and the Quiet Intervention, 1964*. Austin: University of Texas Press, 1979.

Rabe, Stephen G. *The Most Dangerous Area in the World: John F. Kennedy Confronts Communist Revolution in Latin America*. Chapel Hill: University of North Carolina Press, 1999.

Schoultz, Lars. *That Infernal Little Cuban Republic: The United States and the Cuban Revolution*. Chapel Hill: University of North Carolina Press, 2009.

Taffett, Jeffrey F. *Foreign Aid as Foreign Policy: The Alliance for Progress in Latin America*. New York: Routledge, 2007.

Wickham-Crowley, Timothy P. *Guerrillas and Revolution in Latin America: A Comparative Study of Insurgents and Regimes since 1956*. Princeton: Princeton University Press, 1992.

Wright, Thomas C. *Latin America in the Era of the Cuban Revolution and Beyond*. Third ed. Santa Barbara: Praeger, 2018.

NOTES

1. "Sierra Maestra Manifesto," July 12, 1957 (accessed at http://www.latinamericanstudies.org/cuban-rebels/manifesto.htm).

2. Jorge I. Domínguez, *Cuba: Order and Revolution* (Cambridge: Harvard University Press, 1978), 144.

3. Fidel Castro and Ignacio Ramonet, *Fidel Castro: My Life, a Spoken Autobiography*, trans. Andrew Hurley (New York: Scribner, 2008), 247.

4. Lee Lockwood, *Castro's Cuba, Cuba's Fidel*, second ed. (Boulder: Westview Press, 1990), 147.

5. Lars Schoultz, *That Infernal Little Cuban Republic: The United States and the Cuban Revolution* (Chapel Hill: University of North Carolina Press, 2009), 174.

6. Lockwood, *Castro's Cuba*, 160.

7. William Taubman, *Khrushchev: The Man and his Era* (New York: W. W. Norton, 2003), 427.

8. The Constitution of the Republic of Cuba, 1976 (accessed at https://constitutionnet.org/sites/default/files/Cuba%20Constitution.pdf); articles 5, 52, 61.

9. The difference between black market and official exchange rates precludes offering a dollar equivalent.

10. The [1976] Constitution of the Republic of Cuba; articles 45, 45, 46, 50, 51, 48, respectively.

11. Herbert Matthews, *The Cuban Story* (New York: George Braziller, 1961), 185.

12. Fidel Castro, *The First and Second Declarations of Havana: Manifestos of Revolutionary Struggle in the Americas Adopted by the Cuban People*, ed. Mary-Alice Waters, third ed. (New York: Pathfinder Press, 2010), 72–73.

13. Hal Brands, *Latin America's Cold War* (Cambridge: Harvard University Press, 2010), 27.

14. Mark Eric Williams, *Understanding U.S.-Latin American Relations: Theory and History* (New York: Routledge, 2012), 191.

15. Peter Dorner, *Latin American Land Reform in Theory and Practice: A Retrospective Analysis* (Madison: University of Wisconsin Press, 1992), 11.

16. E. Bradford Burns, *A History of Brazil*, third ed. (New York: Columbia University Press, 1993), 444.

17. Ministerio de Educación, Bellas Artes y Culto, *Constitución de la República Dominicana proclamada el 29 de abril de 1963*, various articles.

18. Abraham F. Lowenthal, *The Dominican Intervention* (Cambridge: Harvard University Press, 1972), 27.

19. Howard Jones, *Crucible of Power: A History of American Foreign Relations from 1945* (Lanham, MD: Rowman & Littlefield, 2009), 151.

20. Since Costa Rica had abolished its army, it sent twenty-one police to the Dominical Republic.

21. Constitution of Venezuela, 1961 (accessed at https://pdba.georgetown.edu/Constitutions/Venezuela/ven1961.html); author's translation of title III, chapter V, article 105.

Chapter 6

Three Truncated
Revolutions, 1968–1990

Despite the best efforts of the U.S. government and the Latin American militaries to quell the revolutionary impulse unleashed by the Cuban Revolution, three revolutionary governments came to power between 1968 and 1979. The three had characteristics in common. All traced their origins to domestic issues exacerbated by fidelismo. All carried out profound democratizing change. The United States opposed all three revolutions and played a decisive role in terminating two of them. And all ended before meeting their objectives.

Their differences were also apparent. The revolution in Peru (1968–1975) was carried out by the national armed forces following a coup. Reflecting the strength of the country's consolidated political democracy, the Chilean revolution (1970–1973) came to power through the ballot box. And the Nicaraguan revolution (1979–1990) resulted from the only guerrilla insurrection to take power after Castro's. The Peruvian military pursued socioeconomic democratization in a unique manner; the Chilean presidency of Salvador Allende carried out socioeconomic change within a politically democratic setting; and the Sandinistas in Nicaragua set out to construct both socioeconomic and political democracy from the ashes of the forty-three-year Somoza family dictatorship.

PERU: A MILITARY REVOLUTION

The self-named "Revolutionary Government of the Peruvian Armed Forces," headed by General Juan Velasco Alvarado, carried out profound reforms that transformed Peru's economy and society. Prior to its 1968 coup, the military had been anything but progressive; its primary political role since the 1920s had been to block democratization by repressing the country's main threat to the oligarchy, the APRA (chapter 2). Progressive military-led governments, including those led by Toro and Busch in Bolivia, the Febreristas in Paraguay, and Juan Perón in Argentina, had appeared in the 1930s and 1940s, but in the Cold War, and particularly following the Cuban Revolution, the Latin American militaries' political posture was decidedly reactionary. Thus the Peruvian military as driver of socioeconomic democracy was an anomaly.

Under the impact of fidelismo, Peru in the 1960s appeared to be ripe for revolution. Per capita income was $338 per year, in the middle of the range for Latin America, but distribution of this modest income was extremely skewed. Forty percent of the country's 1960 population spoke Quechua, Aymara, or another native tongue as their first language. Adult illiteracy was over 50 percent nationally but much higher in the Indian strongholds of the Andes. Symptoms of the impact of fidelismo included increased strikes and street demonstrations, creation of pro-Cuban groups, guerrilla movements, and Indian invasions and occupation of haciendas.

The Peruvian revolutionary government coincided with other military dictatorships in South America—those in Brazil, Uruguay, and Chile—and ended just seven months before the Argentine military seized power. All of these other dictatorships were reactionary in the extreme. The Peruvian military bucked that trend owing to several circumstances. The continuation of oligarchic rule into the 1960s fed frustration with civilian politicians for their failure to enact significant reforms over time. The notorious subservience of Peruvian governments to the U.S. government and U.S. corporations was increasingly unacceptable to the military—an institution that was intrinsically nationalistic. In defeating guerrilla outbreaks in 1963 and 1965, officers encountered the harsh reality of Peru's poverty and the marginalization of the indigenous population in the Andes; as a result the military leadership engaged sociologists and others to school the officer corps in Peruvian reality. As in most of the earlier reformist military regimes, power rested with the colonels, not the generals; in Peru, General Velasco, himself a man of modest origins, was advised and supported by a council of colonels that pushed for reform. Finally, the threat of revolution was growing but not imminent, allowing the military to act preemptively, with a minimum of repression, to undercut the appeal of the Cuban Revolution as well as the lingering power of APRA.

The military seized power in October 1968 after botched negotiations between President Fernando Belaúnde Terry and the International Petroleum Company (IPC)—a subsidiary of Standard Oil of New Jersey—over the corporation's legal status and exploitation rights. A leaked copy of the draft agreement revealed major concessions to IPC, the number one symbol of Yankee imperialism to many Peruvians. This damaged the Belaúnde presidency beyond repair. When it overthrew Belaúnde, the new military government immediately nationalized IPC.

The expropriation was not unexpected, given the circumstances. What was not anticipated, in light of its history of upholding oligarchic rule, was the military's pivot to a thoroughgoing revolution. From the outset, the Velasco government prioritized socioeconomic over political democracy. Through agrarian reform, worker co-ownership of enterprises, and a grand scheme to socialize the entire economy, the military regime sought to incorporate the majority of Peruvians who were marginalized by race, language, poverty, illiteracy, and geography into the national polity. Rather than create a social-ist, state-owned economy as in Cuba, the aim was to build an economy based on cooperatives and worker ownership that would be neither communist nor capitalist. During its seven years in power, Velasco's government remained a dictatorship. But since Velasco estimated that it would require at least until 1990, or twenty-two years, to complete the envisioned transformation of Peru, it is unclear whether in its projected later stages the dictatorship would have attempted to create a politically democratic system of governance.

Typically of Latin America, land distribution in Peru was character-ized by extremes, with latifundia dominating. On irrigated coastal lands, modern capitalist enterprises owned by both Peruvian and foreign interests produced primarily sugar and cotton for both domestic and export markets. The coastal haciendas were one of the pillars of the Peruvian oligarchy. In the Andes, haciendas had been carved out of indigenous communal proper-ties, or ayllus, over the centuries. Resident workers on these underproductive haciendas often toiled in subhuman conditions and were paid primarily in land use rights, while millions of largely indigenous peasants were landless. Intellectuals and politicians had long critiqued the Andean landholding pat-tern for its economic and social backwardness.

The military launched its agrarian reform program in June 1969 on the "day of the peasant." Velasco proclaimed that the law "will end forever the unjust social order that impoverished and oppressed the millions of land-less peasants who have always been forced to work the land for others." He added, "the landlord is no longer going to eat from your poverty."[1] While these words seemed directed at the backward Andean haciendas, Velasco first expropriated the modern coastal plantations. This was a blow directed at Peru's oligarchy and an important segment of foreign capital. When agrarian reform reached the Andes several months later, the emphasis was on ending the backward system of land tenure and social domination. The challenge in the Andes was not simply redistribution of land; in contrast to the modern, productive coastal enterprises, land in the Andes would need major invest-ment to afford even a modest standard of living for its inhabitants.

In both regions, the regime placed reformed agricultural property under cooperative ownership rather than individual plots or state farms. On the expropriated coastal plantations, particularly those with industrial components such as rum production or paper manufacturing from sugar cane, conflict ensued along several axes: resident versus non-resident workers; skilled versus unskilled workers; and workers versus professionals such as agronomists, accountants, and chemists. In the Andes, resident workers on expropriated haciendas were challenged by neighboring ayllus, many of which were overpopulated and/or had long-standing claims against the haciendas for illegally appropriating their land. The many landless peasants also pressed claims. The competing claims to land unleashed waves of mobilization that led to an extension of the agrarian reform beyond the government's blueprint.

By the end of Velasco's regime in 1975, both the large, privately owned coastal plantation and the traditional Andean hacienda had virtually disappeared, and between 25 and 40 percent of the rural population had received land, primarily in cooperatives; much of the remaining Andean land was held by ayllus. Population pressures, shortages of usable land in parts of the Andes, and lagging technical and financial assistance to the new cooperatives limited the government's ability to satisfy the manifest land hunger, one unfortunate result of which was the *Sendero Luminoso*, or Shining Path, a Maoist guerrilla movement that wracked the country from 1980 to 1992, remnants of which survive today in the Peruvian Amazon. Despite the evident shortcomings of the agrarian reform, the military government ended a backward and exploitive land tenure system in the Andes and delivered a blow to the oligarchy by eliminating the private coastal plantations.

The General Law of Industries, announced in July 1970, launched reform of the industrial sector. Industrial firms with a minimum of six employees or an annual income of approximately U.S. $25,000 were required to establish a *comunidad industrial*, or industrial community consisting of all employees, who were to receive 15 percent of the companies' income each year in the form of shares until reaching 50 percent ownership of the firms. The industrial community was designed to increase productivity by tying worker income to company profits while dampening class conflict and weaning workers away from unions. As stated in the law's preamble: "Capitalist exploitation will cease. . . . Class struggle will be a thing of the past."[2] Implementation of the law faced obstacles in owners' hiding profits and otherwise resisting workers' inclusion, so that the goal of 50 percent worker ownership was rarely realized. As of September 1974 there were 3,446 registered communities with some 200,000 worker-owners. Similar communities were established in mining, telecommunications, and other economic sectors.

The most comprehensive formulation of the revolutionary government's vision of worker ownership and self-management was the Social Property

Law of May 1974. Reflecting the influence of Christian Democratic communitarianism and the Yugoslav practice of worker self-management, the Social Property Law established the basis for the intended future primary sector of the economy. The social property sector would consist of worker-managed firms in any economic enterprise, the ownership of which would reside in the entire social property sector. Growth of the sector would be financed by diversion of part of the income of each firm into a fund for creating new enterprises, all overseen by a government-appointed council. Along with the social property sector would be the state-owned mining, petroleum, and other basic industries; the industrial communities; and the private sector of small businesses. This complex blueprint for the economy did not have time to develop before the regime's end.

The Velasco government carried out its far-reaching transformation of the country with a minimum of repression—particularly by comparison with contemporaneous military regimes that ruled through state terrorism. It marginalized or dismantled institutions that openly opposed it, including the National Agrarian Society, a large landowner group, and some political parties and labor unions, but normally without persecuting members. But despite the advances made for workers and peasants and the light hand of military rule, the government was unable to achieve broad political support. In 1971 it established an agency tasked with mobilizing popular support, but the effort bore little fruit.

The nationalistic military government focused on reducing Peru's traditional dependence on and subservience to the United States, resulting in conflict with Washington. Velasco established diplomatic relations with the USSR and Communist China, and, flaunting an OAS ban on members establishing relations with Castro's regime, with Cuba. It also joined the Nonaligned Movement, a group of countries that distanced themselves from both the United States and the USSR. Peru's claim of a two hundred nautical mile exclusive fishing zone resulted in several U.S. commercial fishing boats being seized. Velasco refused to compensate the expropriated IPC, claiming the corporation owed more in back taxes than its assets were worth. In building the cooperative and state sectors, the government expropriated a range of other U.S. holdings. Most troubling to Washington was Peru's trade agreement with the USSR that involved major supplies of weaponry, including MiG fighter planes; this gave the Soviets their second military presence in Latin America, after Cuba. The United States ended military aid, and Peru expelled the U.S. military mission. Assessing his nationalistic policies, Velasco said: "Peru was no longer a subjugated country [*un país vendido*], a nation that had to kneel down."[3]

This series of provocations, combined with the military's socioeconomic revolution, would normally have provoked forceful U.S. intervention, as had happened often during the Cold War and would occur again in the other countries undergoing democratization, Chile and Nicaragua. The Peruvian situation was different: The revolutionaries wore military uniforms. As a result, the U.S. offensive was a quiet one, primarily a series of economic pressures against the regime. By 1974, economic problems forced the adoption of unpopular austerity measures, and public discontent mounted as General Velasco suffered serious health problems. The more conservative wing of the military asserted itself and overthrew Velasco in August 1975. The revolutionary military's complex and idealistic vision of Peru's future socioeconomic democracy—a country neither communist nor capitalist with broad inclusion—did not survive the 1975 regime change. Yet in seven years, the Velasco government led one of Latin America's most ambitious attempts to address underdevelopment and social injustice.

CHILE: REVOLUTION BY THE BALLOT BOX

Like the Peruvian military government, the administration of Salvador Allende (1970–1973), a medical doctor and a longtime leader of the Socialist Party, focused on socioeconomic democratization. In contrast to neighboring Peru, the Chilean revolution unfolded within the framework of a consolidated political democracy. Along with Uruguay and Costa Rica, Chile boasted one of Latin America's longest and strongest traditions of political democracy. The oligarchy lost its monopoly of power in the 1920s, and by the late 1930s parties of the left, center, and right were fairly evenly represented in Congress. But beginning in the early 1960s, the impact of fidelismo upset that balance of power as pressure for change mounted.

The presidency of Christian Democrat Eduardo Frei (1964–1970) brought advances in democracy, both political and socioeconomic (chapter 5), along with a realignment of political forces. The 1965 Congressional elections confirmed the rapid leftward movement of the country's political landscape and landowners' loss of their traditional control of their workers' votes: The right-wing Liberal and Conservative parties together won only 7 of 45 seats in the Senate and merely 9 of 147 in the Chamber of Deputies. With a negligible presence in Congress and reformist Frei in the presidency, the power of the Chilean right had virtually evaporated. Meanwhile the left became more radical. An anti-system party that embraced violence for taking power, the Movement of the Revolutionary Left (MIR), was founded by university students in Concepción in 1966. The following year the Socialist Party, historically a broad-based reformist party, declared itself Marxist-Leninist and, like the MIR, accepted the validity of revolutionary violence in pursuit of power.

Even before Allende's election, the institutions of political democracy faced unprecedented challenges. Chile was primed for revolution.

In reaction to Frei's reforms, particularly his agrarian reform that stripped many elite families of their treasured rural estates, the right-wing Conservative and Liberal parties recouped much of the loss they suffered in the 1965 election in the 1969 congressional election. Buoyed by this rebound, they coalesced into the new National Party (PN) and selected former president Jorge Alessandri (1958–1964) as its candidate for the September 1970 presidential election. The left, a coalition of the Socialist and Communist Parties and four small non-Marxist parties, nominated Salvador Allende for his fourth presidential bid under the banner of Unidad Popular (People's Unity, UP). The PDC nominated Radomiro Tomic. With Tomic placing third, Allende narrowly defeated Alessandri, 36.5 to 35.2 percent. The stock market fell by half overnight. An elderly Alessandri supporter interviewed for international television said resignedly, "One must know how to lose."[4] Fear and resignation marked the right's initial response to Allende's victory. That would soon change.

A traditional socialist, Allende believed that socioeconomic democracy could be achieved only through state ownership of the economy. His platform called for acceleration of agrarian reform, expropriation of private-owned industry and business, and income redistribution in order to move the country as quickly as possible toward socialism within the framework Chile's democratic political institutions. Prior to Allende, transitions from capitalism to socialism had occurred in one of two ways: revolutionary insurrection, as in Russia, China, and Cuba or conquest, as was the case of the Eastern European countries that fell under Soviet control following World War II. As a result, the world's eyes were on the Chilean experiment of establishing socialism within a political democracy, which raised the critical question: "Is there a peaceful road to socialism?"

As it did in 1964, the U.S. government invested heavily to prevent Allende's election in 1970. Having failed in that, it focused on the two-month period between the election and Allende's scheduled November inauguration. President Richard Nixon exhorted the CIA to "leave no stone unturned" to prevent his taking office.[5] He and his national security advisor, Henry Kissinger, immediately launched a two-track strategy to stop Allende.

Track 1 involved Congress. The Chilean constitution required Congress to elect the president when no candidate received a majority of the vote—a normal occurrence in Chile's multiparty elections. This was traditionally a formality, as Congress had never failed to elect the candidate who received the plurality of the popular vote. Track 1 aimed to get Congress, where Allende partisans were in the minority, to elect second-place finisher Alessandri, who would resign following his inauguration to permit Frei, who was barred from succeeding himself, to run for a second term. Frei and the Christian Democrats, who would have benefited from the scheme, rejected the proposition, leading to Track 2—a military coup. Given the Chilean military's record of distancing itself from overt political involvement, this too failed and Salvador Allende was inaugurated on November 3, 1970. Kissinger then warned that "the election of Allende as President of Chile poses for us one of the most serious challenges ever faced in this hemisphere."[6] U.S. intervention loomed over Allende from the beginning of the election campaign throughout his tenure as president.

Allende's ambitious agenda faced daunting obstacles: an opposition majority in Congress and a judiciary steeped in conservative values. Nonetheless Allende's first year in office was, as he labeled it, "a revolution *a la chilena* with red wine and *empanadas*" (meat and onion pies)—the food and drink consumed by the *pueblo* on festive occasions.[7] His populist measures put money in the pockets of the working and the middle classes. He nationalized the remaining U.S.-owned copper mines without compensation and accelerated the agrarian reform begun by Frei. Expansion of state ownership of the economy proceeded quickly, as nervous foreign and domestic owners accepted low buyout offers and Allende used an obscure law from the 1932 Socialist Republic to expropriate firms that failed to meet rigid production criteria. Extensive expropriations in banking, communications, insurance, transportation, and manufacturing, combined with the copper nationalization, gave the state control of critical sectors of the economy within the UP's first year. Allende also reestablished diplomatic relations with Cuba, in defiance of the OAS prohibition.

The second year was much less festive for Allende and the UP. Expropriations and populist programs nearly depleted Chile's hard currency reserves, and the PN and PDC formalized an alliance that opposed the government's every initiative. The Nixon administration initiated a credit boycott and the CIA was funneling millions of dollars to opposition parties and media. Chile's Congress rejected Allende's budgets and began impeaching his cabinet ministers. The country's chronic inflation accelerated, and a three-week visit by Fidel Castro alarmed the opposition. The result was constant confrontation and growing polarization.

Stoking the polarization was a growing mass mobilization for accelerating reform. In rural areas, hacienda workers, often supported by the MIR and UP parties, occupied the estates they worked rather than waiting for a legal expropriation to give them the land. Impatient urban workers likewise seized factories and businesses that had not been expropriated. This breakdown of order posed a difficult dilemma for the government. The president was responsible for upholding the law, which protected private property barring a valid expropriation order, but the backbone of Allende's support was

Figure 6.1 Salvador Allende wearing the Chilean presidential sash

the working class, and he was understandably reluctant to use force against it. Government response reflected Allende's ambivalence: some properties remained under worker control, while others were returned to their owners.

In October 1972, Chile's economic elites declared war on Allende. The economic associations representing large mining, industrial, agricultural, and commercial interests, which had historically acted as pressure groups in the political arena, dramatically raised the pressure on Allende and his socioeconomic program. In response to Frei's reforms and the collapse of right-wing power in the 1965 congressional election, leaders of the economic associations had determined to fill the void of conservative political power. They began recruiting smaller-scale capitalists into their organizations, thereby inflating their membership and hence their leverage while keeping control in the hands of the large-scale capitalists. A government proposal to nationalize the trucking industry prompted the associations, known as *gremios* (guilds), to action. They joined striking truck owners in a mass movement similar to a workers' general strike. The "bosses' strike," clandestinely subsidized by the CIA, virtually shut down the economy, creating shortages of food and other essentials throughout the country. Women in upper-class neighborhoods, blaming the government for the crisis, protested with "marches of the empty pots." After a month, the government agreed to appoint three military officers to Allende's cabinet, ending the strike.

Both the right-wing opposition and the UP hoped to resolve the growing polarization and violence in the March 1973 congressional election. The PN-PDC coalition sought to reach the two-thirds necessary to remove

Allende from office, while the UP hoped to gain the majority and protect the president. The election resolved nothing: Opposition candidates received 56 percent of the vote to the UP's 44 percent of the vote—a significant improvement over Allende's 36.5 percent in the presidential election but not enough to end the deadlock in Congress. Having failed to unseat Allende at the ballot box, the opposition shifted tactics to end Allende's six-year term prematurely.

In his annual address to Congress in May 1973, the president touted the progress made on his goal of moving the country toward socialism: two hundred of the country's largest enterprises nationalized, accounting for a third of national production; government ownership of 90 percent of banking and a third of wholesale distribution; and 3,570 large rural properties expropriated, leaving few that exceeded the legal size limit. But economic conditions continued to deteriorate. Runaway inflation, mounting fiscal deficits, and shortages of essential goods drove the economy toward collapse. Rising street violence, assassinations, sabotage, and the formation of a right-wing militia signaled further trouble for the administration. In June, a small military revolt, although easily suppressed by the military command, put citizens on notice that the military's tradition of non-intervention hung in the balance. The sense of crisis was palpable.

The gremios launched a second bosses' strike on July 25, 1973, again with covert U.S. support. Their intention was clear: destabilize the country to force the military to take power and restore order. By August army commander General Carlos Prats, a firm constitutionalist and upholder of the non-interventionist tradition, was the sole obstacle to a coup. Increasingly isolated within the military establishment, he resigned on August 22 after officers' wives threw chicken feed on his lawn. The same day, the Chamber of Deputies of Congress passed a resolution encouraging military action. Allende replaced Prats with General Augusto Pinochet, who dutifully swore to uphold the constitution. As the downward spiral continued, Allende decided on September 10 to hold a plebiscite on whether he should continue as president or resign his office. But before he could announce his decision, the army under Pinochet, along with the air force, navy, and national police, rose in a bloody coup that cut short the Chilean experiment and offered a resounding "NO" to the question, "Is there a peaceful road to socialism?" Chilean political democracy and the socioeconomic democracy under construction succumbed to a brutal military dictatorship on September 11, 1973—known by some as the "first 9-11."

NICARAGUA: REVOLUTION BY INSURRECTION

The Sandinista National Liberation Front (Sandinistas, FSLN) in Nicaragua faced a double challenge: It embraced both forms of democratization in a country that had experience with neither. Nicaragua had unstable elite governments in the nineteenth century, when military coups were the standard form of regime change. This was followed by a U.S. occupation from 1909 to 1933, with two brief interruptions. The U.S.-created National Guard, meant to be apolitical, soon became the instrument of the first Somoza dictator, Anastasio Somoza García. The forty-three-year Somoza family regime, as many dictatorships did, featured elections, a Congress, and a court system, but these were trappings of democracy without substance (chapter 3). The drivers of democracy—labor unions, progressive parties, and university student federations—were either absent or tightly controlled by the Somozas. The task confronting the Sandinistas was similar to that faced earlier by Juan Bosch in the Dominican Republic (chapter 5); the main difference was that Bosch had to deal with Trujillo's intact military, whereas upon defeating Anastasio "Tachito" Somoza Debayle in July 1979, the Sandinistas abolished his National Guard and replaced it with the Sandinista People's Army.

The timing of the Sandinistas' victory was notable. By 1979 both the Peruvian and Chilean revolutions had ended. In response to the wave of revolutionary mobilization set off by the Cuban Revolution, a powerful wave of reaction, abetted by the United States, had swept Latin America. State terrorist regimes (chapter 7) were firmly established in Brazil, Uruguay, Chile, and Argentina and were in formation in Guatemala and El Salvador. Only five Latin American countries were not ruled by military governments when the Sandinistas took power. In view of this dystopian panorama, the installation of a government committed to democratization was an anomaly—an anomaly that soon drew the fury of the hemispheric hegemon.

The FSLN was established by three friends in 1961, following a visit to Cuba by one of them, Carlos Fonseca Amador, a former member of Nicaragua's illegal Communist Party. Named for Augusto C. Sandino, the hero of the resistance to the U.S. Marines' occupation of Nicaragua in the 1920s and early 1930s, the FSLN was fidelista, Marxist, and nationalist. Inspired by Castro's guerrilla war and Che Guevara's book *Guerrilla Warfare*, the Sandinistas adopted rural guerrilla warfare as their modus operandi. Defeated twice in skirmishes by Somoza's National Guard, the Sandinistas learned the hard way what Che Guevara omitted in his story of the Cuban insurrection: the importance of urban resistance. In contrast to Cuba, where a strong urban resistance kept Batista busy and allowed Castro to build up his guerrilla force, there was almost no active opposition in Managua or the other cities; this enabled the National Guard to focus on the FSLN. Rather than give up, the Sandinistas turned from the Guevara playbook, postponed fighting, and patiently built a network of peasant support—a task they referred to in borrowed Maoist terms as "gathering forces in silence." In his memoir of the struggle, Omar Cabezas wrote: "We were trying to awaken the *campesino* to his own dream."[8]

The Sandinistas' cause was aided by a 1972 earthquake that killed some ten thousand people and leveled much of Managua. The earthquake's aftermath exposed the Somoza regime's corruption and venality. Rather than tend to victims, the National Guard openly looted businesses and sold donated relief supplies. Tachito Somoza, the current dictator, added to his immense fortune with huge profits from reconstruction and land deals, one of which involved the purchase of a plot for $30,000 which he subsequently sold for $3 million in U.S. relief funds to his government's Urban Housing Institute; no housing was built on the land. These actions created for the first time an upper- and middle-class civic opposition, organized in 1974 as the Democratic Liberation Union (UDEL), led by newspaper publisher Pedro Joaquín Chamorro.

Following a long period of clandestine recruiting and organizing, the Sandinistas sprang into action in December 1974, again departing from the rural guerrilla script. They captured the guests at a Somoza cabinet minister's Christmas party and held them until the dictator paid a ransom, freed some prisoners, and required newspapers to publish an FSLN manifesto. While demonstrating the Sandinistas' strength and the regime's vulnerability, the Christmas raid also brought on heightened repression. Stymied by the regime's crackdown, the Sandinistas split into three factions, each following a different strategy: One continued the rural guerrilla approach; a second focused on organizing in the cities; and the third recruited more moderate, non-Marxist opponents of Somoza.

Somoza henchmen assassinated the popular UDEL leader Chamorro in January 1978. This action unleashed riots and uprisings across the country, which Somoza met with the full power of his National Guard: shelling of cities and towns, air strikes, and ground offensives killed thousands while creating legions of new enemies of the regime. Somoza was literally at war with his countrymen. At this point the FSLN factions reunited, recruited aggressively, and in May announced a "final offensive" which initially failed. As the regime teetered, U.S. President Jimmy Carter pressured Somoza to resign in order to find a pro-U.S. replacement, but Somoza refused. The FSLN regrouped, and as its fighters approached Managua, Tachito fled.[9] After eighteen years of struggle, the FSLN took the capital on July 19, 1979.

Somoza was gone, the National Guard was disbanded, and the FSLN was intact. With the popularity and prestige they gained from overthrowing the Somozas' dictatorship, a close U.S. ally, the Sandinistas were in a position

Figure 6.2 FSLN leader Daniel Ortega addressing students in Managua

similar to Castro's following Batista's defeat: They could take the country in almost any direction. Most observers anticipated that the FSLN would follow the Cuban blueprint of radical economic change, authoritarian governance, and a foreign policy aligned with the Soviet Union. Instead, the Sandinista revolution was moderate compared not only to Cuba but also to the thwarted Peruvian and Chilean revolutions.

Several factors account for the Sandinistas' moderation. One was timing: By 1979, there was growing skepticism within the socialist bloc about Soviet-style economics, leading to *perestroika*, or economic reforms in the USSR and its Eastern European allies. By the early 1980s, privatization of state-owned assets was beginning to occur in some Latin American countries as the doctrine of neoliberalism spread (chapter 8). Based on Cuba's anemic record of economic development following 1959, Castro reportedly advised the Sandinistas against expropriating the entire privately owned economy as he had done. The Sandinistas' moderation also reflected their recruitment of more pragmatic, less radical members as they broadened their coalition following 1974. Among these were several priests and lay persons inspired by liberation theology, a doctrine of solidarity with the poor and humble that gained followings in several Latin American countries in the 1970s. Finally, there was the practical matter of the United States' hard line against reform in Latin America. When Ronald Reagan assumed the presidency in January 1981, he viewed Nicaragua through Cold War lenses. The unrelenting pressure his administration would apply counseled moderation.

In pursuing political democratization, the Sandinistas proclaimed two central principles: pluralism and participatory democracy. These principles, along with the party's heterogeneity, moderated the power that the FSLN was capable of exercising and resulted in considerable flexibility. The first post-Somoza provisional government, the Governing Junta of National Reconstruction, reflected the commitment to pluralism: its five members included two from the moderate opposition, two from independent pro-Sandinista organizations, and Daniel Ortega of the FSLN's National

Directorate. The Governing Junta was advised by a second transitory political body, the Council of State, which was also broadly representative.

The FSLN formalized its governance in the November 1984 general election, which took place under open U.S. interference and international scrutiny. The Reagan administration declared in advance that the election would be rigged and pressured the right-wing opposition to boycott so that the elected government would be seen as illegitimate. Despite the boycott, three-fourths of registered voters participated in the election that international observers certified as fair. Daniel Ortega was elected president with 63 percent of the vote and the FSLN secured 61 of the 96 National Assembly seats. Three right-wing parties that participated won 29 seats, while three Marxist parties, including the Communist Party, won 6.

Following the election, political opposition to the FSLN continued to be vigorous and relatively free. Twenty-one political parties were registered in Nicaragua; a range of economic interest associations existed, headed by the Superior Council of Private Enterprise (COSEP); and opposition-controlled newspapers, magazines, and radio stations promoted alternative viewpoints. The pressure applied by opposition groups, combined with the Sandinistas' openness to compromise, resulted in policies that were often more pragmatic than dogmatic. Although the FSLN did not have a perfect record of safeguarding all rights of the opposition, the pluralist political system that developed was clearly at odds with Reagan's repeated assertions that Nicaragua's was a "communist totalitarian state."[10]

The second of the FSLN's guiding political principles was participatory democracy. This was exercised in large part within the party itself, through the mass organizations the Sandinistas had created to broaden the struggle against Somoza. These included women's, youth, labor, and farmers' organizations along with the Sandinista Defense Committees, which had security functions and served as neighborhood organizations with various tasks. One of the most important exercises in participatory democracy preceded the adoption of a new constitution in 1987. Prior to writing a draft document, the government held open community meetings (*cabildos abiertos*) throughout the country over nearly two years.

Along with constructing political democracy, the Sandinistas implemented their version of socioeconomic democracy. As it did in constructing the new political order, the FSLN used moderation in effecting economic and social change. From the outset, it broadcast its intention to preserve a significant part of the privately owned economy. The state sector expanded initially with the expropriation of Somoza family properties and those of Somoza collaborators in exile, which included extensive agricultural holdings, processing and manufacturing plants, urban real estate, construction firms, the national airline, and other properties. These properties accounted for approximately a quarter of the value of the national economy. Further nationalizations followed in the banking, insurance, mining, foreign trade, and other sectors, with the government taking the largest holdings and preserving small and medium private property. Through these measures the state sector grew from approximately 15 to 45 percent of the national economy—a normal share in Latin America prior to the onset of neoliberalism.

An examination of changes in agriculture, which employed around half of the country's economically active population, illustrates the Sandinistas' approach. Having nationalized Somoza's agricultural properties, the transitional government issued a conservative agrarian reform order in 1981 that targeted large inefficiently exploited and abandoned holdings and those leased or share-cropped, while guaranteeing the integrity of efficiently run properties of any size. As this failed to satisfy peasant demands for land, a second agrarian reform followed in 1985. This law liberalized the criteria for expropriations and de-emphasized state farms and cooperatives. As a result, by 1988 the state sector had shrunk from 20 to 13 percent of total agricultural land, large private owners held 12 percent, cooperatives held 15 percent, and small- and medium-sized farmers controlled 60 percent of all agricultural land. The power of one of the Sandinista mass organizations, the National Union of Farmers and Cattlemen (UNAG), with some 125,000 members, along with the shrinkage of the formerly Somoza-owned state sector, reflected the dominant position of peasants and small entrepreneurs in a primarily capitalist agricultural economy—a clear contrast with Cuba.

The FSLN government's commitment to socioeconomic democracy involved redistributing income, goods, and services by two methods. One was the empowerment of citizens to advocate for their needs through membership in the Sandinista mass organizations, which exerted pressure on policy formation on their members' behalf. The more direct method of fostering social change was government investment in social services and subsidies. The government made good progress in redistributing societal goods through food subsidies, rent controls, and increased expenditure on education, housing, public health, and a social security system. Free elementary schools and clinics proliferated throughout previously neglected rural areas.

Nicaragua's 1987 constitution reflected the construction of democracy that had been underway since the 1979 victory. It defined the country as a social democracy featuring an elected government, political pluralism, nonalignment in foreign affairs, and a mixed state-private economy. In contrast to Cuba's 1976 constitution, the Nicaraguan constitution enumerated inviolable civil and individual liberties as well as socioeconomic rights. The new constitution embodied the goals of the Nicaraguan revolution and made it clear that the country had chosen a new path to the future—a much more moderate one than Fidel Castro followed in Cuba.

The Sandinistas' moderation failed to shield Nicaragua from the colossus of the north. To Reagan, Nicaragua's establishment of diplomatic relations with Cuba and the Soviet Union—consistent with its stated policy of non-alignment in foreign affairs—was proof that the country was communist and a tool of Moscow and Havana. He stopped all aid, pressured international agencies to cut off loans to Nicaragua, and ordered the mining of Nicaragua's harbors. He began financing the counterrevolutionaries, or "Contras," many of whom were former members of the Somozas' National Guard, to serve as U.S. proxies in an undeclared war against a country with which the United States continued to have diplomatic relations. He praised the Contras, whom he financed illegally through the bizarre Iran-Contra affair after Congress cut funding for his war, as "freedom fighters" and "the moral equivalent of our Founding Fathers."[11]

By 1982, the Contras were attacking from their refuge in neighboring Honduras, and in the following years targeted not only people but also the new rural clinics and schools that were hallmarks of the revolution. The U.S. conducted over forty military exercises in Honduras whose purpose, in addition to intimidating the Sandinista government, was to take massive amounts of weaponry and supplies that the departing troops left behind for the Contras. By 1987 the Contras had some fifteen thousand fighters inside Nicaragua, forcing the government to beef up its army to sixty thousand troops and create a large militia. These measures were effective in containing the invasion, but they also drained the treasury and forced the government to divert resources from its socioeconomic projects. The war produced mounting casualties, forcing the government to institute a draft and leaving many families grieving and war weary.

Reagan's proxy war was effective in eroding the majority of Nicaraguans' enthusiasm for the revolution. To further undermine the government, the U.S. openly invested at least $7.7 million from the congressionally funded National Endowment for Democracy and covertly spent another $5 million to support Daniel Ortega's conservative opponent in the 1990 presidential election, Violeta Chamorro. The U.S. investment of $8.50 per voter paid off: Chamorro, the widow of the publisher murdered by Somoza in 1978, handily defeated Ortega, 55 to 41 percent. Just as surely as if the CIA had orchestrated a coup or the Marines had invaded again, U.S. economic, military, and electoral intervention ended an experiment in political and socioeconomic democratization which, ironically, had followed the script of the long-abandoned Alliance for Progress.

Despite unwavering U.S. opposition to revolution and a rising tide of reaction throughout Latin America, three revolutionary governments came to power between 1968 and 1979. The revolutionary regimes in Peru, Chile, and

Nicaragua were unable to consolidate power and succumbed to internal opposition and overt or covert U.S. intervention. What began as promising progress in democratization in the three countries ended with the bitter realization that revolution could not succeed in Latin America during the Cold War.

SUGGESTIONS FOR FURTHER READING

Aguirre, Carlos and Paulo Drinot, eds. *The Peculiar Revolution: Rethinking the Peruvian Experiment under Military Rule.* Austin: University of Texas Press, 2017.

Berryman, Phillip. *Liberation Theology: Essential Facts about the Revolutionary Movement in Latin America—and Beyond.* Philadelphia: Temple University Press, 1987.

Bitar, Sergio. *Chile: Experiment in Democracy.* Translated by Sam Sherman. Philadelphia: Institute for the Study of Human Issues, 1986.

Burns, E. Bradford. *At War in Nicaragua: The Reagan Doctrine and the Politics of Nostalgia.* New York: Harper and Row, 1987.

Cabezas, Omar. *Fire from the Mountain: The Making of a Sandinista.* Translated by Kathleen Weaver. New York: New American Library, 1985.

Grandin, Greg and Gilbert M. Joseph, eds. *Century of Revolution: Insurgent and Counterinsurgent Violence during Latin America's Long Cold War.* Durham: Duke University Press, 2010.

Gustafson, Kristian. *Hostile Intent: U.S. Covert Operations in Chile, 1964–1974.* Washington, DC: Potomac Books, 2007.

Harmer, Tanya. *Allende's Chile and the Inter-American Cold War.* Chapel Hill: University of North Carolina Press, 2011.

Haslam, Jonathan. *The Nixon Administration and the Death of Allende's Chile: A Case of Assisted Suicide.* London: Verso, 2005.

McClintock, Cynthia and Abraham F. Lowenthal, eds. *The Peruvian Experiment Reconsidered.* Princeton: Princeton University Press, 1983.

Morley, Morris H. *Washington, Somoza, and the Sandinistas: State and Regime in U.S. Policy Toward Nicaragua, 1969–1981.* Cambridge, UK: Cambridge University Press, 1994.

Philip, George. *The Rise and Fall of the Peruvian Military Radicals, 1968–1976.* London: Athlone Press, 1978.

Prevost, Gary and Harry E. Vanden, eds. *The Undermining of the Sandinista Revolution.* New York: St. Martin's Press, 1997.

Ramírez, Sergio. *Adios Muchachos: A Memoir of the Sandinista Revolution.* Trans. Stacey Alba D. Skar. Durham: Duke University Press, 2012.

Sigmund, Paul E. *The Overthrow of Allende and the Politics of Chile, 1964–1976.* Pittsburgh: University of Pittsburgh Press, 1977.

Valenzuela, Arturo. *The Breakdown of Democratic Regimes: Chile.* Baltimore: Johns Hopkins University Press, 1978.

Vanden, Harry E. and Gary Prevost. *Democracy and Socialism in the Sandinista Revolution*. Boulder: Lynne Rienner, 1993.
Walker, Thomas W., ed. *Revolution and Counterrevolution in Nicaragua, 1979–1990*. Boulder: Westview, 1991.

NOTES

1. Juan Velasco Alvarado, "The Master Will No Longer Feed Off Your Poverty," in Orin Starn, Carlos Iván Degregori, and Robin Kirk, eds., *The Peru Reader: History, Culture, Politics* (Durham: Duke University Press, 1995), 279–80; and Enrique Mayer, *Ugly Stories of the Peruvian Agrarian Reform* (Durham: Duke University Press, 2009), 20.

2. Dirk Kruijht, *Revolution by Decree: Peru, 1968–1975* (Amsterdam: Thela Publishers, 1994), 73.

3. Lourdes Hurtado, "Velasco, Nationalist Rhetoric, and Military Culture in Cold War Peru," in Carlos Aguirre and Paulo Drinot, eds., *The Peculiar Revolution: Rethinking the Peruvian Experiment under Military Rule* (Austin: University of Texas Press, 2017), 181.

4. The author viewed the telecast on September 5, 1970.

5. Michael Mann, *The Sources of Social Power: volume 4, Globalizations, 1945–2011* (Cambridge: Cambridge University Press, 2012), 112.

6. Kristian Gustafson, *Hostile Intent: U.S. Covert Operations in Chile, 1964–1974* (Washington, DC: Potomac Books, 2007), 139.

7. Paul E. Sigmund, *The Overthrow of Allende and the Politics of Chile, 1964–1976* (Pittsburgh: University of Pittsburgh Press, 1977), 131.

8. Omar Cabezas, *Fire from the Mountain: The Making of a Sandinista*, trans. Kathleen Weaver (New York: Crown, 1985), 210.

9. After a brief stay in Miami, Somoza settled in Asunción, Paraguay, under the protection of dictator Alfredo Stroessner. An FSLN team assassinated him in September 1980.

10. E. Bradford Burns, *At War with Nicaragua: The Reagan Doctrine and the Politics of Nostalgia* (New York: Harper & Row, 1987), 35.

11. Burns, *At War*, 35.

Chapter 7

The Eclipse of Democracy, 1969–1990

The high point of political democracy in Latin America, prior to the contemporary period, was the late 1950s–early 1960s. With the fallout of the Cuban Revolution, political democracy began to wane. As the impact of fidelismo continued and spread, political democracy became increasingly rare as the military took power in order to fight the influence of pro-Castro groups. With the collapse of political democracy, the drivers of socioeconomic democratization were suppressed, and with that many of the advances made over long years of struggle were rolled back.

STATE TERRORISM

The rise of fidelismo following Fidel Castro's 1959 accession to power led to a revision of Cold War thinking about hemispheric security. The threat was no longer only communists, but also radicalized groups seeking to replicate the Cuban Revolution in their countries. The prevalence of political democracies in Latin America during the early 1960s allowed fidelista groups to form and, in some cases, become strong enough to destabilize governments. The initial response to that threat was to replace democracies with military dictatorships, as occurred with U.S. support in Guatemala, Ecuador, the Dominican Republic, and Honduras in 1963 and Brazil in 1964 (chapter 5).

While this solution stopped the immediate threat of the spread of Cuban-style regimes, revolutionary activity continued to intensify. Che Guevara opened a guerrilla front in Bolivia in 1967 that was designed to train guerrilla fighters to "liberate" several South American countries. Although Che's capture and execution ended that threat after a few months, a new, more effective form of insurrection developed in South America in the 1960s, first in Uruguay, then in Brazil and Argentina: urban guerrilla warfare. Revolutionary governments came to power in Peru, Chile, and Nicaragua between 1968 and 1979; all established diplomatic relations with Cuba and, by their examples, provided inspiration for revolutionaries throughout the region (chapter 6). The *Sendero Luminoso*, or Shining Path, launched a powerful rural guerrilla movement in Peru in 1980 that eventually threatened to topple the government. This never-ending assault on the status quo, which many among the elites considered an existential threat, made a longer term, preferably a permanent solution to the threat of revolution attractive to Latin American military leaders and to the U.S. government.

They found this solution in National Security Doctrine (NSD). Along with counterinsurgency warfare, NSD was taught at the U.S. School of the Americas in the Panama Canal Zone and in dozens of service schools at military installations in the United States, which hosted thousands of Latin American officers over the years. The purpose of NSD was to insulate countries against revolution. This required rapid economic development which, over the long run, would presumably reduce or eliminate poverty. In the short term, national security involved the elimination of Marxists and others considered "subversive," by whatever means necessary—a task that could only be accomplished under military rule. The perceived threat of revolution was so widespread that only five countries avoided military control during the 1970s and 1980s: Mexico, Costa Rica, the Dominican Republic, Venezuela, and Colombia.

In several countries, the armed forces seized power, curtailed civil liberties, and repressed the left. In some cases, the armed forces and civilian collaborators determined that it was necessary to completely eliminate political democracy because civil and political rights, elections, and civilian authority allowed the subversives to exist and even thrive. Once democracy was replaced by military regimes committed to eliminating the threat of revolution, the new masters could forcibly reeducate the population to root out the Marxist concept of class conflict and replace it with ideas of class harmony, respect for authority, and nationalism. Only then would the *patria* be safe from Cuban-style revolution.

The methodology adopted by the regimes that terminated democracy was state terrorism. Among the many definitions of terrorism, that offered by Frederick H. Gareau is among the more inclusive:

> Terrorism consists of deliberate acts of a physical and/or psychological nature perpetrated on select groups of victims. Its intent is to mold the thinking and behavior not only of these targeted groups, but more importantly, of larger sectors of society that identify [with] or share the view and aspirations of the targeted groups or who might easily be led to do so. The intent of the terrorists

is to intimidate or coerce both groups by causing them intense fear, anxiety, apprehension, panic, dread, and/or horror.[1]

This definition applies to terrorism against the state, as practiced in the past by the Irish Republican Army (IRA), the Basque separatist Euskadi Ta Askatasuna (ETA), and more recently by Al-Qaeda and the Islamic State in Iraq and Syria (ISIS). It applies equally to terrorism by the state. It is much more difficult to defend against terrorism by the state than against terrorism directed at the state, as the following case studies demonstrate.

State terrorism was adopted in half of Latin America's countries that accounted for well over half of the region's population. Paraguay under the long rule of General Alfredo Stroessner (1954–1989), Bolivia under General Hugo Banzer (1971–1978), Peru under President Alberto Fujimori (1989–1999), and Haiti under Raoul Cedras (1991–1994) are cases of state terrorism worth studying. But in the interest of effectively exposing the workings of state terrorism, we will examine six cases where state terrorism was long-lasting, highly institutionalized, deadly, and U.S.-supported, except under President Jimmy Carter (1977–1981).

The restriction or elimination of political democracy under military rule had serious implications for Latin America's working and middle classes, the growing underclass of marginalized urban slum dwellers, and in some cases, rural workers. For to secure their control, the armed forces needed to suppress the institutions and individuals who advocated for socioeconomic democracy: left and moderate political parties, labor unions, university student organizations, and progressive clergy, which were the principal driving forces of social progress. Thus along with the loss of political democracy, socioeconomic democracy in Latin America suffered crippling setbacks during the period of severe repression and state terrorism.

BRAZIL

A new type of military government began to develop in Latin America with the March 1964 military coup in Brazil which ended the formal but not inclusive political democracy that had existed since the end of Vargas's Estado Nôvo in 1945. Initially, the military opted to marginalize the more radical left and work with the remaining civilian politicians in a hybrid form of governance, with a military president, civilian-controlled Congress, and civilian state governorships with restricted powers. But facing unexpected resistance, the military soon tightened its control over what it began calling "manipulated democracy." By 1968, student unrest and illegal worker strikes led the military to suspend its own 1967 constitution. When an urban guerrilla movement appeared the following year, the military dictatorship responded even more forcefully, shutting down the remaining civilian governmental institutions and ending any pretense of democracy by 1969.

In addition to targeting the urban guerrillas, the military focused its repression on potential as well as actual supporters of the guerrillas—in other words, on those considered "subversives." Arbitrary arrest, torture, and murder became the standard method of fighting subversion. Those arrested faced military rather than civilian justice: A military officer later admitted, "Torture was an essential part of the military justice system."[2] Government-sanctioned private death squads supplemented the soldiers and police. Because the small urban guerrilla movement was easily defeated, the dictatorship did not use its powers of repression to the full extent possible: A 2014 Truth Commission report listed 434 persons murdered or disappeared by the regime. In routinizing severe repression against broadly defined enemies of the state, the Brazilian military was the first in Latin America to embrace and systematically apply state terrorism.

URUGUAY

In contrast to Brazil, Uruguay had a long tradition of both political and socioeconomic democracy (chapter 2). Yet that tradition did not spare the small country from state terrorism. A crisis of Uruguay's agriculturally based export economy that began in the 1950s, along with the impact of fidelismo, set the stage for Latin America's pioneering urban guerrillas. Founded in 1963, the Tupamaros had become sufficiently powerful by 1970 to threaten the government's survival. Nonetheless, an intense counterinsurgency campaign under a "state of internal war" essentially defeated the Tupamaros by 1972. That did not satisfy the military establishment which, guided by NSD, then turned to rooting out what the officers believed to be the underlying cause of the guerrilla war: the presence of Marxists and subversives and the political system that allowed them to exist.

The state terrorist regime began with a "soft" coup in February 1973. Four months later Congress was dissolved and the public administration was brought under military control. The military followed the Brazilian pattern of gradually eliminating all substantive civilian roles in government. As in Brazil, left parties, labor unions, and universities were the military's prime targets. The regime carried out arbitrary arrests, torture, and murder of dissidents and suspects and drove tens of thousands into exile. An officer reported, "everyone arrested in Uruguay is tortured. There is no one who is not tortured."[3] Before retreating to the barracks, the military had killed or disappeared over 250 individuals. While torture was ubiquitous, the toll in murder and disappearance in Uruguay, as in Brazil, was low in comparison with the harvest of state terrorism in Chile, Argentina, El Salvador, and Guatemala.

CHILE

Unlike most of their Latin American counterparts, the Chilean armed forces had a history of respect for constitutional order. But with the country's extreme polarization, the rising violence, and the breakdown of order, few Chileans were surprised by the September 11, 1973, coup led by army General Augusto C. Pinochet. They expected a standard Latin American coup in which, with little violence, deposed leaders are exiled, the military holds power for a year or two, and elections return civilians to power. Thus the extreme violence and brutality of the coup were shocking.

When President Allende refused to leave the historic La Moneda presidential palace, the air force bombed and set it on fire. Allende shot himself to death during the attack. UP officials and collaborators, whose political affiliations had been perfectly legal until the morning of September 11, became ex post facto criminals and enemies of the new state. The commanders ordered hundreds of persons associated with the UP government to report to the new authorities; having committed no crime, they believed, some turned in themselves to clear their names and were never seen again. Thousands of real and suspected Allende supporters were rounded up and detained in Santiago's National Stadium, other soccer stadiums, military installations, police stations, and other makeshift prisons where they were tortured and hundreds were killed. Photos depicting long lines of prisoners chained together, bodies lying in streets and floating in rivers, and soldiers burning books circulated internationally. Improvised military tribunals sentenced scores of leftists to death. Expropriated landowners exacted retribution on agrarian reform beneficiaries in parts of the countryside. In the regime's first four months, over 1,800 persons were killed or disappeared by government agents or by vigilantes, and thousands took refuge in embassies or escaped across borders on their way to a lengthy exile.

Following the NSD prescription, the Chilean military went beyond dealing with the immediate situation that motivated its seizure of power—the disintegration of democracy under assault by the Chilean elites and the United States. Within hours of taking power, the military junta, comprised of the commanders of the national police, navy, and air force and led by Pinochet of the army, decreed a state of siege befitting "a state or time of war" and vowed to extirpate the "Marxist cancer."[4] To find a final solution to the threats of communism and "subversion," the regime developed powerful and sophisticated tools for physically eradicating the left, eliminating all traces of

Figure 7.1 Tanks in front of La Moneda presidential palace during the 1973 military coup
Getty Images/Horacio Villalobos/Contributor

Marxism, and destroying the democracy that had allowed revolutionary ideas and groups to operate and flourish. In this endeavor, the regime framed itself as a heroic combatant in defense of the traditional values of family, religion, and fatherland against godless Marxists and subversives, and glorified its actions as saving the patria.

The UN and dozens of governments condemned the coup and its extreme violence, while the Nixon administration promptly extended diplomatic recognition to the military regime. Nixon's action had ramifications far beyond Chile's borders. The message from Washington was that anti-communist regimes employing repression, even state terrorism, could rely on U.S. support. It was a green light to Latin America's right wing and armed forces to use any means to destroy political democracy, eradicate the left, and in so doing, erase the socioeconomic gains that workers and, in some countries, campesinos had made through prolonged struggles.

The junta consolidated power by shuttering Congress, dissolving the political parties, imposing strict censorship, and removing university and labor union leadership. It also purged the military ranks of officers considered insufficiently enthusiastic about the unfolding mission of cleansing Chile of Marxism and subversion. In an act that underscored Pinochet's repudiation of Chile's long democratic tradition and his determination to destroy it, he ordered the national voter registry to be burned.

The dictatorship's March 1974 "Declaration of Principles," which labeled the regime "anti-Marxist," revealed the military's design for a new Chile. The military would hold power indefinitely "because the task of reconstructing the country morally, institutionally, and materially requires profound and prolonged action." It would be "absolutely necessary to change the mentality of Chileans" by replacing Marxism and its credo of class struggle with the values of class harmony, obedience to authority, conservative Catholicism, and Chilean nationalism.[5]

After a few months Pinochet placed the "Chicago Boys," students of University of Chicago free market economist Milton Friedman, in charge of economic policy. The scheme involved replacing state direction of the economy, as developed in response to the Great Depression and deepened under Presidents Frei and Allende, with free market policies, or neoliberalism. Neoliberalism undermined the progress toward socioeconomic democracy that began in the 1920s and accelerated after 1964; it impoverished millions of Chileans and would have consequences well into the twenty-first century (chapter 8).

The Directorate of National Intelligence (DINA), led by Pinochet confidante General Manuel Contreras, was a secret police force comprised of military, police, and civilians whose task was to hunt down and eradicate the Chilean left. Pinochet's close relationship with Contreras and the DINA enabled him to consolidate his power and rise in only fifteen months from head of the junta to assume the title of president of the republic and dominate the four-man junta that governed from 1973 to 1990.

The DINA set up secret detention centers where leftists were tortured and often killed by specialized DINA operatives. Villa Grimaldi, a confiscated villa outside of Santiago, was one of the largest and most notorious of such facilities. Gladys Díaz, a Villa Grimaldi survivor, recalled her experience of torture: "Sometimes it's electricity, sometimes drugs . . . the submarine, when they stick your head in sewer water until you almost drown, they take you out, they stick you in again. . . . When there wasn't physical torture there was psychological torture. . . . They put on tapes of voices of children to make me think that my son had been captured."[6] The DINA's priority targets were the clandestine units of the MIR and the Communist and Socialist parties that had formed after the coup, following the murder or forced exile of most of their leadership. By 1976, the left underground was defeated and Pinochet's control over Chile was absolute.

Even before Pinochet achieved total control of Chile, he looked beyond the country's borders to extend his war on Marxism and democracy. In November 1975, DINA head Contreras hosted representatives of Uruguay, Argentina, Paraguay, and Bolivia at the "First Inter-American Conference on National Intelligence," where Operation Condor, a state-sponsored international terrorist network, was born. Contreras told his guests, "Subversion does not recognize borders or countries, and the infiltration permeates all levels of national life."[7] Operation Condor, named for Chile's national bird, soon expanded to include Brazil. It involved cooperation across borders to hunt, torture, and usually kill "subversives" who left their home country for shelter or exile, not only in one of the member countries but even in Europe and the United States.[8] The U.S intelligence agencies aided Operation Condor in various ways.

At the time of the coup, Chile had no human rights organizations to defend citizens against state terrorism and the consequences of Chicago School economics. The Catholic Church, in conjunction with other religious groups and international humanitarian agencies, improvised emergency programs to fight hunger as well as to support families of torture and murder victims. In 1976, the Archdiocese of Santiago established its Vicaría de la Solidaridad

Figure 7.2 General Augusto Pinochet following the overthrow of the Allende government
Getty Images/Staff

(Vicariate of Solidarity), the largest and most active of a dozen human rights organizations that functioned under extremely difficult circumstances. The Vicaría provided aid and solace to impoverished shantytown dwellers, victims of torture, and families of the murdered and disappeared. Despite its dedication, the human rights movement was unable to rein in the repression: Vicaría lawyers filed some nine thousand writs of habeas corpus with the courts to free arrested persons, but judges sympathetic to or intimidated by the regime rejected almost all of them. Following the dictatorship's end, these court filings would prove invaluable for bringing hundreds of former practitioners of state terrorism to justice.

Some two hundred thousand Chileans were forced into exile in countries throughout the world. Despite their dedicated efforts to generate support for restoring democracy, international opposition to the regime, primarily from Europe, was largely ineffectual. The 1976 election of U.S. President Jimmy Carter, who made human rights a centerpiece of his foreign policy, temporarily ended the unwavering U.S. support that Pinochet had enjoyed. However, by making superficial changes such as replacing the notorious DINA with a nearly identical secret police under a different leader and name, the dictator avoided serious conflict with the Carter administration.

In 1980, the general attempted to legitimize the dictatorship by endowing it with a constitution. The draft of his "Constitution of Liberty" was approved in a plebiscite conducted without an electoral registry, which he had burned, and without independent verification. The constitution legalized his dictatorial powers for eight more years and laid out a "protected democracy" to follow the dictatorship's eventual end. It called for a plebiscite after eight years to determine whether Pinochet, or another candidate chosen by the military junta, should receive yet another eight-year term.

The Chilean economy began to contract in late 1981, driving up unemployment and poverty. Spontaneous protests in the Santiago *poblaciones* (slums) were followed by demonstrations organized by emboldened leaders of the outlawed political parties, aimed at forcing Pinochet out of office before the end of his term. Pinochet responded to this first open opposition to his regime with heightened repression. After a failed 1986 assassination attempt against him, Pinochet applied more severe repression that forced the pro-democracy movement to abandon the push to force him from office and to focus instead on defeating him on his own terms: by the plebiscite required by his constitution. Just as Chileans had launched Salvador Allende's revolution at the ballot box, so they would terminate state terrorism at the ballot box after sixteen and a half years (chapter 8).

Reports of successive truth commissions revealed that by the dictatorship's end in 1990, the state terrorist regime had killed or disappeared over 3,200 people and tortured over 38,000.

ARGENTINA

Unlike Uruguay and Chile, Argentina had not consolidated political democracy prior to the rise of state terrorism but had experienced intermittent periods of democratically elected civilian governments dating to the Radical Party ascendancy of 1916–1930 (chapter 2). On the other hand, socioeconomic democratization had advanced notably under Juan Perón's presidency (1946–1955), primarily through the robust state-promoted expansion of unions and generous benefits to the working and middle classes. As noted, Perón left as a legacy an irreconcilably divided, virtually ungovernable country (chapter 3). After Perón's overthrow, the military and the economic elites worked to marginalize Perón's powerful bloc of loyalists, anchored in the labor movement, while the Peronists demanded that their leader be permitted to return from exile and run again for the presidency.

A new element altered the political equation in 1969 when, following a failed popular uprising in the industrial city of Córdoba against the repressive government of General Juan Carlos Onganía (1966–1970), an urban guerrilla movement emerged and rapidly expanded. The six original groups coalesced into two major organizations: the People's Revolutionary Army (ERP) and the *Montoneros*, both inspired by the Tupamaros in neighboring Uruguay. By 1973, four short-lived military regimes had demonstrated conclusively the military's inability to govern. This, combined with the heightened power of the Peronist unions and radicalized youth, and the continuing activity of the urban guerrillas, convinced the military that Perón was the best hope for peace and stability.

Perón returned from his Spanish exile and was elected president in September 1973 with 62 percent of the vote. His presence, however, failed to quell the guerrilla violence and general turmoil. He died less than a year later, leaving his widow and vice president, Isabel Perón, in nominal charge of the fractured country. The next two years saw a major increase in guerrilla actions and right-wing armed response led by the Argentine Anticommunist Alliance (AAA), resulting in an alarming rise in the death toll; among the victims were Uruguayan and Chilean leftists who had fled after their countries' 1973 coups, seeking refuge in Argentina.

The military overthrew the inept Isabel Perón government on March 24, 1976. Army commander General Jorge Rafael Videla and navy commander Admiral Emilio Massera, leaders of the governing junta, initially appeared to be pragmatists intent only on saving the patria from the violence and disorder that had escalated under Isabel Perón. Accustomed to coups and military governments, many Argentines welcomed the military takeover, anticipating the restoration of order. According to the *Buenos Aires Herald*, "The entire nation responded with relief. . . . This was not just another coup, but a rescue operation."[9] But even as the commanders consolidated the new regime, which they named The Process of National Reorganization (*El Proceso*), they were unleashing a lethal assault on civil society: the "Dirty War."

As in the other NSD-inspired military regimes, state terrorism in Argentina was not only a response to the immediate threat of revolution—in this case, the urban guerrillas and mobilized Peronists—but also the instrument for imposing a final solution to the intractable problem of Marxism and subversion. From the peak of their power in 1973, the urban guerrillas had been weakened by police crackdowns and the work of the AAA; by the time of the military takeover their ranks had thinned substantially. Only two months before the coup, General Videla had written that the guerrillas were "absolutely impotent," had "little fighting capability," and were unable to "reach a military level."[10] Their fighting ability continued to decline until the ERP ordered its surviving cadre to abandon Argentina in 1977 and the Montoneros followed suit two years later. Yet the Dirty War continued, as the military used an increasingly fictitious war against the guerrillas as cover for its commitment to physically eliminating Marxists and "subversives," their supporters, and anyone they might influence, thus permanently ending the threat of revolution.

The Argentine military commanders had decided prior to their coup to use state terrorism to eradicate the left. Like their counterparts in Brazil, Uruguay, and Chile, they closed Congress; militarized the public administration; shut down political parties; imposed censorship; and purged universities and unions. But they had learned from the nearly universal denunciation of the Chilean coup and the military regime it installed that open, undisguised state terrorism carried a price in the form of international condemnation and sanctions. Therefore in Argentina, disappearance was the military's primary means of eliminating the threat of revolution.

The regime jailed, tortured, and exiled its enemies while also murdering individuals whose bodies were recovered, but the Dirty War became synonymous with disappearances; in Argentina, the term "disappear" became a sinister transitive verb. Making a person disappear is a particularly heinous variant of murder: It denies loved ones a body to bury and a grave to visit; mourning is perpetual; and the disappeared person's family can never achieve closure. By disappearing their victims, leaving neither arrest records nor corpses, the repressors enjoyed plausible deniability. The horror of disappearances also intensified and prolonged the general state of terror that settled over Argentina and discouraged even minor acts of resistance to the regime.

In Argentina there were no limits to who might be murdered or disappeared, in contrast to Chile where the DINA focused primarily, but not exclusively, on militants of the MIR and the Socialist and Communist parties. In addition to targeting the guerrillas, whose numbers quickly faded, the leaders of the Proceso broadcast the narrative that the country was besieged by "subversives" who must be eliminated to save the patria. Who were these subversives? For Videla, they were those who embraced "ideas contrary to our western, Christian civilization." For General Reynaldo Bignone, subversives were "anti-fatherland" and agents of the "anti-Christ."[11] These definitions were sufficiently elastic that, applied with a broad brush, they could implicate almost anyone, such as a person whose name appeared in the phone book of a detained "subversive" or the owner of money or property that the terrorists could steal.

Public pronouncements such as the following, while tacitly admitting the disappearances, further heightened the sense of terror and demoralized the populace while offering chilling insights into the thinking that underpinned the Dirty War. According to General Ibérico Saint Jean, "First we will kill all the subversives, then we will kill their collaborators, then . . . their sympathizers, then . . . those who remain indifferent; and, finally, we will kill the timid."[12] General Luciano Menéndez quantified the war on subversion: "We are going to have to kill 50,000 people: 25,000 subversives, 20,000 sympathizers, and we will make 5,000 mistakes."[13]

To execute its ambitious plan, the junta divided the country into large "zones," smaller "subzones," and even smaller "areas" and placed them under military or police command. Those commanders set up task groups of between half a dozen and a dozen police and military personnel to carry out the disappearances. Victims were abducted at their homes, workplaces, or even in public spaces. They were not taken to police stations, where their detention would become a matter of record, but to one of over 400 secret detention centers established around the country that were equipped with torture chambers and space for holding persons prior to their disposal. Many of these facilities were located within police stations and military bases; others were built into commercial buildings, such as Automotores Orletti, an auto repair garage in a residential neighborhood and Galerías Pacífico, an upscale mall on a main shopping street, both in Buenos Aires.

In the centers, abducted persons were assigned numbers and delivered to the torture chamber, where they were normally subjected to a week or more of intense physical and psychological torture. Then they were taken to a holding area where, in some facilities, they were handcuffed and shackled in spaces so tiny that they were called "tubos," or tubes, where the physical and psychological abuse and degradation continued. One of the largest and most notorious of the detention centers was located in the Naval Mechanics' School (ESMA) in Buenos Aires. Known as the "Argentine Auschwitz," it hosted over 5,000 prisoners, few of whom left alive.

Pregnant women and Jews were subjected to especially barbaric treatment. After giving birth, the women were either killed or held for later disposal. Their babies were given for adoption to military families and others considered politically safe. Jews suffered disproportionately because of virulent antisemitism in the military and the right in general. They were also overrepresented in some professions that the military considered hotbeds of subversion, particularly psychiatry and academia. Although less than 1 percent of the Argentine population, Jews constituted some 10 percent of the disappeared. According to witness accounts, they suffered even greater humiliation and dehumanization than others.

Prisoners were ranked according to the danger they presumably posed to the mission of El Proceso: potentially dangerous, dangerous, and extremely dangerous. Some of the "potentially dangerous" were transferred to public prisons or freed; almost all the others were marked for death. Murders were normally carried out by shooting or by dropping live, drugged prisoners from aircraft into the Río de la Plata or the Atlantic; after bodies washed up on the Uruguayan shore of the Río de la Plata, death flights went further out over the Atlantic Ocean to dispose of their victims.

At the time of the coup, Argentines had no defense against the reign of terror unleashed upon them. In contrast to its Chilean counterpart, the Argentine Catholic Church hierarchy did not oppose the Proceso; in fact, many of the bishops and archbishops supported the Dirty War and some priests served as chaplains to the corps that conducted state terrorism. Meanwhile, priests inspired by liberation theology worked, at their peril, to aid victims and their families. The Center for Legal and Social Studies (CELS) used legal approaches to protect individuals, with almost no success. However, like the Chilean Vicaría, CELS filed thousands of writs of habeas corpus that eventually became critical evidence in the trials of hundreds of repressors.

The best-known Argentine human rights organization was the Madres de Plaza de Mayo (Mothers of the Plaza de Mayo), a group of women who first met making their dreary rounds of searching police stations and morgues for their disappeared children. These brave women gathered in the Plaza de Mayo in front of the presidential palace on Thursday afternoons, carrying placards with their children's photographs and the phrase "*¿donde están?*" (where are they?). They were vilified and beaten, and some were murdered, but they persisted and became the public face of resistance to state terrorism. They continued their quest long after the dictatorship's end in 1983.

Figure 7.3 Madres de Plaza de Mayo demonstrate for the return of their disappeared children.

The number of victims of state terrorism in Argentina will never be known. The truth commission established under the post-Proceso democratic government documented 8,960 disappearances; however, it acknowledged that its count was far from complete owing to military obfuscation and time constraints. Human rights organizations estimate that thirty thousand were disappeared. Victims include people of both sexes, all ages, various occupations, foreigners as well as Argentines, and at least a dozen disabled persons—some completely paralyzed.

EL SALVADOR

In close alliance with the economic elite—the owners of large coffee plantations that supplied the country's main export—military officers served as presidents of El Salvador from 1931 until 1979, with one brief interval. They governed under a façade of political democracy by holding regular elections from which the poor rural majority was excluded. In the 1960s, the impact of the Cuban Revolution stirred labor and student unrest and introduced landless peasants to the idea of land reform. Anticipating trouble, right-wing elements in 1964 formed the first of several militias that would evolve into death squads. The first of several minor guerrilla movements appeared in 1970. But the initial serious challenge to the status quo occurred within the political system.

José Napoleón Duarte, the popular former mayor of the capital, San Salvador, and a member of the moderate reformist Christian Democratic Party, ran for president in 1972. Duarte was denied the office through fraud, and the military-oligarchy candidate was seated. In the 1977 election the military-oligarchy alliance retained power through even more open, blatant fraud, making it clear that in El Salvador, reform could not be achieved by peaceful means. Unrest mounted, new guerrilla groups formed, and the military and death squads responded with heightened repression in cities and countryside.

The years 1979 and 1980 intensified the Salvadoran conflict and laid the groundwork for greater U.S. intervention against the guerrillas. The July 1979 Sandinista victory in neighboring Nicaragua raised hopes for the guerrillas and grave concern within the ruling cabal. The military included civilians in a new junta in an effort to set a reformist tone, but hard-liners continued to exercise the real power behind the scenes. Meanwhile, right-wing hostility to the Catholic Church grew as many of the clergy embraced liberation theology, which the oligarchy and the military viewed as a danger to their control. The Archbishop of San Salvador, Oscar Arnulfo Romero, insistently called for reining in the death squads and ending the growing repression: "In the name of God, in the name of this suffering people whose cries rise up more and more loudly to heaven, I ask you, I beg you, I order you in God's name: Stop the repression."[14] On March 24, 1980, he was murdered while saying mass in a hospital. This was the boldest step to date in the military's campaign of intimidation and assassination of priests, nuns, and lay religious workers who were or were suspected of being adherents of liberation theology.

The same month, the government instituted a nation-wide stage of siege, which suspended civil liberties and enhanced governmental powers. In October 1980, the disparate guerrilla groups united as the Farabundo Martí National Liberation Front (FMLN), named for the communist leader of the agricultural workers' 1932 strike that provoked La Matanza (chapter 3). Within a year, the FMLN had five thousand fighters and El Salvador was wracked by civil war as well as state terrorism.

Under President Ronald Reagan, U.S. engagement expanded. On one hand, Reagan pushed for a moderate government that would institute reforms to quell support for the FMLN. The other side of U.S. policy reflected Reagan's Cold War view that the FMLN was a tool of a communist Moscow-Havana-Managua axis. This required fortifying the Salvadoran military with equipment and training in counterinsurgency warfare; military aid rose from $6 million in 1980 to $197 million in 1984.

The conflict intensified as the U.S.-financed and trained counterinsurgency battalions and the death squads, following the playbook of the South American terrorist regimes, turned their fire on noncombatants suspected of supporting or even sympathizing with the guerrillas. While repressing in the cities, they focused on the rural areas where the FMLN was most active. Massacres of peasants proliferated, one of the most notorious of which occurred in December 1981 when the U.S.-trained Atlacatl Battalion rounded up and killed between eight hundred and a thousand men, women, and children in the village of El Mozote. When reports of the event appeared in the U.S. press, official denials followed. Ambassador Deane Hinton claimed that the villagers were "either willing or unwilling guerrilla collaborators" who did not die "as a result of systematic massacre."[15] Assistant Secretary of State Thomas Enders assured two U.S. congressional committees that "there is no evidence to confirm that government forces systematically massacred civilians."[16] Neither denied that massacres occurred, only that they were systematic.

By the mid-1980s, the government controlled the main cities and kept the important highways open by day, while the FMLN held large amounts of territory and operated freely at night. This equilibrium was shattered on November 12, 1989, when soldiers of the same Atlacatl Battalion murdered six Jesuits, their housekeeper, and her daughter in the Jesuit-run Central American University in San Salvador. Carried out in the capital, this heinous act of state terrorism could not be effectively denied by Salvadoran or U.S. authorities, and it swayed U.S. public opinion, the U.S. Congress, and President George H. W. Bush toward ending support for the Salvadoran

Figure 7.4 El Salvador army's notorious Atlacatl Brigade
Getty Images

military and government. Meanwhile, the Sandinistas' 1990 electoral defeat, the collapse of the Soviet Union the following year, and the resulting economic crisis in Cuba undercut foreign support for the FMLN. The war and state terrorism created hundreds of thousands of refugees and precipitated a wave of migration that made Salvadorans the fastest-growing Latino population in the United States in the late twentieth century. A UN-brokered 1992 peace accord ended the armed conflict after at least seventy-five thousand people, primarily poor mestizo noncombatants, had lost their lives.

GUATEMALA

Unlike El Salvador, Guatemala had experienced a period of political and socioeconomic democratization during the governments of Juan José Arévalo (1945–1951) and Jacobo Árbenz (1951–1954) (chapter 4). The U.S.-orchestrated overthrow of Árbenz restored the elites to power under a succession of military presidents. However, the democratic experience was not forgotten, and the under the impact of fidelismo a group of young army officers attempted a coup in November 1960. Undaunted by their failure, coup leaders Marco Antonio Yon Sosa and Luis Turcios Lima in 1962 formed a guerrilla movement, the Rebel Armed Forces (FAR), a mix of officers, progressive civilians, reformers, communists, and peasants. Thereafter, guerrilla activity varied in intensity but, unlike the Salvadoran FMLN, never gained the strength to threaten the government's survival.

Despite the guerrillas' limited impact, the military-led regimes of the 1960s adopted the response followed by other state terrorist regimes: severe repression against all potential guerrilla collaborators or sympathizers, including left and moderate political parties, union leaders, students, and especially the Mayan peasantry. In addition to army troops, including U.S.-trained ranger units, governments used death squads comprised largely of army and police personnel to do the repressing. These forces carried out assassinations and kidnappings in the cities and large-scale massacres of the predominantly Mayan peasantry in the countryside.

Colonel Carlos Arana Osorio, elected president in 1970, promised to eliminate the guerrillas even "if it is necessary to turn the country into a cemetery."[17] By the time of his pronouncement, the deadly cycle of guerrilla activity and state terrorism was entrenched. For the next two decades, with military men in the presidency or exercising the real power over weak civilian presidents, the U.S.-trained and supplied army and the death squads intimidated, assassinated, and massacred in the name of anti-communism whenever new guerrilla activity occurred. A particularly bloody 1978 massacre in the northern town of Panzós spurred Mayan peasants to protest and guerrillas to renew their struggle.

General Fernando Romeo Lucas García, president from 1978 to 1982, escalated the repression against leftists, trade unionists, and especially Mayan peasants. By this time, state terrorism in Guatemala had developed into a race and class war against the Maya Indian peasants that led to some of the worst atrocities committed in Latin America, including genocide. Human rights groups reported over three hundred massacres of Mayan peasants during Lucas García's term. The 1979 Sandinista victory in Nicaragua stoked hopes for change in Guatemala, as elsewhere in Central America, adding to the ferment caused by the savage repression.

General Efraín Ríos Montt, an evangelical Protestant who succeeded Lucas García and served as president for seventeen bloody months, further escalated the war on the Maya. Facing a revival of guerrilla activity led by the newly formed Guatemalan National Revolutionary Unity (URNG), an amalgam of several small groups, Ríos Montt unleashed his troops and death squads in a genocide in which women were raped, men tortured and killed, and babies bayoneted or smashed with rocks. Government forces annihilated some six hundred Mayan villages, killed thousands, and drove over one hundred thousand across the border into Mexico.

Figure 7.5 Belated funeral for indigenous victims of the Guatemalan genocide
Getty Images/Andrea Nieto/Stringer

Upon assuming the presidency in January 1981, Ronald Reagan affirmed U.S. support of state terrorism and genocide. He visited Guatemala in an effort to offset negative coverage in the U.S. media and declared that the Guatemalan government had been getting a "bum rap" on human rights and that Ríos Montt was "totally dedicated to democracy in Guatemala."[18] He restored military aid to Guatemala that had been suspended by President Jimmy Carter and thus enabled the government's violent repression.

The strongest voice of indigenous protest was that of Rigoberta Menchú, a Quiché Maya woman who became an activist for Indian and women's rights from an early age. After government forces murdered her parents and brother, she was forced to flee to Mexico. For her activism, she received the Nobel Peace Prize in 1992. She related her brother's torture and death in a book: "When they'd done with him he didn't look like a person any more. His whole face was disfigured . . . they'd even forced stones into his eyes. My brother was tortured more than sixteen days. They cut off his fingernails, they cut off his fingers. . . . They cut the skin off his head and pulled it down on either side and cut off the fleshy part of his face."[19]

State-perpetrated violence declined after 1985 under civilian governments, but the war on the Maya continued until UN-brokered talks between the government and the URNG led to a peace agreement in 1996. A truth commission found that "agents of the state . . . committed acts of genocide against groups

Figure 7.6 Rigoberta Menchú, leading advocate for indigenous and women's rights
Carlos Rodriguez

of Mayan people."[20] It established that over two hundred thousand people were killed in the protracted conflict, 83 percent of them Mayan; government forces and death squads committed 93 percent and the guerrillas 3 percent of the human rights violations.[21] State terrorism in Guatemala accounted for over half of the total slaughter carried out by Latin American state terrorist regimes in their war on democracy, both political and socioeconomic.

The period between 1969 and 1996 was the darkest time in modern Latin American history. The wave of revolutionary activity emanating from Cuba created a powerful counter-wave of repression, supported by the United States—a foreseeable outcome of NSD. State terrorism extinguished democracy—both political and socioeconomic—where they existed and took a huge toll in murder, disappearance, and genocide in the name of insulating Latin America against revolution. In addition to the hundreds of thousands murdered and disappeared, state terrorism left huge numbers of people physically and emotionally scarred by torture and displaced by exile. The ensuing years would bring the challenge of rebuilding political and socioeconomic democracy, or building them from scratch, while coping with the legacies of state terrorism and the human rights crisis it created.

SUGGESTIONS FOR FURTHER READING

Americas Watch. *El Salvador's Decade of Terror: Human Rights since the Assassination of Archbishop Romero*. New Haven: Yale University Press, 1991.
Binford, Leigh. *The El Mozote Massacre: Human Rights and Global Implications*. Second ed. Tucson: University of Arizona Press, 2016.
Bouvard, Marguerite Guzmán. *Revolutionizing Motherhood: The Mothers of the Plaza de Mayo*. Wilmington: Scholarly Resources, 1994.
Brett, Roderick Leslie. *Origins and Dynamics of Genocide: Political Violence in Guatemala*. London: Palgrave Macmillan. 2016.
Carothers, Thomas. *In the Name of Democracy: U.S. Policy toward Latin America in the Reagan Years*. Berkeley: University of California Press, 1991.
Constable, Pamela and Arturo Valenzuela. *A Nation of Enemies: Chile under Pinochet*. New York: W. W. Norton, 1991.
Dinges, John. *Condor Years: How Pinochet and His Allies Brought Terrorism to Three Continents*. New York: New Press, 2004.
Feitlowitz, Marguerite. *A Lexicon of Terror: Argentina and the Legacies of Torture*. Revised and updated ed. New York: Oxford University Press, 2011.
Gill, Lesley. *The School of the Americas: Military Training and Political Violence in the Americas*. Durham: Duke University Press, 2004.

Grandin, Greg and Gilbert Joseph, eds. *Century of Revolution: Insurgent and Counterinsurgent Violence during Latin America's Long Cold War*. Durham: Duke University Press, 2010.

Jonas, Suzanne. *The Battle for Guatemala: Rebels, Death Squads, and U.S. Power*. Boulder: Westview, 1991.

Kornbluh, Peter. *The Pinochet File: A Declassified Dossier on Atrocity and Accountability*. New York: New Press, 2003.

Lewis, Paul H. *Guerrillas and Generals: The "Dirty War" in Argentina*. Westport, CT: Praeger, 2002.

Loveman, Brian. *Por la Patria: Politics and the Armed Forces in Latin America*. Lanham, MD: Rowman & Littlefield, 1999.

Menchú, Rigoberta. *I, Rigoberta Menchú: An Indian Woman in Guatemala*. Second English ed. Trans. Ann Wright. London: Verso, 2009.

Muñoz, Heraldo. *The Dictator's Shadow: Life under Augusto Pinochet*. New York: Basic Books, 2008.

Sanford, Victoria. *Buried Secrets: Truth and Human Rights in Guatemala*. New York: Palgrave Macmillan, 2003.

Skidmore, Thomas E. *The Politics of Military Rule in Brazil, 1964–1985*. New York: Oxford University Press, 1988.

Timerman, Jacobo. *Prisoner Without a Name, Cell Without a Number*. Trans. Tony Talbott. New York: Vintage Books, 1988.

Verbitsky, Horacio. *The Flight: Confessions of an Argentine Dirty Warrior*. Trans. Esther Allen. New York: New Press, 1996.

Whitfield, Teresa. *Paying the Price: Ignacio Ellacuria and the Murdered Jesuits in El Salvador*. Philadelphia: Temple University Press, 1995.

NOTES

1. Frederick H. Gareau, *State Terrorism and the United States: From Counterinsurgency War to the War on Terrorism* (London: Zed Books, 2004), 14.

2. Archdiocese of São Paulo, *Torture in Brazil: A Report by the Archdiocese of São Paulo*, trans Jaime Wright (New York: Vintage Books, 1986).

3. Alain Rouquié, *The Military and the State in Latin America*, trans. Paul Sigmund (Berkeley: University of California Press, 1987), 256.

4. Thomas C. Wright, *State Terrorism in Latin America: Chile, Argentina, and International Human Rights* (Lanham, MD: Rowman & Littlefield, 2007), 60.

5. Thomas G. Sanders, "Military Government in Chile," in *The Politics of Antipolitics: The Military in Latin America*, ed. Brian Loveman and Thomas M. Davies Jr., First ed. (Lincoln: University of Nebraska Press, 1978), 274.

6. Thomas C. Wright and Rody Oñate, *Flight from Chile: Voices of Exile* (Albuquerque: University of New Mexico Press, 1998), 82.

7. Hal Brands, *Latin America's Cold War* (Cambridge: Harvard University Press, 2010), 160.

8. Pinochet did not need Condor's help in DINA's assassination of Orlando Lete-lier, a former Allende cabinet member and his aide Ronni Moffitt, by car bomb on Washington's Embassy Row in September 1976. A memorial to the two is located in Sheridan Circle near the bombing site.

9. *Buenos Aires Herald*, March 25, 1976.

10. *Clarín* (Buenos Aires), January 31, 1976.

11. Marguerite Feitlowitz, *A Lexicon of Terror: Argentina and the Legacies of Tor-ture*, revised and updated ed. (New York: Oxford University Press, 2011), 27.

12. Feitlowitz, *Lexicon*, 32.

13. Paul Lewis, *Guerrillas and Generals: The "Dirty War" in Argentina* (Westport, CT: Praeger, 2002), 147.

14. Jeffrey Davis, *Justice Across Borders: The Struggle for Human Rights in U.S. Courts* (New York: Cambridge University Press, 2008), 44.

15. Leigh Binford, *The El Mozote Massacre: Human Rights and Global Implica-tions*, Second ed. (Tucson: University of Arizona Press, 2016), 74.

16. Russell Crandall, *The Salvador Option: The United States in El Salvador, 1977–1992* (New York: Cambridge University Press, 2016), 227.

17. Jim Handy, *Gift of the Devil: A History of Guatemala* (Boston: South End Press, 1984), 167.

18. Thomas Carothers, *In the Name of Democracy: U.S. Policy toward Latin America in the Reagan Years* (Berkeley: University of California Press, 1991), 62.

19. Rigoberta Menchú, *I, Rigoberta Menchú: An Indian Woman in Guatemala*, ed. Elisabeth Burgos-Debray, trans. Ann Wright, Second ed. (London: Verso, 2009), 203, 204. Menchú has admitted that she did not witness her brother's death but learned the details from her mother.

20. Daniel Rothenberg, ed., *Memory of Silence: The Guatemalan Truth Commis-sion Report* (New York: Palgrave Macmillan, 2012), 77.

21. Responsibility for the remaining 4 percent could not be established.

Chapter 8

Democratic Progress and Regression, 1978–2000

The period from 1978 to 2000 brought both advances and setbacks for Latin American democracy. During the dark days of repression and state terrorism, only five countries escaped military rule. Most Latin Americans lived under military dictatorships for varying periods and of those, the great majority lived under state terrorism. Then a powerful wave of political democratization swept the region, beginning in 1978 with a milestone of democratic progress in the Dominican Republic when, following a decade of elected but authoritarian government, the country experienced for the first time in its history a peaceful transfer of power from government to opposition after an election. The following year, dictatorships began to fall. The first to go was the forty-three-year Somoza dynasty in Nicaragua, overthrown by the Sandinistas. Democratization accelerated with the end of a military junta in Ecuador later that year, the restoration of civilian rule in Peru in 1980, and three more democratic transitions in 1982. Even chronically authoritarian Haiti experienced a brief democratic transition in 1990, which lasted only eight months. The cycle ended in 2000 when the iron grip of Mexico's PRI was broken after seventy-one years.

This wave created the most politically democratic period in Latin American history, with more democratically elected governments than in the late 1950s–early 1960s, when several dictatorships persisted (chapters 4 and 5). However, socioeconomic democracy faltered as the region embraced political democracy. Developments in the world economy, the imposition of neoliberalism, and policies left over from military dictatorships suppressed hard-won socioeconomic gains in many countries. In sum, the period brought both gains to celebrate and losses to lament.

A WAVE OF POLITICAL DEMOCRATIZATION

The surge of political democratization was not the first wave of political change that had affected democracy in Latin America. In the 1930s and 1940s, nearly half of the Latin American countries experienced governments that either proposed, or in some cases, were able to implement policies that furthered socioeconomic democracy. Inspired largely by the victory of the Western democracies over the Axis powers in World War II, a brief tide of political democratization began in 1945. The onset of the Cold War brought dictators to power in almost half of the Latin American countries beginning in 1948. Next, a new period of political democratization dating from the mid-1950s duplicated the earlier peak of 1948. Beginning in 1959, a wave of revolutionary activity inspired by the Cuban Revolution swept the region; but rather than bringing revolutionary change or reform, with two exceptions, the revolutionary impulse created a counterwave of militarization and extreme repression that began in 1963 and continued into the 1990s, crushing political and setting back socioeconomic democracy. The wave of political democratization that began in 1978, examined here, continued the post-1930 pattern of alternation between authoritarianism and political democracy and between advances and setbacks in socioeconomic democracy.

Latin America's trend toward democratic governance coincided with a global wave of democratization, according to political scientist Samuel P. Huntington.[1] The wave began with the fall of dictatorships in Portugal and Greece in 1974 and Spain the following year. Democratization accelerated in 1989 with the fall of several communist governments in Eastern Europe, followed by the 1991 collapse of the Soviet Union and the 1991–1992 breakup of Yugoslavia. Some of the former communist countries embarked on the path of political democratization; others continued with authoritarian rule.

Geography was a primary determinant of the political direction followed in the post-communist countries. Those located in Europe had a strong incentive to establish democratic institutions. For them, the European Union (EU) was a magnet, largely for economic reasons. Even the poorest EU member states were wealthy in comparison with those of the former Yugoslavia and Soviet Union. Membership in the EU meant help with the transition from socialist to capitalist economies and direct economic aid for new members. Anticipating expansion to the former communist countries, the EU in 1993 adopted its Copenhagen Criteria that required new members to establish political democracy, follow the rule of law, and protect human rights. After a period of preparation, eight post-communist countries joined in 2004, and by 2020 the majority of Europe's former communist-run countries had either joined or applied for membership in the EU. Meanwhile, the Eurasian and

Central Asian countries of the former Soviet Union had little incentive to democratize, and few have done so.

In contrast to the post-communist countries of Europe, Latin America had no external prod to democratize. The democratic wave in Latin America was citizen-driven. Although accustomed to longer or shorter periods of dictatorship, Latin America as a whole had never lived under the severe repression and state terrorism that peaked in the 1970s and 1980s. Almost all of the region's countries had experienced at least brief interludes of political democracy prior to the onset of state terrorism in 1969 and a few had established strong democratic roots. Thus political democracy was not a foreign concept in Latin America, and for a majority of its citizens the choice between democracy and authoritarianism was clear-cut.

Nonetheless, Latin America's transition to political democracy faced numerous obstacles. One of these was the implementation of neoliberal economic policies, which increased poverty and income inequality (see below). Another was the lack of democratic experience and culture in many countries, some of which had been ruled by caudillos, military officers, or oligarchies during much of their history since independence. Uruguay, Chile, and Costa Rica were the main exceptions, and in the first two, state terrorist regimes attempted but failed to extinguish democratic cultures and values. Raúl Alfonsín, Argentina's first democratically elected president following the end of the Dirty War, explained the challenge facing his country, and indeed most of Latin America: "It was not a matter of reconstructing a system that was functioning well until it was interrupted by authoritarianism, but of establishing new foundations for an authentic democratic system."[2]

Moreover, the tradition of authoritarianism, the nemesis of political democracy, was not dead. Peru's elected President Alberto Fujimori (1990–2000) in 1992 shuttered Congress, suspended the constitution, and assumed dictatorial powers. Alfonsín's successor in Argentina, Carlos Menem (1989–1999) did not go as far as Fujimori but stacked the Supreme Court with unqualified cronies in order to further his agenda. In Mexico, authoritarianism continued to underpin the one-party political system.

Powerful militaries were another issue for some of the new political democracies. Most countries had been under military rule for varying lengths of time, and in some instances, after the establishment of elected governments the officers refused to accept civilian control of their institutions. Such was the case most clearly in Guatemala and El Salvador, where the military commanders exercised more power than the presidents, and in Chile, where former dictator Pinochet used his position as commander of the army to harass and intimidate presidents to the end of his tenure in 1998. Establishing firm civilian control of the military was a delicate matter in several other countries.

The legacy of state terrorism was another challenge. The civilian governments that followed the terrorist regimes faced profoundly divided societies. On one side were the military and the civilians who supported their policy of exterminating the left; on the other were victims of torture, families of the murdered and disappeared, and the human rights movements formed during the dictatorships. The most divisive issue was justice versus impunity. Would military-issued amnesties protect human rights violators from prosecution under civilian rule? Would truth commission reports satisfy victims, their families, and the human rights movements, or would they demand investigations and trials? How would the militaries react to prosecution when, in their view, they had heroically saved their countries from Marxism and subversion? These were some of the burning questions facing the new civilian governments intent on protecting their fragile democracies. Two countries have had some success in meeting this challenge: In Argentina and Chile, hundreds of human rights violators have been tried and convicted since 2000, while the divisive legacy of state terrorism is largely unresolved elsewhere.

DEMOCRATIZATION IN MEXICO

Almost all of Latin America's democratic transitions involved civilians replacing military dictatorships. Mexico, along with the Dominican Republic (see above), followed a different trajectory: transforming an undemocratic civilian regime into a democracy. President Lázaro Cárdenas (1934–1940) implemented sweeping socioeconomic reforms as prescribed by the revolutionary 1917 constitution and sought to build a unique corporatist form of single-party political democracy by restructuring the dominant party, previously run essentially by generals (chapter 3). Known since 1946 as the PRI, the party under Cárdenas expanded its base exponentially by incorporating the national labor confederation and the beneficiaries of agrarian reform while limiting military involvement. Over time, the intended mass democracy evolved into a top-down, authoritarian structure controlled by the party hierarchy that monopolized political power. Despite holding regular elections at the local, state, and federal levels, Mexico was not a democracy, as the elections did not pass the most basic test of "fair, free, and open." Commenting in 1990, Peruvian novelist and Nobel Laureate Mario Vargas Llosa called this system "the perfect dictatorship."[3]

By the 1980s, recurring economic problems, increased repression, heightened and undisguised corruption, and a blatantly fraudulent 1988 presidential election eroded the PRI's legitimacy, leading to the party's first-ever loss of a state governorship in 1989. The 1990s brought drug wars, political assassinations, another financial crisis, and in 1994, a popular insurrection led by the Zapatista National Liberation Army (EZLN) in the poor, largely Mayan state of Chiapas.

In response to these developments and to the wave of democratization that had swept Latin America, Mexico's political landscape underwent a profound change. Following the corrupt 1988 presidential election, public pressure forced the government to reform the electoral system. The cornerstone of the new system is the Federal Electoral Institute (IFE), which went through a series of reforms until by 1996 it was separated from the executive branch and staffed by non-partisan citizens, eliminating the PRI's ability to manipulate elections. The same year, the Electoral Court was established to adjudicate electoral disputes and certify elections. With the resulting enhanced transparency in elections, the PRI lost its majority in the federal Chamber of Deputies in 1997 and in 2000 gave up the presidency to conservative Vicente Fox of the National Action Party (PAN).

ECLIPSE OF THE STATE TERRORIST REGIMES

Argentina was the first country ruled by state terrorism to transition to political democracy. Because the military expected to hold power until its mission of making the country safe from revolution was complete, at some indefinite time in the future, it developed no plans for an eventual return to civilian government. However, a series of unforeseen developments began to unravel the regime four years after its inception. President Jimmy Carter pressured the regime by withholding financing for infrastructure projects in exchange for permission for the Inter-American Commission on Human Rights to conduct an on-site investigation of disappearances in 1980. Underestimating the emerging clout of the OAS's principal human rights arm, the Proceso leaders reluctantly accepted the deal but attempted to sabotage the investigation by disguising the torture and death facilities and threatening retaliation against anyone who testified before the Commission. Despite the pressure, hundreds of brave Argentines spoke with the Commission's investigators.

The Human Rights Commission's damning report was banned in Argentina but circulated clandestinely. It demonstrated what was widely suspected: that the individuals who were missing had not fled the country nor were they "terrorists" killed in confrontations with police, as the military consistently claimed. They were victims of state terrorism. An economic crisis in 1981 sparked the beginnings of active opposition to the regime. The following year, in an effort to rally public support for its faltering government, the military invaded the Malvinas/Falkland Islands, claimed by Argentina but long occupied by Britain. The brief war, a disaster for Argentina, quickly eroded any lingering support for the regime.

Figure 8.1 Argentine military during the 1982 Falklands/Malvinas War

Having been exposed as the instrument of mass disappearances and demonstrated ineptness at managing the economy and fighting a war, the military beat a hasty retreat to the barracks. The regime granted itself an amnesty and published a document justifying its actions as a patriotic service that saved the country from Marxists and subversives, then surrendered power to civilians. After almost eight years of state terrorism, President Raúl Alfonsín of the moderate Radical Party (UCR) and a new Congress took office on December 10, 1983.

Uruguay followed. Just as state terrorism in Uruguay was established incrementally, so did it end. Most fundamentally, as heirs to Latin America's first political and socioeconomic democracy, many Uruguayans held onto the country's traditional political values despite the military's efforts to stamp them out. Miscalculating public sentiment, the military called for a referendum on institutionalizing the political system it had devised, which amounted to military governance with minimal civilian participation. In the November 1980 referendum, 57 percent of the voters voted against the new regime, launching a four-year process of military withdrawal. An economic downturn in 1982 brought a high social cost in falling wages and the doubling of unemployment, further eroding support for the government. Political parties were reauthorized in 1982, and elections were scheduled for November 1984. Following the elections, after twelve years of military governance and state terrorism, civilian rule returned to Uruguay in March 1985 under the leadership of President Julio Sanguinetti of the Colorado Party.

Fifteen years after they overthrew President Goulart (chapter 5), the Brazilian armed forces could be confident that their mission of sanitizing

Brazil against revolution had been fulfilled. Thus when he took office in March 1979, General João Baptista Figueiredo publicly expressed the armed forces' desire to return to the barracks. Yet despite the absence of revolutionary threats, the process of returning power to civilians took a full eleven years.

The return to civilian rule was a phased-in process, beginning with the restoration of party rights and elections for state governors in 1982, which opposition groups won. The military decided to install the first civilian president in twenty-one years in the 1985 presidential election, but fearing the outcome of a free and direct popular election, the administration prescribed an indirect election procedure that ensured acceptable results. A new constitution in 1988 and the first direct presidential election in three decades, with an expanded electorate that included illiterates and sixteen-year-olds, finished the process: After twenty-one years of direct military rule and five of close military oversight, with the inauguration of President Fernando Collor de Mello in March 1990 Brazil emerged with a more inclusive political democracy than the one it had lost in 1964.

In Chile, dictator Augusto Pinochet was bound by his own 1980 "Constitution of Liberty" to hold a plebiscite no later than 1988 on whether to extend his presidency for eight more years. As the other South American state terrorist regimes had ended, leaving Chile as the lone holdout during a strong region-wide wave of democratization, he faced considerable pressure to conduct a clean election. Satisfied that the threat of revolution was over, the Reagan administration pressured Pinochet to hold a legitimate plebiscite to avoid a potential leftist resurgence in reaction to a rigged one. Many among the Chilean elites, the political right, and ranking military officers also felt that it was safe to return power to civilians after sixteen and a half years, should Pinochet lose. Forced to allow the opposition to organize and campaign, the overconfident Pinochet was stunned at the plebiscite's outcome: He was rejected, 55 to 43 percent. Fellow junta members had to restrain the enraged dictator from annulling the results.

In contrast to Argentina, Uruguay, and Brazil, the end of the dictatorship in Chile did not lead to a transition to political democracy. According to his constitution, Pinochet had a year and a half left in his term after the plebiscite, with full dictatorial powers intact. While the constitution laid out the general outlines of the post-Pinochet government, Pinochet used this time to dictate *leyes de amarre* (tie-up laws). The constitution and the tie-up laws were designed to ensure impunity for Pinochet and the armed forces, keep the free market economy intact, and prevent the left from coming to power. The impediments to political democracy included: nine of the forty-seven senators appointed directly or indirectly by Pinochet, among them former commanders of the army, navy, air force, and national police; Pinochet himself as a senator-for-life; an electoral system that strongly favored the right; a Supreme

Court packed with Pinochet loyalists; and a statute that made the armed forces virtually autonomous. For the icing on the cake, Pinochet extended his commandership of the army for eight years, to 1998, ensuring his continuing ability to intimidate and threaten the elected governments that succeeded him. This was the "protected democracy" that Pinochet bequeathed Chile.

El Salvador was the next country to exit state terrorism. Unlike the South American terrorist regimes, El Salvador was gripped by both civil war and state terrorism during the 1980s. A turning point in the conflict came in November 1989, when the cold-blooded murder of the Jesuits in the Central American University began to erode U.S. support for the government. The FMLN lost the active support of the Sandinistas and of Cuba in the following months. The result was peace negotiations held under UN auspices in Mexico City, beginning in April 1991. The Chapultepec Agreement was signed in January 1992.

The peace agreement reflected the near-parity of government and rebel military forces, as evidenced by its provisions relating to the army and other government-sponsored armed groups. The army was to be reduced in size and budget, be responsible only for external defense, and be replaced in domestic jurisdiction by a new civilian police force. The army was also to be placed under civilian authority, its intelligence department abolished, and human rights violators within its ranks cashiered. The rapid deployment units such as the Atlacatl Batallion and the private death squads were to be abolished. Detailed instructions on the makeup and functions of the new civilian police and on sweeping judicial reform were included. In addition, the Chapultepec Agreement called for action on one of the most important underlying causes of the conflagration: agrarian reform. It also required aid for rebuilding areas most affected by terrorism and civil war. Finally, and very importantly, it called for the integration of the FMLN into the country's "civil, institutional, and political life" and legalized the FMLN as a political party.[4]

The agreement, of course, was only as good as its implementation. The restructuring of the armed forces proceeded expeditiously, as did the creation of the civilian police force, but not without hitches. Agrarian reform was enacted slowly through the 1990s, and money for rebuilding was sparse. Moreover, there was no accountability for human rights violations committed during the conflict: Five days after the release of a UN-sponsored Truth Commission report, which attributed 80 percent of such violations to government forces, the conservative-controlled National Assembly passed a bill of absolute amnesty. The amnesty stood until the Supreme Court reversed it in July 2016. On the political front, however, change soon became evident. An FMLN-backed candidate became mayor of San Salvador in 1997; FMLN candidates gained seats in the national Congress, at one point becoming the largest bloc; but it was not until the next century that FMLN candidates twice won the presidency, in 2009 and 2014. El Salvador appeared to be moving toward a two-party democracy, a process interrupted a few years later (chapter 9).

The Guatemalan peace accords of December 1996 were also brokered by the UN. They resembled the Salvadoran peace agreement in provisions for demilitarizing the country; calling for reducing the size and budget of the military; limiting the military's role to defending borders; creating a new civilian police force; and eliminating the paramilitary forces, or death squads. The accords included an amnesty for all crimes except genocide, forced disappearance, and torture—the common practices of the state terrorism unleashed on the country. They also required judicial reforms and recognized the distinct identity of indigenous peoples. They failed to address socioeconomic reforms, in particular the agrarian reform as mandated by the Salvadoran accord. The insurgent URNG became a political party in 1998 but, reflecting its weakness compared to El Salvador's FMLN, fared poorly at the polls.

Despite the similarities, the context in which the Guatemalan accords were reached was very different from that in El Salvador. In the latter, the two sides negotiated from a position of rough parity in military strength; in Guatemala, the URNG never attained the power to seriously threaten the Guatemalan army or government. Thus the outcome in Guatemala was essentially a ceasefire, not an attempt to address the underlying causes of the thirty-six-year conflict. The sense that things had not changed was underscored in April 1997 when the Catholic Church released the report of its truth commission, the "Recovery of Historical Memory" (the UN released its own report in 1999): Monsignor Juan José Gerardi, the primary author of the Church's report, was brutally murdered days after its release, and the perpetrator was never identified. As in El Salvador, the value of the peace accords was in their implementation. On the tenth anniversary of the accords, Amnesty International reported: "The goal of the December 1996 Peace Accords was a state based on the rule of law, but today Guatemala continues to be crushed by the rule of impunity."[5]

A few Guatemalan military men were eventually tried and sentenced for the crimes not covered by the amnesty, but most observers found this to be tokenism. When general and former President Efraín Ríos Montt (chapter 7), the ultimate state terrorist who was responsible for the most brutal period of the violent repression, was convicted of genocide and crimes against humanity in 2013, the country's highest court overturned the verdict.

With the end of state terrorism, Latin America emerged from the most fraught period in its recent history. Conflict resolution moved from torture centers and Mayan villages to national Congresses and the courts. While some repression continued, as it does everywhere, the dread of being tortured, raped, murdered, massacred, and disappeared by state agents dissipated.

Attention turned to protecting human rights and fortifying the fragile democracies that followed the period of heightened repression and state terrorism.

SOCIOECONOMIC DEMOCRACY IN
THE LATE TWENTIETH CENTURY

While the late twentieth century was a banner period for political democracy,
it was a time of regression for socioeconomic democracy. This negative turn
resulted from developments in the world economy and their repercussions in
Latin America, and from the widespread application of neoliberal policies.

The Great Depression of the 1930s had brought new economic policies to
the larger, more developed Latin American countries. To counter the crisis,
these countries abandoned nineteenth-century laissez-faire economics, promoted rapid industrialization through protective tariffs and subsidies, and
embraced state-driven economic development, including government ownership of important economic assets (chapter 3). Half a century later, a new
economic crisis forced another change of course.

The new economic crisis—the "lost decade" of the 1980s—was part of
a global pattern of economic recession. As international demand for Latin
America's commodities fell sharply, per capita gross domestic product (GDP)
contracted by around 10 percent and unemployment soared. The remedy for
this crisis would be to reverse the policies adopted half a century earlier. The
new economic model was neoliberalism, so called because it was essentially
a reversion to nineteenth-century liberal, free market, free trade, laissez-faire
economics. This time, the radical shift of economic policy affected not just
the larger, more developed countries but all of Latin America except Cuba.

The change in direction first occurred in Chile under the Pinochet dictatorship, when the so-called Chicago Boys—disciples of Milton Friedman,
a University of Chicago professor of economics—took charge of economic
policy (chapter 7). Chile had followed the general pattern of state-driven economic development since the 1930s, and under Presidents Frei and Allende,
state control of the economy had increased substantially. Friedman's free
market economics dictated that the economy be freed from state intervention and allowed to operate virtually without constraints. The changes that
ensued were so radical and so painful to many Chileans that they could
not have occurred while the country was still a democracy, as working and
middle-class parties would have blocked them. It required a military dictatorship, which answered only to itself, to implement neoliberalism in Chile.

The Chicago Boys' formula was to roll back the layers of government
involvement in the economy. With the country under strict military control,
they did this through a "shock" treatment that initially drove the economy

down to near-Depression levels, creating mass unemployment and poverty as price controls over goods and services were eliminated, government spending was slashed, and state-owned enterprises of all kinds were privatized, sold at bargain prices. The public social security system that had been in place for decades was dismantled, replaced by private companies. The public health system was defunded and partially replaced by private health insurance companies. Funding for public education was drastically curtailed while subsidies were offered to private schools, and expensive for-profit universities proliferated. The protective tariffs that had promoted industrialization were eliminated, resulting in a flood of imports that drove manufacturing firms into bankruptcy. A draconian labor code erased the decades of progress that many workers had enjoyed, while much of the agrarian reform was reversed, restoring landowner control over agricultural land and workers. Through these policies, the Chicago Boys essentially rejected the state's responsibility for citizens' welfare that had become explicit in Chile's reformist 1925 constitution.

After the initial contraction, the economy boomed from 1979 to 1982, propped up by massive borrowing. This "Chilean miracle" crashed in 1982 but revived after three years. With this recovery, unemployment eased and poverty levels declined, but privatization of pensions, health, and education greatly exacerbated economic inequality. Impressed by the macroeconomic picture and ignoring its negative effects, many economists touted the Chilean way as Latin America's future. Due to unforeseen circumstances, this future became reality.

Whereas the Pinochet dictatorship freely chose the neoliberal model of economic development, neoliberalism was forced upon the rest of Latin America, save Cuba. The roots of the neoliberal imposition are found in the 1973 "oil shock," when the Middle Eastern members of the Organization of Petroleum Exporting Countries (OPEC) sought to punish countries, especially the United States, that supported Israel in the 1973 Arab-Israeli War. OPEC restricted members' production, quadrupling petroleum prices. This move flooded OPEC countries, including Venezuela and, to a lesser extent Ecuador, with "petrodollars" while causing economic pain in the majority of Latin American countries that relied on imported oil. This bonanza was deposited in U.S. and other banks which, to put their cash to work, offered generous loans to Latin American governments and private firms struggling with the OPEC effect. As a result, total Latin American external debt rose dramatically from around $29 billion in 1970 to some $372 billion in 1982.

The worldwide recession of the 1980s depressed the prices of Latin American exports and halted the region's economic growth. This raised the specter of defaulting on the massive loans. When the Mexican government announced in 1982 that it could not meet its payment obligations, the international financial institutions took action to prevent Mexico and other Latin American countries from defaulting. Led by the International Monetary Fund (IMF) and the World Bank, the lenders offered to renegotiate the loans to reduce interest rates and payments as a way to prevent a major catastrophe for international lenders and the world economy. They also offered bridge loans, further indebting Latin America.

As the condition for refinancing billions of dollars of debt and offering emergency loans, the lending institutions demanded implementation of radical policy changes such as those applied earlier in Chile. Given the United States' paramount influence within these international organizations, the neoliberal policies they prescribed were also known as the "Washington Consensus." Intended to stabilize the heavily indebted Latin American economies, the imposed measures were also designed to benefit multinational companies and ensure that the lenders would be repaid. The lenders demanded fiscal austerity and balanced budgets; the opening of closed or protected economies to foreign investment and international trade; elimination of price controls; and privatization of state-owned assets. Budgets, government services, and subsidies to the poor were slashed almost everywhere; protective tariffs were cut or eliminated; labor rights were restricted under the euphemistic term "labor flexibilization"; and domestic and transnational corporations bought up the public sectors at bargain prices. In effect, Latin American countries were forced to surrender national control over economic policy to the international lenders and, indirectly, to U.S. capital.

Mexico's President Carlos Salinas de Gortari (1988–1994) and Argentina's President Carlos Saúl Menem (1989–1999) set the pace in privatizations. In Mexico, the number of state-owned firms fell from 1,155 in 1982 to 158 in 1993; *Forbes* magazine reported that as a result of the corrupt disposal of state assets, the number of billionaires in Mexico rose from one in 1987 to twenty-four in 1995.[6] Among those acquiring these companies was Mexican Carlos Slim, who was periodically the world's richest person. In Argentina, the Menem administration privatized the country's railways, airports, subways, ports, and the oil, gas, power, water, and telecommunications sectors. Other countries followed suit.

In the many instances of foreign companies buying state-owned companies, the majority of the profits went abroad. Typical of privatizations throughout Latin America, corrupt officials negotiated such transfers in ways that enriched themselves and sold assets at bargain basement prices. Privatization also had negative socioeconomic consequences. As state enterprises, the companies were not always expected to be profitable as they could often rely on government subsidies, allowing them to employ personnel in excess of need. Under private ownership, however, these companies' primary concern was profit; in pursuit of greater efficiency, they shed hundreds or thousands of redundant employees, raising levels of unemployment and poverty.

Latin America's economic contraction in the "lost decade" of the 1980s, exacerbated by the implementation of neoliberal policies, had severe human consequences. Together, they jeopardized or erased the gains made by many middle- and working-class people over the preceding decades and drove up poverty levels. Jobs were lost due to the contraction of government employment, privatization of state-owned enterprises, and the new competition of imported consumer goods that negatively impacted the manufacturing sectors. Already weakened by the 1970s and 1980s dictatorships, labor's bargaining power could not recover due to the contraction of manufacturing and public sector employment along with labor flexibilization, leaving workers vulnerable to unemployment and declining wages and benefits. By 1990, an estimated 50 percent of the region's population lived in poverty, many of whom lived in extreme poverty on one dollar per person per day or less. These developments also redistributed income and wealth in favor of the elites, worsening Latin America's chronic wealth and income inequality that ranked as the world's most extreme.

Many who lost their jobs or suffered wage cuts joined the masses surviving in the informal economy, which by 2000 included half of the region's urban population. They lived by hawking cheap goods on the streets, guarding parked automobiles, or offering their labor on an ad hoc basis; they lacked union representation, the protection of labor regulations, and social security benefits. In this period of heightened need, reductions in government spending on health, education, and subsidies for transportation and food were particularly onerous, as illustrated by sporadic and often violent protests against austerity measures and price increases. Elimination of the *tortilla* subsidy in Mexico contributed to the sharp contraction of real wages that propelled millions of desperate Mexicans northward seeking survival in the United States. Millions of Latin Americans fell into poverty, and millions more perched precariously just above the poverty line. Economic growth resumed in the 1990s, but in most countries it was erratic and punctuated by sporadic financial crises.

The effects of neoliberalism reached beyond the urban population. First the Mexican Revolution, then the Cuban Revolution made agrarian reform a key political issue in much of Latin America, and revolutionary governments in Peru, Chile, and Nicaragua carried out extensive land redistribution programs. The Pinochet dictatorship reversed agrarian reform in Chile, and Mexico terminated its seven decades of agrarian reform in 1992. Under neoliberalism, austerity and the emphasis on economic rather than social development kept the agrarian reform issue off political agendas in most countries. Moreover, as Latin America's urban population mushroomed from under 50

Chapter 8

Figure 8.2 A favela housing Brazil's urban poor

percent in 1960 to around 70 percent in 1990, political power shifted to the cities and urban priorities took precedence over those of the rural poor and landless. Thus rural poverty continued unabated or worsened across most of Latin America.

The deleterious effects of neoliberalism did not go unnoticed. Fidel Castro, progressive politicians, academics, even conservative Pope John Paul II spoke out against the social impact of neoliberalism. The Latin American Council of Bishops condemned "economism," or "the absolutizing of market forces and the power of money, forgetting that the economy is to be at the service of the people and not the other way around."[7] By the end of the 1990s, the World Bank, a chief architect of the neoliberal policies imposed on Latin America and much of the rest of the world, began advocating measures to reverse the social damage it had caused. Renowned Mexican man of letters Carlos Fuentes wondered how political democracy could survive neoliberalism: "From the Caribbean to the Southern Cone, the question is, How much poverty can democracy sustain?"[8]

RESISTANCE TO NEOLIBERALISM

In December 1991, as the vogue of neoliberalism was sweeping Latin America, the Uruguayan Congress enacted a law that provided for privatization of several state enterprises, including the national telecommunications and petroleum companies, which had been under government ownership for decades. Citizens opposed to the dismantling of Uruguay's traditional state role in the economy mobilized against the measure and gathered the signatures of 25 percent of the electorate as required for a referendum. In the December 1992 referendum, 82.8 percent of eligible voters turned out, and 73 percent voted to repeal the law. By that action, Uruguayans reaffirmed an essential part of the socioeconomic democracy initiated under Jorge Batlle y Ordóñez in the early twentieth century.

Other instances of resistance to neoliberalism were not as peaceful as the Uruguayan referendum. After years of frustration with their marginalization and poverty, Mayan Indians in the southern Mexican state of Chiapas organized as the EZLN and rose in rebellion on January 1, 1994. Not coincidentally, that was the day that the North American Free Trade Agreement (NAFTA), which linked Mexico with the United States and Canada in a free trade zone, took effect. This treaty culminated the imposition of neoliberalism in Mexico. NAFTA threatened to further impoverish the Maya farmers facing competition with more efficient U.S. agricultural producers. The rebels captured and briefly held the state capital, San Cristóbal de las Casas; skirmished with government forces; then settled into a protracted war that relied more on websites than bullets. The movement's agenda later broadened to include a pro-indigenous platform, but it clearly began as a protest against aggressive neoliberalism.

In 1997, the World Bank offered Bolivian President Gonzalo Sánchez de Lozada $600 million of debt relief. In exchange, pushing its neoliberal agenda of privatization of government enterprises, the Bank required the sale of the public water system in the city of Cochabamba, Bolivia's fourth largest, to investors. The arrangement gave *Aguas de Tunari*, a joint venture of transnational corporations Bechtel and Edison International, a forty-year concession not only for the city water system but also for rights to ground, well, and irrigation water.

After implementation, water rates increased some 200 percent, consuming 25 to 30 percent of typical poor families' income. Popular resistance to the concession began in November 1999 under the leadership of a Coordinating Committee of Water and Life. Initial discussions with authorities were unproductive, and popular mobilization followed; the "Cochabamba water war" was on. A massive demonstration in February 2000 was repressed by soldiers and police. This was followed by open meetings throughout the city that drew huge crowds demanding termination of the concession. In early April, demonstrators erected barricades to repel the forces sent to disperse them. In response, the government declared martial law and pursued the Coordinating Committee's organizers. The random murder of a young man by government forces was a tipping point: On April 10, 2000, the concession was annulled and the state utility company resumed control of Cochabamba's water. As in Uruguay and in contrast to Mexico, popular opposition to neoliberalism succeeded in Cochabamba, but these victories could not stop the march of the new, old economic doctrine.

The value of the restoration of political democracy cannot be overstated. Democratization dissipated the black cloud of fear under which millions of people had lived and many had died. Latin Americans celebrated the end of severe repression, especially of state terrorism, with their commitment to democracy and human rights strengthened. At the same time, the "lost decade" of the 1980s and the imposition of neoliberalism halted or reversed the socioeconomic democratization that had occurred in many countries over the decades. Moving in opposite directions, political and socioeconomic democracy parted ways, putting in place during the last two decades of the century an unprecedented political democracy, but a hollow one.

SUGGESTIONS FOR FURTHER READING

Barahona de Brito, Alexandra. *Human Rights and Democratization in Latin America: Uruguay and Chile*. New York: Oxford University Press, 1997.
Berry, Albert, ed. *Poverty, Economic Reform, and Income Distribution in Latin America*. Boulder: Lynne Rienner, 1998.
Bethell, Leslie, ed. *Latin America: Economy and Society since 1930*. Cambridge, UK: Cambridge University Press, 1998.
Camp, Roderic Ai and Shannan L. Mattiace. *Politics in Mexico: The Path of a New Democracy*. Seventh ed. New York: Oxford University Press, 2020.
Domínguez, Jorge I. and Michael Shifter, eds. *Constructing Democratic Governance in Latin America*. Baltimore: Johns Hopkins University Press, 2008.
Gillespie, Charles Guy. *Negotiating Democracy: Politicians and Generals in Uruguay*. Cambridge, UK: Cambridge University Press, 1991.
Hagopian, Frances and Scott P. Mainwaring, eds. *The Third Wave of Democratization in Latin America: Advances and Setbacks*. Cambridge, UK: Cambridge University Press, 2005.
Huntington, Samuel P. *The Third Wave: Democratization in the Late Twentieth Century*. Norman: University of Oklahoma Press, 1991.

Kingstone, Peter R. *The Political Economy of Latin America: Reflections on Neoliberalism and Development*. New York: Routledge, 2011.

Montgomery, Tommie Sue. *Revolution in El Salvador: From Civil Strife to Civil Peace*. Second ed. Boulder: Westview Press, 1995.

Schultz, Jim and Melissa Crane Draper, eds. *Dignity and Defiance: Stories from Bolivia's Challenge to Globalization*. Berkeley: University of California Press, 2008.

Smith, Peter H. with Cameron J. Sells. *Democracy in Latin America: Political Change in Comparative Perspective*. Third ed. New York: Oxford University Press, 2017.

Walker, Thomas W. and Ariel C. Armony, eds. *Repression, Resistance, and Democratic Transition in Central America*. Wilmington: Scholarly Resources, 2000.

Winn, Peter, ed. *Victims of the Chilean Miracle: Workers and Neoliberalism in the Pinochet Era, 1972–2002*. Durham: Duke University Press, 2004.

Wright, Thomas C. *Impunity, Human Rights, and Democracy: Chile and Argentina, 1990–2005*. Austin: University of Texas Press, 2014.

NOTES

1. Samuel P. Huntington, *The Third Wave: Democratization in the Late Twentieth Century* (Norman: University of Oklahoma Press, 1991). Note that Huntington's book, published in 1991, does not cover most of the developments in the former Soviet bloc, the former Soviet Union, and the former Yugoslavia.

2. Rebecca Bill Chávez, *The Rule of Law in Nascent Democracies: Judicial Politics in Argentina* (Stanford: Stanford University Press, 2004), 29.

3. Jonathan Schlefer, *Palace Politics: How the Ruling Party Brought Crisis to Mexico* (Austin: University of Texas Press, 2008), 1.

4. "Chapultepec Agreement" (accessed at https://peacemaker.un.org/elsalvador -chapultepec92).

5. Amnesty International, "Guatemala Human Rights" (accessed at Amnestyusa. org/countries/guatemala).

6. Greg Grandin, *Empire's Workshop: Latin America, the United States, and the Rise of the New Imperialism* (New York: Metropolitan Books, 2006), 188.

7. Thomas W. Walker, *Nicaragua without Illusions: Regime Transition and Structural Adjustments in the 1990s* (Wilmington: Scholarly Resources, 1997), 300.

8. Carlos Fuentes, *A New Time for Mexico*, trans. Marina Gutman Castañeda (New York: Farrar, Straus, and Giroux, 1996), 110.

Chapter 9

Democracy in the New Millennium, 2000–Present

The turbulent and bloody era of revolution and reaction launched by the 1959 Cuban Revolution was drawing to a close by the early 1990s. With the end of the Pinochet dictatorship in Chile in 1990, state terrorism continued only in El Salvador and Guatemala but was winding down in both countries. The 1991 collapse of the USSR ended the Soviet subsidy that had sustained Cuba for thirty years and funded much of Castro's support for hemispheric revolution, forcing the Cuban Revolution to turn inward for survival. And the 1992 capture of Abimael Guzmán, leader of Peru's *Sendero Luminoso* insurrection, left Colombia, where the Revolutionary Armed Forces of Colombia (FARC) and smaller groups were still active, as the only country with sustained guerrilla warfare.[1]

With the violent clash between political democracy and authoritarianism largely resolved, advocates of democracy had new agendas for the new millennium. One was to shore up the political democracies that had emerged from repression and state terrorism over the past two decades. The other was to respond to the soaring levels of poverty produced by neoliberalism and the depressed prices of Latin America's exports in the 1980s and 1990s.

FORTIFYING POLITICAL DEMOCRACY

Between 1978 and 2000, most Latin American countries underwent democratic openings (chapter 8). Many of the new democracies appeared in countries with little or no democratic experience and culture. The challenge facing all was to consolidate their fledgling democracies; one approach followed in almost all countries was to make their political systems more inclusive.

Expanding the electorate was not a new development. Indeed, the history of political democracy in Latin America is largely the story of building

Table 9.1 Evolution of the Latin America Electorate*

Country	Year	Population in millions	Percentage of Population Registered	Percentage of Registered Voters Voting	Percentage of Population Voting
Argentina	1916	8.3	14.3%	62.7%	9.0%
	1946	15.8	21.6%	83.4%	18.0%
	1973	23.4	61.1%	85.5%	52.3%
	2003	38.7	65.8%	78.2%	51.4%
Bolivia	1951	2.8	7.2%	61.6%	4.4%
	1966	3.9	32.3%	86.6%	27.9%
	1980	5.6	35.9%	74.3%	26.6%
	2002	8.8	47.0%	72.1%	33.9%
Brazil	1930	33.6			5.6%
	1950	51.9	22.1%	72.1%	15.9%
	1989	147.5	55.6%	85.6%	47.6%
	2002	174.6	66.0%	79.5%	52.5%
Chile	1920	3.8	9.8%	45.1%	4.4%
	1946	5.6	11.2%	75.9%	8.8%
	1970	9.4	37.8%	83.5%	31.5%
	2000	15.2	53.1%	90.5%	48.1%
Colombia	1918	5.9			6.9%
	1949	11.4	25.2%	39.8%	10.0%
	1974	22.7	39.5%	58.1%	23.0%
	2002	43.8	55.3%	46.5%	25.7%
Costa Rica	1913	.41	20.0%	78.0%	15.6%
	1944	.73	22.5%	43.2%	9.7%
	1974	1.9	45.0%	79.9%	35.9%
	2002	4.0	56.7%	60.2%	34.2%
Cuba	1901	1.7	20.0%	63.5%	12.7%
	1936	4.1	40.8%	67.1%	27.3%
	1948	5.2	48.5%	78.7%	38.2%
Dominican Republic	1962	3.4	47.9%	64.7%	31.0%
	1974	4.5	44.1%	71.7%	31.6%
	1990	7.0	46.6%	59.9%	27.9%
	2004	8.9	56.2%	72.8%	41.0%
Ecuador	1901	1.27			5.8%
	1933	2.6			2.5%
	1968	5.6	21.2%	77.5%	16.4%
	2002	12.1	67.4%	71.2%	48.0%
El Salvador	1931	1.4	27.4%	58.3%	16.0%
	1967	3.2	40.2%	38.8%	15.6%
	1984	4.8	54.0%	59.0%	31.9%
	1999	6.2	51.2%	38.5%	19.8%

Guatemala	1944	2.4	13.0%	97.6%	12.7%
	1966	4.6	20.5%	50.0%	11.3%
	1985	8.0	34.6%	69.3%	24.0%
	2003	13.9	36.5%	58.9%	21.1%
Haiti	Insufficient data				
Honduras	1916	.67			12.8%
	1948	1.3	22.7%	86.0%	19.5%
	1971	2.6	34.2%	67.5%	23.1%
	1985	4.4	43.5%	84.0%	36.6%
	2001	6.6	52.4%	66.3%	34.7%
Mexico	1917	13.4			13.4%
	1982	73.0	43.2%	74.8%	32.2%
	1994	87.4	52.3%	77.2%	40.4%
	2000	97.4	60.4%	64.0%	38.6%
Nicaragua	1924	0.7	18.3%	69.8%	12.7%
	1963	1.5	37.1%	79.1%	29.4%
	1984	3.2	49.0%	75.4%	37.0%
	1996	4.7	51.4%	76.4%	39.3%
Panama	1948	0.8	40.1%	70.9%	28.4%
	1968	1.4	40.3%	60.1%	24.2%
	1989	2.3	51.0%	64.0%	32.5%
	2004	2.9	68.0%	76.9%	52.3%
Paraguay	1943	1.2			10.0%
	1963	1.9	38.7%	85.1%	32.9%
	1983	3.5	32.6%	92.6%	30.2%
	2003	5.8	41.5%	64.3%	26.7%
Peru	1931	6.1		82.5%	5.2%
	1956	8.9	17.7%	84.0%	14.9%
	1980	17.3		79.1%	29.6%
	2001	26.3	56.6%	81.4%	46.3%
Uruguay	1920	1.3			13.8%
	1950	2.2	54.3%	70.5%	38.3%
	1984	2.9	75.2%	87.9%	66.0%
	2004	3.7	66.9%	89.6%	60.0%
Venezuela	1947	4.5	36.9%	72.1%	26.6%
	1963	8.2	41.3%	92.3%	38.1%
	1983	17.3	44.9%	87.3%	39.2%
	2000	24.2	48.4%	56.6%	27.4%
United States (for comparison)	1900	76.1			18.4%
	1936	128.2			35.6%
	1968	200.7			36.5%
	1996	265.6			36.3%

Source: Dieter Nohlen, ed. *Elections in the Americas: A Data Handbook*, vols. 1 and 2 (Oxford, UK: Oxford University Press, 2005).

* These are presential elections, sometimes combined with congressional elections. Where more than four such elections are reported in the source, the elections in the table are spaced as equally as possible between the earliest and latest. Availability of data varies among countries.

inclusion over time. Most income and wealth qualifications for voting ended before 1900. Paraguay in 1961 was the last country to enfranchise women, and Brazil in 1985 was the last to offer illiterates the vote. Over a period of years, countries lowered the voting age to eighteen, and in a few to sixteen. Compulsory voting was another means of expanding political participation—a scheme adopted in several countries but widely abandoned as ineffective.

In recent years, most Latin American countries have made their politics more inclusive by empowering women. Women's suffrage, enacted between 1929 and 1961, had not done so. As late as 1989, Latin America had had no elected women presidents and very few members of national legislatures, cabinet members, or high court judges. This began to change in the 1990s and accelerated in the 2000s as women, abetted by supportive male politicians, broke down barriers to attaining higher office. This gave them a greater stake in their countries' political systems and made politics more inclusive while further legitimizing the fragile democracies emerging from the period of military dictatorship and state terrorism.

In 1991, Argentina became the world's first country to enact a gender quota law. This legislation mandated that a fixed percentage of all political parties' candidates for the national Congress be women. The Argentine innovation spread throughout the region until by 2022, only Cuba and Guatemala had failed to enact gender quotas.

The mandates of gender quotas have become broader over time. Several countries have extended quotas to regional and local elections. Nearly half require gender parity in party lists for national office. Most other countries that have adopted gender quotas require that women constitute between 30 percent and 40 percent on party lists, and some require alternation of female and male candidates on the lists in order to enhance women's chances for election. Numerous political parties have voluntarily adopted quotas for party offices. As a result of this dynamic, Latin America is the world's region with the greatest concentration of gender quotas.

Women's representation in national legislatures has greatly benefited from the quotas. From fewer than 1 percent of seats in 1979, they held 19 percent in 2012, ranging from a high of 40 percent in Nicaragua to a low of 4 percent in Haiti. In 2022, women held 35.8 percent of all congressional seats, making Latin America the region with the highest percentage of women in national legislatures, narrowly edging Europe. For comparison, in 2022 women held 27.0 percent of the seats in the U.S. Congress and 24.5 percent of parliamentary seats worldwide.

Women have held the office of president in several countries. Isabel Perón (1974–1976), Juan Perón's vice president, succeeded him upon his death (chapter 8). The second woman president was Lidia Gueiler Tejada, who served eight months as Bolivia's interim president (1979–1980). Latin

Table 9.2 Percentage of Women in National Legislatures, 2022

Country	Percentage of seats held by women
Argentina	44.2%
Bolivia	48.2%
Brazil	15.2%
Chile	32.7%
Colombia	20.2%
Costa Rica	45.6%
Cuba	53.4%
Dominican Republic	25.7%
Ecuador	38.7%
El Salvador	27.4%
Guatemala	19.4%
Haiti*	0.0%
Honduras	27.3%
Mexico	49.8%
Nicaragua	50.5%
Panama	22.5%
Paraguay	16.8%
Peru	40.0%
Uruguay	26.9%
Venezuela	22.2%
Latin America	35.8%
United States	27.0%
World	24.5%

Sources: Latin America and United States, retrieved from https://data.ipu.org/women-ranking; World, retrieved from http://archive.ipu.org/wmn-e/world.htm

*Haiti has not had a functioning parliament since 2019.

America's first elected woman president was Violeta Chamorro of Nicaragua (1990–1997). Women presidents have become more common in the new millennium: Mireya Moscoso of Panama (1999–2004); Michelle Bachelet of Chile (2006–2010 and 2014–2018); Cristina Fernández de Kirchner of Argentina (2007–2015); Laura Chinchilla of Costa Rica (2010–2014); Dilma Rousseff of Brazil (2010–2016); and Jeanine Áñez, interim president of Bolivia (2019–2020). The most recent woman to be elected president is Xiomara Castro of Honduras (2022–2026). Bachelet, Fernández, and Rousseff were elected to second terms. There seems to be no pattern of political orientation among the women presidents, as they have come from their countries' left, right, and center parties and coalitions.

Women's empowerment has extended beyond electoral offices. In 2018, women in their countries' highest courts ranged from 11.1 percent in Panama to 62.2 percent in Cuba, with women holding at least one third of positions in seven other countries. In the same year, the percentage of women in cabinet posts ranged from 4.9 in Brazil to 56.3 in Nicaragua, with women holding

Figure 9.1 Michelle Bachelet, president of Chile, 2006–2010 and 2014–2018
Getty Images/MARTIN BERNETTI/Staff

at least one third of cabinet positions in six other countries. In 2022, women held 50 percent or more of cabinet positions in Nicaragua, Costa Rica, and Colombia; Chile had the highest percentage at 58.

Another measure that has expanded the electorate and helped to consolidate democracy is external voting. Expatriates had sought this form of inclusion for some time, but in most countries it has come about only recently despite the fact that the economic crisis of the 1980s and the rise of repressive military dictatorships propelled millions of Latin Americans to North America, Europe, and beyond. Of the seventeen countries that have adopted expatriate voting, thirteen enacted it after 2000. An important factor in this electoral reform in some countries, particularly the poorer ones, is the importance of monetary remittances from those living abroad to family members in the country of origin. The countries most dependent on remittances in 2019 and the percentage of their gross domestic product (GDP) produced by remittances were: Haiti, 39 percent; El Salvador, 20 percent; Honduras, 20 percent; Guatemala, 12 percent; and Nicaragua, 11 percent; all of them have adopted external voting. Another factor in the adoption of external voting is the substantial numbers of exiles from the countries subjected to state terrorism in the 1970s and 1980s who have not returned but retain citizenship in their home countries.

Protecting human rights has also contributed to fortifying democracy. Numerous countries have endeavored to guarantee human rights by legislation and by ratifying international human rights treaties. Having lived through the Dirty War, with its huge toll of disappearances, Argentina went the furthest: In 1994, it incorporated the nine international human rights treaties that the country had ratified into its constitution and declared them superior to domestic law. Many countries have established national human rights commissions and ombudsmen to monitor and report on human rights violations. The OAS, through its Inter-American Commission on Human Rights and Inter-American Court of Human Rights, has added weight to the fight for human rights and, by extension, for political democracy.

Meanwhile, the OAS began promoting political democracy more robustly.[2] In 2001, the organization adopted its Inter-American Democratic Charter, which emphasizes political but reaffirms the commitment to socioeconomic democracy: "The peoples of the Americas have a right to democracy and their governments have an obligation to promote and defend it. Democracy is essential for the social, political, and economic development of the peoples of the Americas."[3] The Charter gave the OAS the power of sanction in the case of "an unconstitutional interruption of the democratic order of a member state."[4] If the rupture cannot be repaired through diplomacy, the OAS can suspend the offending state's membership by a two-thirds vote. The only application of the sanction occurred in 2009, when the president of Honduras was removed by a coup (see below). The country's membership was restored in 2011.

The OAS commitment to political democracy went beyond the words of the Charter and the use of its sanction power against Honduras. One of the OAS's responsibilities is observing elections to assure their fairness. Although the observation missions began in 1962, relatively few occurred until the wave of democratization began in 1978 and accelerated through the 1990s. In the new millennium, the organization's Department of Electoral Cooperation and Observation has a large and sophisticated apparatus to deploy to countries seeking the OAS imprimatur of honest elections as another means of consolidating their democracies. Most Latin American countries have invited OAS electoral observation missions at one time or another after 2000.

THE DISAPPEARING MILITARY DICTATORSHIP

These measures designed to consolidate political democracy would have mattered little if the behavior of Latin America's militaries had not changed. Beginning in the late 1970s and continuing through the 1980s, the generals retreated from presidential palaces to military barracks. Chilean General

Augusto Pinochet, who was voted out of office in 1988 and left the Moneda Palace in 1990, was almost the last to go. General Raoul Cedras's de facto rule in Haiti (1991–1994) was the only case of military governance since Pinochet.

Recent military withdrawal from governing contrasts sharply with historical experience. In the nineteenth century, military men routinely seized and held power in many countries, particularly prior to the rise of stable governments during the period of the export economies (chapter 1). The Great Depression triggered military coups that propelled officers to power and created several long-term military dictatorships. In the wake of the Cuban Revolution, soldiers took power to cleanse their countries of Marxism and "subversion."

In the last few decades, the military has generally refrained from staging coups when irregular situations, such as economic and social crises or interruptions of presidential terms, have arisen. In 2001, Argentina experienced both such crises simultaneously: The national currency lost two-thirds of its value overnight, deadly riots forced the president's resignation, and four interim presidencies followed within twelve days. This multidimensional crisis was an open invitation to military intervention in a country with a lengthy history of coups and military dictatorships, but the armed forces stood aside. Between 1990 and 2019, presidencies were interrupted by resignation or impeachment in Peru, Brazil, Bolivia, Paraguay, and multiple times in Ecuador. As recently as November 2020, Peru had three presidents in one week. These ruptures of presidential continuity offered opportunities for the military to fill vacuums of power, as they formerly tended and were expected to do. Yet almost all of these crises were resolved, without military intervention, by the constitutional prescriptions for succession.

In the new millennium, the militaries have removed only three presidents from office. Ecuadorian officers removed President Jamil Mahuad in 2000. In 2009, the Honduran military ousted and exiled President José Manuel Zelaya. This was not a clear-cut coup, however, as the Supreme Court had ordered Zelaya's detention for defying its rulings and, following the military's action, the Congress voted overwhelmingly to remove him from office. Despite the ambiguity of this presidential interruption, the OAS exercised its sanction power to suspend Honduras's membership in the organization. Following these two coups, the military rejected forming a government and allowed the constitutional order of succession to play out. The outcome of the 2019 coup in Bolivia was different (see below).

There are several reasons for the militaries' refusal to assume the responsibility of governing. Despite the severity of the COVID-19 pandemic, there has been no new crisis as dire as the Great Depression or the revolutionary mobilizations unleashed by the Cuban Revolution—both of which led to an explosion of military dictatorships. Leaders of the new democracies that emerged from the repression and state terrorism of the 1970s and 1980s worked to bring the militaries under civilian control by appointing civilians as ministers of defense and by limiting the militaries' role, by law or constitution, to external defense. Cutting budgets and cadre were common steps, balanced by providing updated materiel to maintain defensive capabilities. The militaries' intelligence services, notorious for spying on civilians and targeting many for persecution, were curtailed or dismantled. Human rights courses were added to military training curricula. Several countries have provided troops for UN peacekeeping missions, giving the armed forces a new role. Finally, the trials and convictions of hundreds of military personnel in Argentina and Chile for human rights violations during the dictatorships provide a cautionary tale.

DEMOCRATIC PROGRESS

Despite the numerous challenges to consolidating political democracy, considerable progress has been made in the early twenty-first century as elections have been held with expanded electorates almost everywhere and with fewer documented instances of electoral fraud. The once-formidable challenge of surrendering power to the opposition following a government's electoral defeat has become a routine occurrence. The expectation of military intervention in times of crisis has virtually disappeared, as has the threat of the military establishing dictatorships. While access to registration and voting still eludes some, and enforcement of campaign finance laws is lax, Latin America enjoys more, and more inclusive political democracy than ever before. Although many do not exercise their right to vote in every election, the vast majority of Latin Americans of the appropriate age are entitled to exercise the franchise—a stark contrast to the first century of independence.

These advances notwithstanding, citizen attitudes toward political democracy are ambivalent, with considerable variation across time, age, and national borders. Young people are less positive about democracy than older citizens who had lived under repressive military dictatorships. And not surprisingly, attitudes are more supportive during periods of greater prosperity than times of economic stagnation or regression.

According to reliable polling, citizens are less enthusiastic for political democracy than they were two decades ago; 61 percent of Latin Americans expressed support for democracy in 2021, down from 68 percent when this polling began in 2004. Reflecting in part the negative economic impact of the collapse of the commodities boom and the COVID-19 pandemic, only 43 percent of Latin Americans were satisfied with democracy in 2021, compared with 52 percent in 2004. Nonetheless, asked whether they would tolerate a military coup, 60 percent in 2021 answered in the negative, compared with only 48 percent who opposed a coup in 2004. These data suggest that while political democracy has less than optimal support, a strong majority prefer it to military rule.[5]

SOCIOECONOMIC DEMOCRACY: BUILDING OR REBUILDING SOCIAL SAFETY NETS

Latin America's new political democracies faced strong headwinds. Not only did many lack democratic experience and culture; they arose during the onslaught of neoliberalism, which drove many workers into the informal economy and exacerbated poverty and inequality (chapter 8). While leaders sought to strengthen the new democracies by making them more inclusive, as noted above, the growth of poverty during the 1980s and 1990s meant that the political democracies of the early twenty-first century lacked firm underpinnings. In addressing poverty, the Latin American countries formed part of a worldwide effort led by the United Nations to drive down or eradicate poverty. The anti-poverty drive has been supported by the World Bank and the IMF, the same institutions that forced neoliberalism upon Latin America and caused poverty to mushroom.

An economic recovery in the early 2000s provided the wherewithal essential to Latin American governments' anti-poverty campaigns. A prolonged decline in the prices of Latin America's raw material exports in the 1980s and 1990s gave way to a "commodities boom" between 2003 and 2014 that boosted demand for Latin America's exports of copper, iron ore, oil, soybeans, grains, and other raw materials to fuel growing economies, particularly that of China. Latin American trade with China ballooned from $10 billion in 2000 to $241 billion in 2011. The terms of trade—the price of Latin America's exports relative to the price of imports—also improved significantly. As exports grew in volume and value, demand for labor stimulated employment and wages, which in turn promoted consumption and drove growth in other economic sectors. Enhanced government revenues led to public investment in infrastructure and other areas, creating further employment opportunities.

Latin American governments did not rely solely on the bounty of the commodities boom to fight poverty and build or rebuild social safety nets. While the drive to reduce poverty accelerated after 2000, a novel approach to poverty reduction dates to 1990, when the government of Honduras, one of poorest countries in the hemisphere, pioneered the conditional cash transfer (CCT), or payments to poor families with conditions attached. From the modest beginning in Honduras, CCTs spread through Latin America. Some programs target families mired in extreme poverty, defined by the World Bank as living on less than U.S. $1.90 per person per day. Others aid families in more moderate poverty, those living on less than U.S. $5.50 per person per day. By 2010, the largest programs served millions of people: Mexico's program was serving five million households, while Brazil's supported eleven million families, nearly a quarter of the country's population.

While the amounts of monthly payments to poor households vary across the region, all CCT programs are focused on the health and education of the recipient families. Pregnant women must have pre- and post-natal medical visits. Babies and young children must have regular medical check-ups and be vaccinated. Nutritional education is often offered. School-age children are required to stay in school through specified grade levels. Success of the CCTs requires the provision of adequate schools, health facilities, and trained personnel for both—a major challenge in the poorer countries.

The CCTs' long-term goal is to promote social mobility by enabling recipients to escape the intergenerational transmission of poverty. According to economist Santiago Levy, the architect of Mexico's anti-poverty program, the objective of CCTs is "to try to help poor families today with investments in their human capital, in nutrition, education and health, with the idea that we won't have to help them tomorrow, because these investments . . . will enable them to gain better salaries and more productive jobs in the future enabling them to leave poverty."[6] In the short term, the CCTs and other governmental anti-poverty programs, combined with the economic stimulus provided by the commodities boom, lifted millions of Latin Americans out of poverty. However, the cooling of the Chinese and other fast-growing economies beginning in 2014 and the impact of the COVID-19 pandemic reversed the downward trajectory of poverty. While CCTs have been effective in poverty alleviation, they are no solid foundation for socioeconomic democracy.

Along with poverty, Latin America suffers great disparities in wealth and income. Inequality is embedded in Latin America's history. Beginning in the colonial period, Europeans and European-descended people (creoles and mazombos) exploited indigenous peoples, held Africans and their descendants as slaves, and ruled over the mixed-race population that developed over the centuries, appropriating property and wealth to themselves along the way. Inequality persisted through the first century of independence and began to change significantly only in the twentieth century as limited social services were instituted, a middle class developed, and workers joined unions. The socioeconomic advances that followed narrowed inequality somewhat, but still left chasms between rich and poor. Blatant inequality has engendered protests and riots in several countries since 2000, including Chile (see below). In 2019, Brazil had the region's highest income inequality while El Salvador had the lowest.[7]

Table 9.3 Poverty and Extreme Poverty in Latin America, select years 1990–2021*

Year	Percentage of people living in poverty**	Number of people living in poverty in millions	Percentage of people living in extreme poverty	Number of people living in extreme poverty in millions
1990	51.2%	212	15.5%	64
2002	45.3%	229	12.2%	62
2010	31.6%	176	8.7%	48
2015	29.1%	171	8.8%	52
2018	29.8%	181	10.4%	63
2020	33.0%	204	13.1%	81
2021 (estimate)	32.1%	201	13.8%	86

Source: Social Panorama of Latin America 2021, retrieved from https://repositorio.cepal.org/bitstream/handle/11362/47719/1/S2100654_en.pdf

*No data for Cuba and Haiti

**The Economic Commission for Latin America and the Caribbean (ECLAC) assesses poverty based on criteria other than U.S. dollars per person per day. Its formula begins with the cost of a basic basket of food and includes costs of necessities and inflation.

THE PINK TIDE

One of the salient political developments of the early twenty-first century was the emergence of a number of leftist governments collectively known as the Pink Tide, which came to power largely through their opposition to neoliberalism. Hugo Chávez, elected president of Venezuela in 1998, pioneered the Pink Tide. He was followed by Brazil's Luiz Inácio Lula da Silva (known simply as Lula) and Argentina's Néstor Kirchner in 2003, by Uruguay's Tabaré Vásquez in 2005, Bolivia's Evo Morales in 2006, Ecuador's Rafael Correa and Nicaragua's Daniel Ortega in 2007, and El Salvador's Mauricio Funes in 2009.

These governments were more moderate than the revolutionary regimes that took power between 1968 and 1979 (chapter 6) and much more so than the Cuban Revolution. Often described or self-identified as "socialist" or proponents of "twenty-first-century socialism," several renationalized industries that had been privatized under neoliberalism but did not take expropriation of the private economy as far as it went in Cuba and, to a lesser extent, in Peru, Chile, and Nicaragua. Rather, the new leftist leaders attempted to humanize neoliberalism, rather than vanquish it altogether, by establishing social safety nets for as many of their citizens as possible. Compared with more conservative contemporary governments, Pink Tide regimes normally expanded anti-poverty programs for broader coverage and took additional measures such as establishing or enhancing old age pensions, raising the minimum wage, and in some cases, carrying out agrarian reform. We will examine three iconic and very different Pink Tide regimes: those of Hugo Chávez in Venezuela (1999–2013), Lula in Brazil (2003–2010), and Evo Morales in Bolivia (2006–2019).

Following a long history of dictatorship, Venezuela launched a promising experiment in democracy in 1958 (chapter 5). The government relied on income from massive petroleum exports for its socioeconomic programs, but in the 1980s falling oil prices and adoption of neoliberal policies drove up poverty and eroded support for political democracy. A colonel in the Venezuelan army, Hugo Chávez achieved prominence as leader of a failed 1992 coup. Despite its failure, the military uprising made Chávez popular among the country's poor majority and positioned him for a future in electoral politics following his 1994 release from prison.

That future arrived in 1998, when Chávez was elected president with 56 percent of the vote on a promise to write a new constitution and change the country's direction. The following year, he secured his new constitution, which called for broad participation in politics and renamed the country the "Bolivarian Republic of Venezuela" after the liberator of South America and founder of Venezuela, Simón Bolívar. In 2000 Chávez was elected to a six-year term. With its Bolivarian majority, the Congress in 2001 granted Chávez decree powers, which he used extensively. As opposition grew and some privately owned media openly called for his ouster, a military coup briefly overthrew him in April 2002, but loyal army units and massive protests by his supporters turned the tide in his favor, and he was back in office within forty-eight hours. Washington denied involvement in the coup. The opposition then turned to the constitution's referendum provision to force a recall election in 2004, but the president prevailed with 59 percent of the vote.

Corresponding with a rebound of oil prices, Chávez ramped up his socio-economic program in 2003. Rather than following the CCT pattern, he developed what he called "missions." This outreach involved promoting grassroots organizations among the poor in line with his emphasis on participatory democracy. Eventually numbering approximately twenty, the missions had specific charges designed to lift people out of poverty and improve their lives in other ways. Among the most important were those aimed at education: literacy, remedial primary and secondary education, and university education through extension programs. Another, *Misión Mercal*, consisted of government-owned supermarkets and cooperatives that distributed heavily subsidized food. *Misión Barrio Adentro* involved the construction and operation of clinics in poor urban and rural areas to provide basic health care. Others focused on housing, land reform, popular culture in the arts, and the creation of a citizen militia. Chávez staffed his missions, in part, by trading oil for Cuban human capital: Some twenty thousand Cuban medical personnel were sent to Venezuela's poorest areas as part of Cuba's "soft power" deployment of medical professionals throughout much of the world. Most estimates indicate that these combined efforts, including an agrarian reform that benefited approximately half of the rural population, cut Venezuela's poverty rate by some 50 percent.

In addition to his outreach to the poor, Chávez increased state ownership of the economy in oil, steel, agriculture, banking, telecommunications, and power by expropriation or purchase, reversing some of the privatizations carried out under the neoliberal policies of the 1980s and 1990s. He also raised the government's share of oil revenues. With Cuba's power in decline, Chávez asserted Venezuela's leadership of Latin America's left in 2005 by forming the Bolivarian Alliance for the Peoples of our America (ALBA, which also means "dawn"), a trade and solidarity agreement with Cuba, Pink Tide–governed regimes in Bolivia, Ecuador, and Nicaragua, and several Caribbean island nations.

Chávez continued to build his personal power through a form of authoritarian creep, winning reelection in 2006 with 63 percent of the vote, forming his United Socialist Party of Venezuela (PSUV) the following year, and in 2009 winning a referendum to allow unlimited presidential reelections. Chávez's authoritarian style was controversial, particularly to the business and conservative political groups that opposed his agenda and to the U.S. government. He was a charismatic leader who developed a cult of personality and established relationships with his followers through his missions and his Sunday

Figure 9.2 Hugo Chávez, Pink Tide pioneer and president of Venezuela, 1999–2013
Agência Brasil

television and radio show, "Aló Presidente" (Hello President). The regime became increasingly authoritarian, with few checks on its power, media freedom under siege, and a thoroughly politicized military. The domestic opposition and U.S. media began labeling Chávez a dictator, despite international observers' validation of all the elections and referenda. The U.S. government invested heavily to shore up the opposition to a regime it considered increasingly hostile, even dangerous, to U.S. interests. Chávez responded by calling U.S. President George W. Bush "the devil" and assailing "American imperialism."

Diagnosed with cancer in 2011, Chávez went to Cuba several times for treatment and died in March 2013 after winning another presidential term in 2012. His remains repose in an impressive mausoleum with an eternal flame and a military guard. He was succeeded in office by his vice president, Nicolás Maduro (see below).

Along with Rafael Correa of Ecuador and Evo Morales of Bolivia, Chávez represented the Pink Tide's more radical, populist wing. Brazil's Lula, a progressive and pragmatic man of modest origins, followed a less flamboyant, more moderate approach to humanizing neoliberalism. As the long Brazilian military dictatorship (1964–1985) began to allow political activity in preparation for returning power to civilians, Lula took advantage of the opening by forming an independent labor union and, in 1980, the Workers' Party (PT). Lula ran unsuccessfully for president in 1990. Fernando Collor de Mello, the winner, embraced the neoliberal trend of austerity, lowered tariffs, and privatization of government-owned enterprises. The persistent Lula lost in the two subsequent elections before winning on his fourth try in 2002 and being reelected in 2006, taking over 60 percent of the vote in both cases.

During his tenure, Lula focused on dual goals: raising Brazil's international stature to a level befitting the world's eighth largest economy and alleviating the country's widespread, persistent poverty. Internationally, he promoted Brazil's newer exports such as airplanes and ethanol. He lobbied unsuccessfully for a permanent seat on the UN Security Council but gave Brazil a prominent role in the new Group of Twenty (G-20), an international forum for major economies. Finally, Lula enhanced Brazil's image by luring the world's greatest sporting events to the country: the World Cup soccer tournament in 2014 and, for only the second time in Latin America, the Olympic Games in 2016, both held after his presidency.

Lula's war on poverty was a multifaceted endeavor that included raising the minimum wage and expanding social security, credit for small farmers, and pensions for workers in the growing informal economic sector. A major infrastructure project created jobs. The centerpiece of the fight against poverty was his version of the CCT approach. He first launched the Zero Hunger (*Fome Zero*) program to combat the malnutrition that accompanied poverty. Then he combined that program with one started by his predecessor, Fernando Henrique Cardoso, that paid cash to families for keeping their children in school and getting them vaccinated. The hybrid Family Stipend (*Bolsa Familia*) eventually reached nearly a quarter of Brazil's population. These combined approaches reduced poverty dramatically; government figures indicate that "extreme poverty" fell from 9 percent to 4 percent by 2012.

Unlike Chávez, who controlled almost all the levers of power in Venezuela, Lula was constrained by the PT's minority status in Congress, which necessitated negotiations and coalitions and ruled out potential radical legislation. He carried out agrarian reform through an existing modest program, primarily on public lands in remote areas, thus avoiding most expropriations. He disappointed Brazil's powerful agrarian reform lobby, the Landless Workers' Movement, by distributing only marginally more land than his predecessor. Lula did not nationalize important parts of the economy. Tapping enhanced income during the commodities boom, he paid off the entirety of Brazil's debt to the IMF in 2006. *The Economist* praised him for pursuing "growth and equality within the confines of a responsible economic policy."[8] Despite his shortcomings in socioeconomic democratization and the disappointment of some within his PT, Lula was very popular; he had an 80 percent approval rating at the end of his second term.

Lula's successor and vice president Dilma Rousseff essentially followed the policy direction of her predecessor. After winning a second term in 2014, Rousseff was impeached and removed from office by Congress amid major

Figure 9.3 Lula, Pink Tide president of Brazil, 2003–2010

corruption scandals. In 2018, Brazil elected conservative former military officer Jair Bolsonaro, who set Brazil on a course radically different from those of Lula and the Pink Tide (see below).

A third Pink Tide regime took power in Bolivia. Elected president with 54 percent of the vote in December 2005, Evo Morales, an Aymara Indian, had achieved prominence as leader of a coca leaf growers' union that fought to stop Bolivian governments' collaboration with U.S. efforts to eradicate the farming of coca—a plant which, in addition to forming the basis of cocaine, has important historic and cultural significance to the Andean peoples. Founded in 1998, Morales's party, the Movement Toward Socialism (MAS), grew out of the *cocaleros'* movement.

Nationalism, *indigenismo*, and efforts to build a social safety net for South America's poorest country were hallmarks of Morales's 2006–2019 tenure.[9] Bolivia's economy, powered by natural gas exports to Brazil and Argentina, benefited from the high prices of the commodities boom. In 2006 he forced the international gas companies to negotiate new contracts, raising the government's share of gas profits to 82 percent. The following year a law gave control of all mineral rights to the state. Although selective nationalizations followed and Morales continually denounced imperialism, substantial new foreign investment flowed into the country. In 2017, Morales emphatically rejected neoliberalism by declaring Bolivia's "total independence" from the World Bank and the IMF. His nationalism was more than economic: In 2008 he expelled U.S. ambassador Philip Goldberg for interfering in Bolivia's internal affairs. He later expelled the U.S. Drug Enforcement Agency (DEA) and the United States Agency for International Development (USAID) for similar reasons. From that low point, U.S.-Bolivia relations gradually improved but U.S. drug policies and some of Morales's domestic initiatives, his alignment with Cuba and Venezuela, and Bolivia's membership in Chávez's ALBA were ongoing controversies.

Morales's indigenismo was on display from the beginning of his tenure. He held two inaugurations: the first at Tiwanaku, a revered native religious site, and the second in the traditional style in the capital, La Paz. Bolivia incorporated the UN's 2007 Declaration on the Rights of Indigenous Peoples as national law. Evo's 2009 constitution created the "Plurinational State of Bolivia," which defines indigenous peoples as "every human collective that shares a cultural identity, language, historic tradition, institutions, territory, and world view, whose existence predates the Spanish colonial invasion." Enumerated rights of indigenous groups include self-determination, cultural identity, religious beliefs, cultural practices and customs, collective land ownership (the ayllu), and seven designated seats in the 173-member Congress, which is renamed the Plurinational Legislative Assembly.[10]

A key aspect of the regime's elevation of native peoples was the notion of "decolonization," or freeing Bolivia from the legacy of centuries of European and creole domination. In Morales's words, "What we want is equality and justice; to repair the damage of five hundred years of colonization."[11] To implement this somewhat vague goal, Morales created a Vice-Ministry of Decolonization in 2009. In practice, decolonization meant making the indigenous equal to the European-derived practices in a number of fields. For example, laws required that traditional native medicine be taught in medical schools and that native languages and cultures be taught in all public schools. In addition, three indigenous universities were established.

The Morales administration pursued a number of initiatives to fight poverty and create an effective social safety net under the rubric of "*Vivir Bien*," or living well. It expanded a CCT measure from the late 1990s into three separate components that reached additional families: pre- and post-natal care for pregnant women; payments to keep children vaccinated and in school through eighth grade; and old age pensions. Price controls were imposed on essential goods and services. A literacy campaign aimed at the illiterate 40 percent of rural and 20 percent of urban Bolivians had some success. Measures to promote health among the poor included the deployment of some nine hundred Cuban doctors and eight hundred paramedics, largely to new clinics in rural areas and urban slums, and scholarships were established for five thousand

Figure 9.4 Evo Morales, Bolivia's indigenous Pink Tide president, 2006–2019
Getty Images/José Luis Quintana/Contributor

Bolivians to study medicine in Cuba. In the rural areas, electrification, road building, and the establishment of schools and clinics improved peasant lives. A 2006 agrarian reform law revived the process launched by the 1952 revolution with significant progress achieved in land distribution. Overall, these initiatives combined with the commodities boom reduced poverty by an estimated 40 percent and extreme poverty by 60 percent.

Despite having a two-thirds majority in Congress after 2009, Morales did not have the degree of control that Chávez achieved in Venezuela. Morales's indigenismo and socioeconomic reforms were embraced by the indigenous population but resisted by the more European and mestizo, more wealthy lowland residents of eastern Santa Cruz department, who constantly pushed for autonomy and resisted most of the president's initiatives. He also faced challenges from supporters who tried to drive him leftward; militant peasant and worker organizations continually used protests, strikes, and highway blockages to press their demands.

Morales won reelection in 2009 with 64 percent of the vote. Thereafter, apparently considering himself indispensable to the success of his revolution, he resorted to manipulating the system to prolong his tenure rather than grooming a successor. In the run-up to the 2014 election, his supporters in the Plurinational Constitutional Court ruled that the constitution's two-term limit did not apply as his first term had begun prior to the constitution's adoption. He won that election with 61 percent of the vote. To pave the way to a yet another term, he called a referendum in 2016 on allowing a fourth term, which was narrowly defeated. Undeterred, Morales turned again to the Plurinational Constitutional Court, which in November 2017, citing the OAS's American Convention on Human Rights, declared term limits a human rights violation—a decision rejected by the OAS Secretary-General.

The October 2019 election was Morales's undoing. The constitution stipulated that if no candidate reached 50 percent of the vote, the leading candidate could win the presidency with 40 percent and a ten-point advantage over the second-place contender. With Morales under 50 percent and leading the second-place contender by fewer than ten points, broadcasting of the results was suspended. When it resumed after twenty hours, after more ballots had arrived from remote, pro-MAS areas, Morales led by slightly over the ten-point threshold for election but with suspicions raised by the suspension of the count, protests mounted. Seeking validation of his victory, Morales invited the OAS to audit the vote. In a controversial report, the OAS alleged that there had been serious irregularities. Facing disorder, a rebellion by the national police, and the military commanders' call for him to go, he resigned on November 10 and flew to Mexico. This was a soft coup, but a coup nonetheless.

As in Ecuadorian and Honduran coups, the Bolivian military rejected taking office. However, in contrast to the other cases, the constitutional order of succession was not followed as violence and threats led the designated successor and others in the line of succession, all members of MAS, to flee. Eventually, with military support, conservative, anti-MAS Jeanine Áñez emerged as provisional president. But eleven months later, economist Luis Arce, the MAS candidate, won the Bolivian presidential election and promised to build on Morales's achievements.

Nearly a quarter century after Hugo Chávez launched the Pink Tide, only one of its original protagonists continued in power but he, Daniel Ortega, had abandoned the socioeconomic objectives common to Pink Tide regimes and ruled Nicaragua as a dictator. Yet the Latin American left was not dead. By 2022, observers had discerned what some were calling a New Pink Tide, consisting of eight left-leaning governments. The new left in power was as disparate as the original Pink Tide. Mexico's Andrés Manual López Obrador (AMLO), elected in 2018, and Argentina's Alberto Fernández (2019, not related to his predecessor Cristina Fernández de Kirchner), pursued relatively moderate change. Luis Arce of Bolivia (2020) basically continued Evo Morales's policies. Honduran Xiomara Castro (2022) ran on a platform of democratic change. The more radical wing, at least in terms of their political programs, consisted of Peruvian Pedro Castillo (2021) and Chile's Gabriel Boric (2022). The election of Colombian leftist Gustavo Petro in June 2022 and Lula of Brazil in October 2022 (see below) added momentum to the leftward tilt of Latin America.

CONTEMPORARY DEVELOPMENTS WITH IMPLICATIONS FOR DEMOCRACY

Dictatorship Redux

Despite the strong trend toward political democracy, authoritarian rule has made a comeback in a few countries, most notably in Venezuela, Nicaragua, and El Salvador while in Brazil, a would-be authoritarian attempted but failed to override constitutional restraints on his powers. In the first three countries, the aspiring dictators followed a similar playbook. Friendly congressional majorities, elected fairly or fraudulently, and high courts were key to their power grabs. One or both of these bodies eliminated constitutional prohibitions of successive presidential reelections. With that check on their powers eliminated, the protagonists were able to consolidate power and establish dictatorships.

Upon Hugo Chávez's death in March 2013, Nicolás Maduro, his vice president, took office. A month later, he won an election, denounced by the opposition as fraudulent, for a full term. Benefiting from the 2009 referendum that abolished term limits, he methodically converted the authoritarian regime he inherited to an outright dictatorship.

In a first step, the pliant National Assembly granted Maduro the right to rule by decree. In a setback to Maduro's ambitions, the opposition gained control of the National Assembly in December 2015 amid growing citizen anger over severe repression, a prolonged recession, and runaway inflation. Before the new legislature was seated, however, the outgoing PSUV-controlled body packed the Supreme Court with Maduro loyalists. By this point, Maduro's deeds and inflammatory words had earned him the unwavering opposition of successive U.S. administrations resolved to undermine his regime.

In July 2017, Maduro created a constituent assembly by referendum. But rather than draw up a new charter, the PSUV-dominated body appropriated the functions of the opposition-controlled National Assembly, rendering it powerless. Maduro's May 2018 reelection, in a poll boycotted by the opposition, was not recognized by the OAS, the European Union, the United States, and a majority of Latin American countries. Against that backdrop, in January 2019 Juan Guaidó, a member of the neutered National Assembly, swore himself in as president of Venezuela and was quickly recognized as the legitimate ruler by the United States and some sixty other countries.

The government met protests against growing poverty and abuse of power with repression, often deadly. Maduro faced heightened economic sanctions, a failing economy, a thwarted plot by Guaidó to foment a military uprising, and a bizarre invasion led by two former U.S. Green Berets. Meanwhile,

Figure 9.5 Nicolás Maduro, Hugo Chávez's successor and dictator of Venezuela, 2013–present
Agência Brasil

millions of Venezuelans voted with their feet in a diaspora that spread throughout Latin America and beyond. Tactical and financial support from Russia, China, and Iran and personnel from Cuba propped up the increasingly isolated regime.

Maduro consolidated his dictatorship in December 2020 when his party regained control of the National Assembly, the last national political institution that he did not dominate. A key element in the dictatorship's survival was the military hierarchy, whose loyalty is based, in part, on the generals' control of lucrative state-owned enterprises. Under Maduro, Venezuela had reverted to its historic pattern of dictatorship.

Former Sandinista commander and president of Nicaragua Daniel Ortega established another dictatorship. Following his loss in the 1990 presidential election to conservative Violeta Chamorro (chapter 6), Ortega ran unsuccessfully in 1996 and 2001, distancing himself further each time from his revolutionary past. He finally prevailed in the 2006 election, winning with only 38 percent of the vote after the conservatives split. The same year the FSLN won a plurality of seats in the National Assembly and gained a comfortable majority in 2011.

In office, Ortega began dismantling institutional checks on presidential power. The FSLN gained control of the Supreme Court after purging its conservative members and lifted the ban on presidential succession in office. Ortega enhanced his authority over governmental institutions, including the military and police forces, and placed family members and allies in key positions. Controlling the electoral machinery, he easily won the 2016 election with his wife, Rosario Murillo, as his running mate.

Facing budgetary problems, Ortega announced cuts in social security benefits in April 2018, resulting in major protests demanding his resignation and restoration of political democracy. A brutal crackdown left over three hundred people dead, over two thousand injured, and hundreds imprisoned. Prior to the November 2021 election, the FSLN-controlled National Assembly gave Ortega the power to ban individuals from running for office for a variety of alleged, mostly vague offenses. Using that power liberally, he detained seven presidential candidates and over thirty other opposition figures, while the electoral court prohibited three parties from contesting the election. Ortega and Murillo won reelection with three-fourths of the vote in the sham election. With Ortega as president, his wife as vice president, and family members strategically placed throughout the government and the economy, Nicaragua appeared poised for a new Somoza-style dynasty.

The 1992 peace accords ended civil war and state terrorism in El Salvador and outlined a political democracy with socioeconomic components. Political democracy functioned relatively well, with conservatives holding power until the former guerrilla group FMLN, reconstituted as a political party, took the presidency in 2009 and 2014. However, gang violence continued, corruption flourished, and the socioeconomic promises of the peace accords remained largely unfulfilled. The new democracy's failure to address these and other issues led to its demise.

Nayib Bukele, the grandson of Palestinian immigrants, was elected mayor of the capital, San Salvador, in 2015. His popularity as mayor led to his election as president in 2019, at age thirty-seven. His party won a majority in the April 2021 legislative election and, in alliance with three small parties, achieved a two-thirds super majority in the National Assembly. The Assembly immediately, and illegally, purged the attorney general's office and the Constitutional Court and packed them with Bukele loyalists, undermining judicial independence—a central element of the peace accords. Bukele called this action "house cleaning," while domestic and international organizations deemed it an illegal power grab. In September 2021 the Constitutional Court ruled that Bukele could run for reelection in 2024, potentially closing out El Salvador's brief interlude of political democracy.

Jair Bolsonaro, a former army captain, was elected president of Brazil in October 2018 following a campaign filled with demagoguery and authoritarian rhetoric. He brought numerous active and retired military men into his administration, raising concern about a reversion to the recent state terrorist dictatorship. He attempted to subvert constitutional restraints on his power but lacking a congressional majority he made little headway. He constantly lashed out at opponents and made the Supreme Court his favorite target, once threatening to dispatch troops to close it. He declared, "I am actually the constitution."[12]

Rather than acknowledge the seriousness of the COVID-19 pandemic, he downplayed the danger. He called his compatriots "a country of sissies" and told them to stop "whining."[13] Bolsonaro's attitude was partially responsible the high number of reported deaths from COVID-19. His autocratic tendencies and inadequate response to the pandemic earned him the sobriquet "Trump of the tropics" and cost him political support.

Former President Lula was convicted of corruption, but, following a year and a half in prison, was freed by the Supreme Court in November 2019 and cleared to run against incumbent Bolsonaro for the presidency. Following an acrimonious and hard-fought campaign, Lula narrowly defeated Bolsonaro, 50.9 to 49.1 percent—a margin of 2.14 million votes—on October 30, 2022. As during his previous presidency (2003–2010), Lula will lack a congressional majority and thus be constrained in the scope of socioeconomic reforms he is able to enact. However, perhaps more importantly, Brazil's young political democracy has apparently survived its most perilous moment.

Chile and Pinochet's legacy

Violent protests, known as *el estallido* (the explosion), erupted in Chile in October 2019 after the right-wing government of Sebastián Piñera imposed a small increase in the fares of the Metro, a transit system that serves Santiago and its suburbs. As hundreds of thousands of people around the country joined the students who initiated the protests, the movement morphed into a protest against Chile's high degree of income and wealth inequality, which had been exacerbated by the neoliberal policies enacted under the Pinochet dictatorship. Protesters targeted sub-standard education, health care, wages, pensions, and opportunities for the poor in the largely privatized economy. Police and army brutality in countering the protests further energized the movement, despite cancellation of the fare increase and other conciliatory moves by the government.

After a few weeks the protesters' focus shifted again, to Pinochet's 1980 constitution. Approved in a bogus plebiscite, and although much amended, the constitution prolongs undemocratic norms and practices and remains a potent symbol of the country's era of state terrorism. Under popular pressure, the authorities agreed to hold a referendum on whether to retain or replace Pinochet's constitution. On October 23, 2020, Chileans voted overwhelmingly, 78 percent to 22 percent, to adopt a new constitution. A constituent assembly with gender parity and a large left-wing contingent was elected in

Figure 9.6 Chileans protesting inequality and Pinochet's 1980 constitution, 2019
Getty Images/SEBASTIAN CISTERNAS/Contributor

April 2021; its product, designed to deepen both socioeconomic and political democracy, was deemed too radical by the Chilean electorate, which overwhelmingly rejected it, 62 to 38 percent, on September 4, 2022. Despite that setback, there was still strong sentiment to draft a more moderate and workable constitution that will erase the remainder of Pinochet's legacy.

DEMOCRACY IN CUBA

The collapse of the Soviet Union in 1991 and the end of the Soviet subsidy led the Cuban economy to contract by one third. Faced with this dire situation, compounded by a tightening of the decades-old U.S. economic embargo, Castro instituted modest economic reforms, including openings for small private businesses and encouragement of foreign investment in tourism. In poor health, Fidel Castro resigned the presidency in 2008 and was succeeded by his younger brother Raúl Castro. More pragmatic than Fidel, Raúl announced his intention to reduce government employment by 20 percent as a step toward a mixed state-private economy. Faced with a growing exodus of Cubans fleeing poverty and lack of opportunity, he carried out additional economic reforms, including legalizing more private businesses and creating a real estate market in houses and apartments.

While fueling modest economic growth, the economic reforms have carried a high price. The revolution's socioeconomic democracy, based on the principle of egalitarianism, has given way to social divisions: Those with access to dollars or euros brought by tourists or remitted by relatives living abroad are able to acquire consumer goods, while those without still depend on low-paying state jobs and the meager goods acquired by the ration card. This has turned professionals such as medical doctors and university professors to waiting tables and driving taxis in order to enter the hard currency economy. The 2015 restoration of U.S.-Cuban diplomatic relations fueled a surge in U.S. tourism that further entrenched the hard currency-ration card divide in Cuban society.

Following Raúl Castro's 2018 retirement from the presidency, the evolving order was formalized in 2019 in a new constitution. This document addresses both political and socioeconomic democracy. It confirms the dictatorship of the Communist Party in terms borrowed from the 1976 constitution (chapter 5). The civil rights intrinsic to political democracies, as before, are subordinated to the party dictatorship: "People's freedom of press is recognized. This right is exercised according to the law and for the good of society." The new constitution's definition of socioeconomic democracy reflects the reforms that moved the country away from the egalitarian model that was the hallmark of the Cuban Revolution. In contrast to the 1976 charter, it recognizes and

Figure 9.7 U.S. President Barack Obama and Cuban leader Raúl Castro restore diplomatic relations, July 2015

protects private property and foreign investment and restates Cuba's commitment to socialist values, but not to classical socialism: the state "guarantees an increasingly just redistribution of wealth in order to conserve the limits that are compatible with the socialist values of equity and social justice."[14]

Raúl resigned as first secretary of the party in April 2021, completing the transition to the post-Castro era. Three months later, unprecedented protests broke out over poverty, food shortages, and general lack of freedom. Police put down the protests with harsh repression. The transition and the protests raised the question: Does the Cuban Revolution have a future without a Castro as leader?

The early twenty-first century has been a banner period for political democracy in Latin America. Since the beginning of the wave of democratization in 1978, the great majority of countries have established and retained democratically elected governments that have become more inclusive by adopting gender quotas. Military coups have become rare, and the armed forces have refrained from taking power when civilian governments are interrupted. However, the tradition of authoritarianism has reasserted itself in a handful of countries. The adoption of Conditional Cash Transfers (CCTs) reduced poverty that had ballooned under the impact of neoliberalism. Several countries elected Pink Tide governments that attacked the social consequences of neoliberalism with particular vigor. The end of the commodities boom and the consequences of the COVID-19 pandemic have stalled progress in socioeconomic democratization, signaling potential problems for the future of political democracy.

SUGGESTIONS FOR FURTHER READING

Adato, Michelle and John Hoddinott, eds. *Conditional Cash Transfers in Latin America*. Baltimore: Johns Hopkins University Press, 2010.
Armendariz, Beatriz and Felipe Larraín B. *The Economics of Contemporary Latin America*. Cambridge: MIT Press, 2017.
Carroll, Rory. *Myth and Reality in Hugo Chávez's Venezuela*. New York: Penguin, 2013.
Cruz-Martinez, Gibrán, ed. *Welfare and Social Protection in Contemporary Latin America*. London: Routledge, 2019.
Ellner, Steve, ed. *Latin America's Pink Tide: Breakthroughs and Shortcomings*. Lanham, MD: Rowman & Littlefield, 2019.
Faletti, Tulia and Emilio A. Parrado, eds. *Latin America since the Left Turn*. Philadelphia: University of Pennsylvania Press, 2018.
Farthing, Linda C. and Benjamin H. Kohl. *Evo's Bolivia: Continuity and Change*. Austin: University of Texas Press, 2014.
Gaudichaud, Franck, Massimo Modonesi, and Jeffery R. Webber. *The Impasse of the Latin American Left*. Durham: Duke University Press, 2022.
Gómez Bruera, Hernán F. *Lula, the Workers' Party, and the Governability Dilemma in Brazil*. New York: Routledge, Taylor and Francis Group, 2013.
Goodale, Mark and Nancy Postero. *Neoliberalism Interrupted: Social Change and Contested Governance in Contemporary Latin America*. Stanford: Stanford University Pres, 2013.
Hellinger, Daniel C. *Comparative Politics of Latin America: Democracy at Last?* New York: Routledge, 2021.
López-Segrera, Francisco. *The United States and Cuba: From Closest Enemies to Distant Friends*. Lanham, MD: Rowman & Littlefield, 2017.
Piatti-Crocker, Adriana. *Diffusion of Gender Quotas in Latin America and Beyond: Advances and Setbacks in the Last Two Decades*. New York: Peter Lang, 2011.
Posner, Paul W., Jean-François Mayer, and Viviana Petroni. *Labor Politics in Latin America: Democracy and Worker Organization in the Neoliberal Era*. Gainesville: University of Florida Press, 2018.
Postero, Nancy. *The Indigenous State: Race, Politics, and Performance in Plurinational Bolivia*. Oakland: University of California Press, 2017.
Silva, Eduardo and Federico M. Rossi, eds. *Reshaping the Political Arena in Latin America: From Resisting Neoliberalism to the Second Incorporation*. Pittsburgh: University of Pittsburgh Press, 2018.
Vanden, Harry E. *Politics of Latin America: The Power Game*. Sixth ed. New York: Oxford University Press, 2018.
Webber, Jeffrey R. and Barry Carr, eds. *The New Latin American Left: Cracks in the Empire*. Lanham, MD: Rowman & Littlefield, 2013.

NOTES

1. The 1994 EZLN uprising in Mexico had only a brief period of armed combat.

2. By the new millennium OAS membership had expanded to all but one of the independent countries in the Americas, including the Caribbean island nations. Expansion beyond the original twenty-one began in 1967 with two island nations, Trinidad and Tobago (two names, one country) and Barbados. The last to join was Guyana in 1991. In 2009, the OAS rescinded its 1962 expulsion of Cuba, but Cuba rejected the opportunity to rejoin.

3. Inter-American Democratic Charter, article 1.

4. Inter-American Democratic Charter, article 21.

5. For greater detail, see https://vanderbilt.edu/lapop/ab2021/2021_LAPOP_AmericasBarometer_2021_Pulse_of_Democracy.pdf.

6. Lauri Heimo, "Domestication of Global Policy Norms: Problematisation of the Conditional Cash Transfer Narrative," in Gibrán Cruz-Martínez, *Welfare and Social Protection in Contemporary Latin America* (London: Routledge, 2019), 139.

7. https://www.statista.com/statistics/1050681/latin-america-income-inequality-country/.

8. Hernán F. Gómez Bruera, *Lula, the Workers' Party, and the Governability Dilemma in Brazil* (New York: Routledge, 2013), 115.

9. There is no direct translation of the term *indigenismo*. "Indianism" or "Indigenism" would be the closest English language translations.

10. Constitution of Bolivia, 2009 (accessed at https://www.constituteproject.org/constitution/Bolivia_2009.pdf).

11. Linda C. Farthing and Benjamin H. Kohl, *Evo's Bolivia: Continuity and Change* (Austin: University of Texas Press, 2014), 3.

12. *The Guardian*, April 20, 2020.

13. *Washington Post*, November 11, 2020 and *The Guardian*, March 5, 2021.

14. The Constitution of the Republic of Cuba, 2019 (accessed at https://constituteproject.org/constitution/Cuba_2019.pdf?lang=en); quotations in order: articles 5, 55, 30.

Final Observations

The state of democracy in Latin America today may be assessed by posing and answering this question: Has the democratic promise of the OAS Charter and the American Declaration of the Rights and Duties of Man been met? Although those lofty goals have not been fully realized, it would be wrong to dismiss the very substantial progress that has been made, both before and after the formal 1948 commitment to democracy in Latin America—and the United States.

Political democracy has remote roots in the ad hoc elections held during the independence movements of the early nineteenth century, which introduced Latin Americans to that method of establishing and changing governments. The adoption of constitutions and legislatures in the new countries put in place additional ingredients of a future political democracy. But the first half century of independence brought little progress toward democratization as, with few exceptions, caudillos ruled. Latin America's integration into the world economy following 1870 created conditions for the emergence of stable governments, both dictatorships and oligarchic regimes with the trappings but not the substance of political democracy. The export economies also created new social classes whose demands for participation in the politics and societal goods of their countries drove the initial democratization early in the twentieth century.

Beyond the goals of fair, free, and open elections and peaceful transfers of power, the history of political democratization in Latin America can be measured by the expansion of the electorate. The nineteenth century witnessed limited progress in this area: A few males benefited from the gradual elimination of income or property requirements almost everywhere and of the literacy requirement in a few countries. The twentieth century witnessed much more movement: Women and illiterates were enfranchised and the age requirement for voting was lowered. More progress has been made on inclusiveness in the early twenty-first century as leaders have sought to consolidate democracies with gender quotas and expatriate voting. Today virtually all Latin Americans aged eighteen and above (sixteen in a few countries) who wish to participate in the political process have the right to do so.

The armed forces' withdrawal from governance, following the dark period of military dictatorships and state terrorism in the 1970s and 1980s, has been a critical factor in the ascendancy of democratic governments in the new millennium.

Socioeconomic democratization in Latin America proceeded slowly. In the nineteenth century, the prevailing laissez-faire ideology left responsibility for socioeconomic welfare to individuals and to charity, often with grim results. Socioeconomic democracy was initially driven by a handful of intellectuals and by workers who joined illegal unions to push for improved wages and working conditions. Starting in the early twentieth century with Batlle y Ordóñez in Uruguay and the Mexican Revolution, states began assuming responsibility for citizens' welfare and over time, labor legislation, social security systems, and free public education appeared in almost every country. The benefits of these advances normally stopped at cities' edge, leaving the masses of rural landless workers at the mercy of landowners until, beginning in Mexico, a few countries implemented agrarian reform.

After slow but real progress in protecting citizens' welfare, Latin America governments in the 1980s and 1990s were forced to adopt neoliberal policies. In doing so, they reneged on the responsibility for citizens' welfare, and social safety nets frayed. Governments introduced conditional cash transfers (CCTs) to counter the impoverishment of the working classes, and beginning in the early 2000s, used the bounty of the commodities boom to lift millions of citizens out of poverty. The Pink Tide regimes took additional steps to provide relief for the poor. With the end of the commodities boom, the passing of Pink Tide governments, and the COVID-19 pandemic, poverty reduction programs suffered and the advances in poverty reduction eroded.

At this moment in time, Latin America faces a critical juncture. As political democracy is challenged around the world, including in the United States, Latin American democracy faces a potential crisis. Buffeted by the sagging prices of its exports and the ravages of the COVID-19 pandemic, the long wave of political democratization that began in 1978 is confronting the erosion of socioeconomic democracy. Authoritarian governance has already returned in a handful of countries. Carlos Fuentes's question about the relationship between the two forms of democracy—"How much poverty can [political] democracy sustain?"—has acquired new relevance.[1]

The answer to Fuente's question will shape the next chapter in the long and convoluted history of Latin America's democratic journey.

NOTE

1. Carlos Fuentes, *A New Time for Mexico*, trans. Marina Gutman Castañeda (New York; Farrar, Straus, and Giroux, 1996), 110.

Select Bibliography: Books in English

Abbott, Elizabeth. *Haiti: The Duvaliers and Their Legacy*. New York: McGraw-Hill, 1988.

Adato, Michelle and John Hoddinott, eds. *Conditional Cash Transfers in Latin America*. Baltimore: Johns Hopkins University Press, 2010.

Aguirre, Carlos and Paulo Drinot, eds. *The Peculiar Revolution: Rethinking the Peruvian Experiment under Military Rule*. Austin: University of Texas Press, 2017.

Albert, Bill. *South America and the First World War: The Impact of the War on Brazil, Argentina, Peru, and Chile*. Cambridge, UK: Cambridge University Press, 1988.

Alexander, Robert J. *Agrarian Reform in Latin America*. New York: Macmillan, 1974.

———, ed. *Aprismo: The Ideas and Doctrines of Víctor Raúl Haya de la Torre*. Kent, OH: Kent State University Press, 1973.

———. *Arturo Alessandri: A Biography*. Ann Arbor: Published for Latin American Institute, Rutgers University, by University Microfilms International, 1997.

———. *The Bolivian National Revolution*. Reprint. Westport, CT: Greenwood Press, 1974.

———. *Rómulo Betancourt and the Transformation of Venezuela*. New Brunswick: Transaction Books, 1982.

Americas Watch. *El Salvador's Decade of Terror: Human Rights since the Assassination of Archbishop Romero*. New Haven: Yale University Press, 1991.

Ameringer, Charles D. *Don Pepe: A Political Biography of José Figueres of Costa Rica*. Albuquerque: University of New Mexico Press, 1978.

———. *The Cuban Democratic Experience: The Auténtico Years, 1944–1952*. Gainesville: University of Florida Press, 2000.

Andersen, Martin Edwin. *Dossier Secreto: Argentina's Desaparecidos and the Myth of the "Dirty War."* Boulder: Westview Press, 1993.

Anderson, Jon Lee. *Che Guevara: A Revolutionary Life*. Second ed. New York: Grove Press, 2010.

Archdiocese of Guatemala, Recovery of Historical Memory Project. *Guatemala Nunca Más: The Official Report of the Human Rights Office, Archdiocese of Guatemala*. Maryknoll: Orbis Books, 1999.

Archdiocese of São Paulo. *Torture in Brazil: A Shocking Report on the Pervasive Use of Torture by Brazilian Military Governments, 1964–1985*. Translated by Jaime Wright. Austin: University of Texas, Institute of Latin American Studies, 1985.

Argentina. Comisión Nacional sobre la Desaparición de Personas. *Nunca más: The Report of the Argentine National Commission on the* Disappeared. First American Edition. New York: Farrar, Straus, Giroux, 1986.

Argote-Freyre, Frank. *Fulgencio Batista*. New Brunswick: Rutgers University Press, 2006.

Armendariz, Beatriz and Felipe Larraín B. *Economics of Contemporary Latin America*. Cambridge: MIT Press, 2017.

Arnson, Cynthia J. *In the Wake of War: Democratization and Internal Armed Conflict in Latin America*. Washington, DC: Woodrow Wilson Center Press, 2012.

Arriagada, Genaro. *Pinochet: The Politics of Power*. Translated by Nancy Morris. Boston: Unwin Hyman, 1988.

Bacchus, Wilfred A. *Mission in Mufti: Brazil's Military Regimes, 1964–1985*. Westport, CT: Greenwood Press, 1990.

Balfour, Sebastian. *Castro*. Third ed. Harlow, UK: Pearson Longman, 2009.

Barahona de Brito, Alexandra. *Human Rights and Democratization in Latin America: Uruguay and Chile*. New York: Oxford University Press, 1997.

Becker, Marc. *Indians and Leftists in the Making of Ecuador's Modern Indigenous Movements*. Durham: Duke University Press, 2008.

Becker, Marjorie. *Setting the Virgin on Fire: Lázaro Cárdenas, Michoacán Peasants, and the Redemption of the Mexican Revolution*. Berkeley: University of California Press, 1995.

Bell, John Patrick. *Crisis in Costa Rica: The 1948 Revolution*. Austin: University of Texas Press, 1971.

Benjamin, Thomas. *La Revolución: Mexico's Great Revolution in Memory, Myth, and History*. Austin: University of Texas Press, 2000.

Bergquist, Charles W. *Labor in Latin America: Comparative Essays on Chile, Argentina, Venezuela, and Colombia*. Stanford: Stanford University Press, 1986.

Berry, Albert, ed. *Poverty, Economic Reform, and Income Distribution in Latin America*. Boulder: Lynne Rienner, 1998.

Berryman, Phillip. *Liberation Theology: Essential Facts about the Revolutionary Movement in Latin America—and Beyond*. Philadelphia: Temple University Press, 1987.

Betancur, Belisario, Reinaldo Figueredo Planchart, and Thomas Buergenthal. *From Madness to Hope: The Twelve-Year War in El Salvador: Report of the Commission on the Truth for El Salvador*. New York: United Nations, 1993.

Bethell, Leslie, ed. *The Independence of Latin America*. Cambridge, UK: Cambridge University Press, 1987.

———. *Latin America: Economy and Society since 1930*. Cambridge, UK: Cambridge University Press, 1998.

———. *Spanish America after Independence, c. 1820–c. 1870*. Cambridge, UK: Cambridge University Press, 1987.

Binford, Leigh. *The El Mozote Massacre: Human Rights and Global Implications.* Second ed. Tucson: University of Arizona Press, 2016.

Bitar, Sergio. *Chile: Experiment in Democracy.* Translated by Sam Sherman. Philadelphia: Institute for the Study of Human Issues, 1986.

Blanchard. Peter. *The Origins of the Peruvian Labor Movement, 1883–1919.* Pittsburgh: University of Pittsburgh Press, 1982.

Blight, James A. and Peter Kornbluh. *Politics of Illusion: The Bay of Pigs Invasion Reexamined.* Boulder: Lynne Rienner, 1998.

Booth, John A. *The End and the Beginning: The Nicaraguan Revolution.* Second ed. Boulder: Westview Press, 1985.

Bouvard, Marguerite Guzmán. *Revolutionizing Motherhood: The Mothers of the Plaza de Mayo.* Wilmington: Scholarly Resources, 1994.

Brands, Hal. *Latin America's Cold War.* Cambridge: Harvard University Press, 2010.

Braun, Herbert. *The Assassination of Gaitán: Public Life and Urban Violence in Colombia.* Madison: University of Wisconsin Press, 2003.

Brenner, Philip et al. *A Contemporary Cuba Reader: The Revolution under Raúl Castro.* Second ed. Lanham, MD: Rowman & Littlefield, 2015.

Brett, Roderick Leslie. *Origins and Dynamics of Genocide: Political Violence in Guatemala.* London: Palgrave Macmillan, 2016.

Brewer, Stewart. *Borders and Bridges: A History of U.S.-Latin American Relations.* Westport, CT: Praeger, 2006.

Brown, Jonathan. *Cuba's Revolutionary World.* Cambridge: Harvard University Press, 2017.

Bulmer-Thomas, Victor. *The Economic History of Latin America since Independence.* Cambridge, UK: Cambridge University Press, 2003.

Burns, E. Bradford. *At War in Nicaragua: The Reagan Doctrine and the Politics of Nostalgia.* New York: Harper and Row, 1987.

———. *The Poverty of Progress: Latin America in the Nineteenth Century.* Berkeley: University of California Press, 1980.

Bushnell, David and Neill Macaulay. *The Emergence of Latin America in the Nineteenth Century.* Second ed. New York: Oxford University Press, 1994.

Bustamante, Michael J. and Jennifer L. Lambe, eds. *The Revolution from Within: Cuba, 1959–1980.* Durham: Duke University Press, 2019.

Cabezas, Omar. *Fire from the Mountain: The Making of a Sandinista.* Translated by Kathleen Weaver. New York: New American Library, 1985.

Calder, Bruce H. *The Impact of Intervention: The Dominican Republic during the U.S. Occupation of 1916–1924.* Princeton: M. Wiener, 2006.

Camp, Roderic Ai. *Politics in Mexico: The Democratic Consolidation.* Fifth ed. New York: Oxford University Press, 2007.

Camp, Roderic Ai and Shannan L. Mattiace. *Politics in Mexico: The Path of a New Democracy.* Seventh ed. New York: Oxford University Press, 2020.

Cardoso, Fernando Henrique and Enzo Faletto. *Dependency and Development in Latin America.* Translated by Marjory Mattingly Urquidi. Berkeley: University of California Press, 1979.

Carothers, Thomas. *In the Name of Democracy: U.S. Policy toward Latin America in the Reagan Years*. Berkeley: University of California Press, 1991.

Carroll, Rory. *Myth and Reality in Hugo Chávez's Venezuela*. New York: Penguin, 2013.

Castro, Daniel, ed. *Revolution and Revolutionaries: Guerrilla Movements in Latin America*. Wilmington: SR Books, 1999.

Castro, Fidel. *The First and Second Declarations of Havana: Manifestos of Revolutionary Struggle in the Americas*. Edited by Mary-Alice Waters. Third ed. New York: Pathfinder Press, 2007.

———. *History Will Absolve Me*. Translator not indicated. Havana: Editorial de Ciencias Sociales, 1975.

———. *Revolutionary Struggle. 1947–1958*. Ed. Rolando Bonachea and Nelson P. Valdés. Cambridge: MIT Press, 1972.

Castro, Fidel and Ignacio Ramonet. *Fidel Castro: My Life, A Spoken Autobiography*. Translated by Andrew Hurley. New York: Scribner, 2008.

Centeno, Miguel Ángel and Agustín E. Ferraro, eds. *State and Nation Making in Latin America and Spain: Republics of the Possible*. Cambridge, UK: Cambridge University Press, 2013.

Child, John. *Unequal Alliance: The Inter-American Military System, 1938–1978*. Boulder: Westview Press, 1980.

Chile. *Report of the Chilean National Commission on Truth and Reconciliation*. 2 vols. Translated by Phillip E. Berryman. Notre Dame: University of Notre Dame Press, 1993.

Chomsky, Aviva. *A History of the Cuban Revolution*. Second ed. Hoboken: John Wiley and Sons, 2015.

Chomsky, Aviva, Barry Carr, and Pamela Maria Smorkaloff, eds. *The Cuba Reader: History, Culture, Politics*. Second ed. Durham: Duke University Press, 2019.

Christie, Jane L. *Negotiating Gendered Discourses: Michelle Bachelet and Cristina Fernández de Kirchner*. Lanham, MD: Lexington Books, 2015.

Ciccariello-Maher, George. *We Created Chávez: A People's History of the Venezuelan Revolution*. Durham: Duke University Press, 2013.

Collier, Simon. *Chile: The Making of a Republic, 1830–1865: Politics and Ideas*. Cambridge, UK: Cambridge University Press, 2003.

Conaghan, Catherine M. *Fujimori's Peru: Deception in the Public Sphere*. Pittsburgh: University of Pittsburgh Press, 2005.

Constable, Pamela and Arturo Valenzuela. *A Nation of Enemies: Chile under Pinochet*. New York: W. W. Norton, 1991.

Cortés Conde, Roberto and Shane J. Hunt, eds. *The Latin American Economies: Growth and the Export Sector, 1880–1930*. New York: Holmes and Meier, 1985.

Costa Pinto, António. *Latin American Dictatorships in the Era of Fascism: The Corporatist Wave*. New York: Routledge/Taylor and Francis Group, 2019.

Crandall, Russell. *The Salvador Option: The United States in El Salvador, 1977–1992*. New York: Cambridge University Press, 2016.

Crassweller, Robert D. *Perón and the Enigmas of Argentina*. New York: W. W. Norton, 1987.

————. *Trujillo: The Life and Times of a Caribbean Dictator*. New York: Macmillan, 1966.

Cruden, Alexander, ed. *Genocide and Persecution: El Salvador and Guatemala*. Detroit: Greenhaven Press, 2013.

Cruz-Martínez, Gibrán, ed. *Welfare and Social Protection in Contemporary Latin America*. London: Routledge, 2019.

Cumberland, Charles C. *Mexican Revolution: Genesis under Madero*. New York: Greenwood Press, 1969.

de Castro, Fabio, Kees Koonings, and Marianne Wiesebron, eds. *Brazil under the Workers' Party: Continuity and Change from Lula to Dilma*. Houndmills, Basingstoke, Hampshire, UK: Palgrave Macmillan, 2014.

de Laforcade, Geoffroy and Kirwin Shaffer. *In Defiance of Boundaries: Anarchism in Latin American History*. Gainesville: University Press of Florida, 2015.

de la Torre, Carlos and Cynthia J. Arnson, eds. *Latin American Populism in the Twenty-First Century*. Washington, DC: Woodrow Wilson Center Press, 2013.

de Vylder, Stefan. *Allende's Chile: The Political Economy of the Rise and Fall of the Unidad Popular*. Cambridge, UK: Cambridge University Press, 1976.

Dean, Warren. *The Industrialization of São Paulo, 1880–1945*. Austin: Published for the Institute of Latin American Studies by the University of Texas Press, 1969.

DeShazo, Peter. *Urban Workers and Labor Unions in Chile, 1902–1927*. Madison: University of Wisconsin Press, 1983.

Dinges, John. *Condor Years: How Pinochet and his Allies brought Terrorism to Three Continents*. New York: New Press, 2004.

Domínguez, Jorge I. *Cuba: Order and Revolution*. Cambridge: Harvard University Press, 1978.

————. *To Make a World Safe for Revolution: Cuba's Foreign Policy*. Cambridge: Harvard University Press, 1989.

Domínguez, Jorge I. and Michael Shifter, eds. *Constructing Democratic Governance in Latin America*. Baltimore: Johns Hopkins University Press, 2008.

Dorner, Peter. *Latin American Land Reforms in Theory and Practice: A Retrospective Analysis*. Madison: University of Wisconsin Press, 1992.

Drake, Paul W. *Between Tyranny and Anarchy: A History of Democracy in Latin America, 1800–2006*. Stanford: Stanford University Press, 2008.

Drinot, Paulo. *The Allure of Labor: Workers, Race, and the Making of the Peruvian State*. Durham: Duke University Press, 2011.

Drinot, Paulo and Alan Knight, eds. *The Great Depression in Latin America*. Durham: Duke University Press, 2014.

Eastman, Scott and Natalia Sobrevilla Perea, eds. *The Rise of Constitutional Government in the Iberian Atlantic World: The Impact of the Cádiz Constitution of 1812*. Tuscaloosa: University of Alabama Press, 2015.

Ellner, Steve, ed. *Latin America's Pink Tide: Breakthroughs and Shortcomings*. Lanham, MD: Rowman & Littlefield, 2019.

————, ed. *Latin America's Radical Left: Challenges and Complexities of Political Power in the Twenty-First Century*. Lanham: Rowman & Littlefield, 2014.

————. *Rethinking Venezuelan Politics: Class, Conflict, and the Chávez Phenomenon.* Boulder: Lynne Rienner, 2008.

Esparza, Marcia, Henry R. Huttenbach, and Daniel Feierstein, eds. *State Violence and Genocide in Latin America: The Cold War Years.* London: Routledge, 2010.

Falleti, Tulia and Emilio A. Parrado, eds. *Latin America Since the Left Turn.* Philadelphia: University of Pennsylvania Press, 2018.

Farthing, Linda C. and Benjamin H. Kohl. *Evo's Bolivia: Continuity and Change.* Austin: University of Texas Press, 2014.

Feitlowitz, Marguerite. *A Lexicon of Terror: Argentina and the Legacies of Torture.* Revised and updated ed. New York: Oxford University Press, 2011.

Fink, Leon and Juan Manual Palacio, eds. *Labor Justice Across the Americas.* Urbana: University of Illinois Press, 2017.

Fleet, Michael. *The Rise and Fall of Chilean Christian Democracy.* Princeton: Princeton University Press, 1985.

Forment, Carlos A. *Democracy in Latin America, 1760–1900.* Chicago: University of Chicago Press, 2003.

Fowler, Will. *Santa Anna of Mexico.* Lincoln: University of Nebraska Press, 2009.

Fraser, Nicholas and Marysa Navarro. *Eva Perón.* Second ed. New York: W. W. Norton, 1996.

French, John D. *The Brazilian Workers' ABC: Class Conflict and Alliances in Modern São Paulo.* Chapel Hill: University of North Carolina Press, 1992.

French, John D. and Daniel James, eds. *The Gendered Worlds of Latin American Women Workers: From Household and Factory to the Union Hall and Ballot Box.* Durham: Duke University Press, 1997.

Gargarella, Roberto. *Latin American Constitutionalism, 1810–2010: The Engine Room of the Constitution.* Philadelphia: Temple University Press, 2013.

Garner, Paul. *Porfirio Díaz: Profiles in Power.* Harlow, UK: Longman, 2001.

Garrard-Burnett, Virginia, Mark Atwood Lawrence, and Julio E. Moreno, eds. *Beyond the Eagle's Shadow: New Histories of Latin America's Cold War.* Albuquerque: University of New Mexico Press, 2013.

Gaudichaud, Franck, Massimo Modonesi, and Jeffery R. Webber. *The Impasse of the Latin American Left.* Durham: Duke University Press, 2022.

Gilbert, Dennis. *Oligarchy and the Old Regime in Latin America, 1880–1970.* Lanham, MD: Rowman & Littlefield, 2017.

————. *Sandinistas: The Party and the Revolution.* New York: Basil Blackwell, 1988.

Gilderhus, Mark T., David C. LaFevor, and Michael J. LaRosa. *The Third Century: U.S.-Latin American Relations since 1889.* Second ed. Lanham, MD: Rowman & Littlefield, 2017.

Gill, Lesley. *The School of the Americas: Military Training and Political Violence in the Americas.* Durham: Duke University Press, 2004.

Gillespie, Charles Guy. *Negotiating Democracy: Politicians and Generals in Uruguay.* Cambridge, UK: Cambridge University Press, 1991.

Gillespie, Richard. *Soldiers of Perón: Argentina's Montoneros.* New York: Oxford University Press, 1983.

Gilmore, Robert L. *Caudillism and Militarism in Venezuela, 1810–1910*. Athens: Ohio University Press, 1964.

Gleijeses, Piero. *Shattered Hopes: The Guatemalan Revolution and the United States*. Princeton: Princeton University Press, 1991.

Gobat, Michel. *Confronting the American Dream: Nicaragua Under U.S. Imperial Rule*. Durham: Duke University Press, 2005.

Gómez Bruera, Hernán F. *Lula, the Workers' Party, and the Governability Dilemma in Brazil*. New York: Routledge, Taylor and Francis Group, 2013.

Gonzáles, Michael J. *The Mexican Revolution, 1910–1940*. Albuquerque: University of New Mexico Press, 2002.

González, Luis J. and Gustavo A. Sánchez Salazar. *The Great Rebel: Che Guevara in Bolivia*. Translated by Helen R. Lane. New York: Grove Press, 1969.

Goodale, Mark. *A Revolution in Fragments: Traversing Scales of Justice, Ideology, and Practice in Bolivia*. Durham: Duke University Press, 2019.

Goodale, Mark and Nancy Postero. *Neoliberalism, Interrupted: Social Change and Contested Governance in Contemporary Latin America*. Stanford: Stanford University Press, 2013.

Gorriti Ellenbogen, Gustavo. *The Shining Path: A History of the Millenarian War in Peru*. Translated by Robin Kirk. Chapel Hill: University of North Carolina Press, 1999.

Grandin, Greg. *Empire's Workshop: Latin America, the United States, and the Rise of the New Imperialism*. New York: Henry Holt, 2007.

———. *The Last Colonial Massacre: Latin America in the Cold War*. Revised ed. Chicago: University of Chicago Press, 2011.

Grandin, Greg and Gilbert M. Joseph, eds. *Century of Revolution: Insurgent and Counterinsurgent Violence during Latin America's Long Cold War*. Durham: Duke University Press, 2010.

Greenfield, Gerald Michael and Sheldon L. Moran, eds. *Latin American Labor Organizations*. New York: Greenwood Press, 1987.

Grieb, Kenneth J. *Guatemalan Caudillo, the Regime of Jorge Ubico: Guatemala, 1931–1944*. Athens: Ohio University Press, 1979.

Guest, Ian. *Behind the Disappearances: Argentina's Dirty War against Human Rights and the United Nations*. Philadelphia: University of Pennsylvania Press, 1990.

Guevara, Ernesto (Che). *Guerrilla Warfare*. Brian Loveman and Thomas M. Davies Jr., eds. Third ed. Wilmington: SR Books, 1997.

———. *Reminiscences of the Cuban Revolutionary War*. Translated by Victoria Ortiz. New York: Monthly Review Press, 1968.

Gustafson, Bret. *Bolivia in the Age of Gas*. Durham: Duke University Press, 2020.

Gustafson, Kristian. *Hostile Intent: U.S. Covert Operations in Chile, 1964–1974*. Washington, DC: Potomac Books, 2007.

Guy, Donna J. *Women Building the Welfare State: Reforming Charity and Creating Rights in Argentina, 1880–1955*. Durham: Duke University Press, 2009.

Gwynne, Robert N. *Industrialization and Urbanization in Latin America*. Baltimore: Johns Hopkins University Press, 1986.

Haber, Stephen et al. *Mexico since 1980.* New York: Cambridge University Press, 2008.

Hagopian, Frances and Scott P. Mainwaring, eds. *The Third Wave of Democratization in Latin America: Advances and Setbacks.* Cambridge, UK: Cambridge University Press, 2005.

Hahner, June E. *Emancipating the Female Sex: The Struggle for Women's Rights in Brazil, 1850–1940.* Durham: Duke University Press, 1990.

Hammond, Gregory. *The Women's Suffrage Movement and Feminism in Argentina from Roca to Perón.* Albuquerque: University of New Mexico Press, 2011.

Hamnett, Brian. *Juárez.* London: Longman, 1994.

Harmer, Tanya. *Allende's Chile and the Inter-American Cold War.* Chapel Hill: University of North Carolina Press, 2011.

Hart, John Mason. *Revolutionary Mexico: The Coming and Process of the Mexican Revolution.* Berkeley: University of California Press, 1987.

Harten, Sven. *The Rise of Evo Morales and the MAS.* London: Zed Books, 2011.

Harvey, Neil. *The Chiapas Rebellion: The Struggle for Land and Democracy.* Durham: Duke University Press, 1998.

Haslam, Jonathan. *The Nixon Administration and the Death of Allende's Chile: A Case of Assisted Suicide.* London: Verso, 2005.

Hellinger, Daniel C. *Comparative Politics of Latin America: Democracy at Last?* Third ed. New York: Routledge, 2021.

Hentschke, Jens R., ed. *Vargas and Brazil: New Perspectives.* New York: Palgrave Macmillan, 2006.

Hershberg, Eric and William M. LeoGrande, eds. *A New Chapter in US-Cuban Relations: Social, Political, and Economic Implications.* New York: Palgrave Macmillan, 2016.

Hodges, Donald C. *Argentina's "Dirty War": An Intellectual Biography.* Austin: University of Texas Press, 1991.

———. *The Latin American Revolution: Politics and Strategy from Apro-Marxism to Guevarism.* New York: William Morrow, 1974.

Horowitz, Louis and Jaime Suchlicki, eds. *Cuban Communism.* Eleventh ed. New Brunswick: Transaction, 2003.

Huntington, Samuel P. *The Third Wave: Democratization in the Late Twentieth Century.* Norman: University of Oklahoma Press, 1991.

Hutchison, Elizabeth A. *Labors Appropriate to Their Sex: Gender, Labor, and Politics in Urban Chile, 1900–1930.* Durham: Duke University Press, 2001.

Immerman, Richard H. *The CIA in Guatemala: The Foreign Policy of Intervention.* Austin: University of Texas Press, 1982.

James, Daniel, ed. *The Complete Bolivian Diaries of Che Guevara and Other Captured Documents.* First Cooper Square ed. New York: Cooper Square Press, 2000.

Jonas, Suzanne. *The Battle for Guatemala: Rebels, Death Squads, and U.S. Power.* Boulder: Westview, 1991.

Joseph, Gilbert M. and Daniela Spenser. *In from the Cold: Latin America's New Encounter with the Cold War.* Durham: Duke University Press, 2008.

Karush, Matthew B. and Oscar Chamoso, eds. *The New Cultural History of Peronism: Power and Identity in Mid-Twentieth Century Argentina*. Durham: Duke University Press, 2010.

Katz, Friedrich. *The Life and Times of Pancho Villa*. Stanford: Stanford University Press, 1998.

Kingstone, Peter R. *The Political Economy of Latin America: Reflections on Neoliberalism and Development*. New York: Routledge, 2011.

Klein, Herbert S. *Parties and Political Change in Bolivia, 1880–1952*. Cambridge, UK: Cambridge University Press, 1969.

Knight, Alan. *The Mexican Revolution*. 2 vols. New York: Cambridge University Press, 1986.

Kohl, James. *Indigenous Struggle and the Bolivian National Revolution: Land and Liberty!* New York: Routledge, 2021.

Kohl, James and John Litt, eds. *Urban Guerrilla Warfare in Latin America*. Cambridge: MIT Press, 1974.

Kornbluh, Peter, ed. *The Bay of Pigs Declassified: The Secret CIA Report on the Invasion of Cuba*. New York: New Press, 1998.

———. *The Pinochet File: A Declassified Dossier on Atrocity and Accountability*. New York: New Press, 2003.

Kruijt, Dirk. *Revolution by Decree: Peru, 1968–1975*. Amsterdam: Thela Publishers, 1994.

Kruijt, Dirk, Rey Tristán, and Alberto Martín Álvarez, eds. *Latin American Guerrilla Movements: Origins, Evolution, Outcomes*. New York: Routledge, 2020.

LaFeber, Walter. *Inevitable Revolutions: The United States in Central America*. Second ed. New York: W. W. Norton, 1993.

Langley, Lester D. *The United States and the Caribbean in the Twentieth Century*. Fourth ed. Athens: University of Georgia Press, 1989.

Larson, Brooke. *Trials of Nation Making: Liberalism, Race, and Ethnicity in the Andes, 1810–1910*. Cambridge, UK: Cambridge University Press, 2004.

Leech, Garry. *The FARC: The Longest Insurgency*. London: Zed Books, 2011.

LeoGrande, William M. *Our Own Backyard: The United States in Central America, 1977–1992*. Chapel Hill: University of North Carolina Press, 1998.

LeoGrande, William M. and Peter Kornbluh. *Back Channel to Cuba: The Hidden History of Negotiations Between Washington and Havana*. Chapel Hill: University of North Carolina Press, 2014.

Leonard, Thomas M. *Fidel Castro: A Biography*. Westport, CT: Greenwood Press, 2004.

Levine, Robert M. *Father of the Poor? Vargas and His Era*. Cambridge, UK: Cambridge University Press, 1998.

Levinson, Jerome and Juan de Onís. *The Alliance that Lost Its Way*. Chicago: Quadrangle Books, 1970.

Levitsky, Steven and Kenneth M. Roberts, eds. *The Resurgence of the Latin American Left*. Baltimore: Johns Hopkins University Press, 2011.

Lewis, Paul H. *Authoritarian Regimes in Latin America: Dictators, Despots, and Tyrants*. Lanham, MD: Rowman & Littlefield, 2006.

————. *Guerrillas and Generals: The "Dirty War" in Argentina*. Westport, CT: Praeger, 2002.

————. *Paraguay under Stroessner*. Chapel Hill: University of North Carolina Press, 1980.

Lockwood, Lee. *Castro's Cuba, Cuba's Fidel*. Second ed. Boulder: Westview Press, 1990.

López-Segrera, Francisco. *The United States and Cuba: From Closest Enemies to Distant Friends*. Lanham, MD: Rowman & Littlefield, 2017.

Loveman, Brian. *No Higher Law: American Foreign Policy and the Western Hemisphere since 1776*. Chapel Hill: University of North Carolina Press, 2010.

————. *Politics and the Armed Forces in Latin America*. Lanham, MD: Rowman & Littlefield, 1999.

Loveman, Brian and Thomas M. Davies Jr. *The Politics of Antipolitics: The Military in Latin America*. Lincoln: University of Nebraska Press, 1978.

Lowenthal, Abraham F. *The Dominican Intervention*. reprint. Baltimore: Johns Hopkins University Press, 1995.

————, ed. *The Peruvian Experiment: Continuity and Change under Military Rule*. Princeton: Princeton University Press, 1975.

Lynch, John. *Argentine Caudillo: Juan Manuel de Rosas*. Wilmington: SR Books, 2001.

————. *Caudillos in Spanish America, 1800–1850*. Oxford, UK: Clarendon Press, 1992.

————. *The Spanish American Revolutions, 1808–1826*. Second ed. New York: Norton, 1986.

Macaulay, Neill. *The Sandino Affair*. Durham: Duke University Press, 1985.

Marel García Pérez, Gladys. *Insurrection and Revolution: Armed Struggle in Cuba, 1952–1959*. Translated by Juan Ortega. Boulder: Lynne Rienner, 1998.

Matthews, Herbert. *The Cuban Story*. New York: George Braziller, 1961.

Mayer, Enrique. *Ugly Stories of the Peruvian Agrarian Reform*. Durham: Duke University Press, 2009.

McClintock, Cynthia and Abraham F. Lowenthal, eds. *The Peruvian Experiment Reconsidered*. Princeton: Princeton University Press, 1983.

McSherry, J. Patrice. *Predatory States: Operation Condor and Covert War in Latin America*. Lanham, MD: Rowman & Littlefield, 2005.

Menchú, Rigoberta. *I, Rigoberta Menchú: An Indian Woman in Guatemala*. Second English ed. Translated by Ann Wright. London: Verso, 2009.

Mesa-Lago, Carmelo and Jorge Pérez-López. *Cuba under Raúl Castro: Assessing the Reforms*. Boulder: Lynne Rienner Publishers, 2013.

Millett, Richard. *Guardians of the Dynasty: A History of the U.S.-Created Guardia Nacional de Nicaragua and the Somoza Family.* Maryknoll: Orbis Books, 1977.

Mitchell, Stephanie E. and Patience A. Shell, *Women's Revolution in Mexico, 1910–1953*. Lanham, MD: Rowman & Littlefield, 2007.

Montgomery, Tommie Sue. *Revolution in El Salvador: From Civil Strife to Civil Peace*. Second ed. Boulder: Westview Press, 1995.

Morley, Morris H. *Washington, Somoza, and the Sandinistas: State and Regime in U.S. Policy Toward Nicaragua, 1969–1981*. Cambridge, UK: Cambridge University Press, 1994.

Morris, James Oliver. *Elites, Intellectuals, and Consensus: A Study of the Social Question and the Industrial Relations System in Chile*. Ithaca: New York State School of Industrial and Labor Relations, Cornell University, 1966.

Muecke, Ulrich. *Political Culture in Nineteenth-Century Peru: The Rise of the Partido Civil*. Pittsburgh: University of Pittsburgh Press, 2004.

Muñoz, Heraldo. *The Dictator's Shadow: Life under Augusto Pinochet*. New York: Basic Books, 2008.

Munro, Dana Gardner. *Intervention and Dollar Diplomacy in the Caribbean, 1900–1921*. Princeton: Princeton University Press, 1964.

Munton, Don and David A. Welch. *The Cuban Missile Crisis: A Concise History*. Second ed. New York: Oxford University Press, 2012.

Nallim, Jorge A. *Transformations and Crisis of Liberalism in Argentina, 1930–1955*. Pittsburgh: University of Pittsburgh Press, 2012.

Nohlen, Dieter. *Elections in the Americas: A Data Handbook*. 2 volumes. New York: Oxford University Press, 2005.

Nunn, Frederick M. *Yesterday's Soldiers: European Military Professionalism in South America, 1890–1940*. Lincoln: University of Nebraska Press, 1983.

O'Brien, Thomas F. *Century of U.S. Capitalism in Latin America*. Albuquerque: University of New Mexico Press, 1999.

———. *The Revolutionary Mission: American Enterprise in Latin America, 1900–1945*. New York: Cambridge University Press, 1996.

Parker, Phyllis R. *Brazil and the Quiet Intervention, 1964*. Austin: University of Texas Press, 1979.

Paterson, Thomas G. *Contesting Castro: The United States and the Triumph of the Cuban Revolution*. New York: Oxford University Press, 1994.

Peloso, Vincent C. *Race and Ethnicity in Latin American History*. New York: Routledge, 2014.

Peloso, Vincent C. and Barbara A. Tenenbaum, eds. *Liberals, Politics, and Power: State Formation in Nineteenth-Century Latin America*. Athens: University of Georgia Press, 1996.

Pérez Jr., Louis A. *Cuba: Between Reform and Revolution*. Fifth ed. New York: Oxford University Press, 2014.

———. *Cuba under the Platt Amendment, 1902–1934*. Pittsburgh: University of Pittsburgh Press, 1986.

Pérez-Stable, Marifeli. *The Cuban Revolution: Origins, Course, and Legacy*. Third ed. New York: Oxford University Press, 2011.

Philip, George. *The Rise and Fall of the Peruvian Military Radicals, 1968–1976*. London: Athlone Press, 1978.

Piatti-Crocker, Adriana. *Diffusion of Gender Quotas in Latin America and Beyond: Advances and Setbacks in the Last Two Decades*. New York: Peter Lang, 2011.

Pion-Berlin, David and Raphael Martínez. *Soldiers, Politicians, and Civilians: Reforming Civil-Military Relations in Democratic Latin America.* Cambridge, UK: Cambridge University Press, 2017.

Porter, Susie S. *Working Women in Mexico City: Public Discourses and Material Conditions, 1879–1931.* Tucson: University of Arizona Press, 2003.

Porzecanski, Arturo C. *Uruguay's Tupamaros: The Urban Guerrilla.* New York: Praeger, 1973.

Posada-Carbó, Eduardo, ed. *Elections before Democracy: The History of Elections in Europe and Latin America.* Houndmills, Basingstoke, Hampshire, UK: Macmillan Press, 1996.

Posner, Paul W., Jean-François Mayer, and Viviana Petroni. *Labor Politics in Latin America: Democracy and Worker Organization in the Neoliberal Era.* Gainesville: University of Florida Press, 2018.

Postero, Nancy. *The Indigenous State: Race, Politics, and Performance in Plurinational Bolivia.* Oakland: University of California Press, 2017.

Prevost, Gary, Carlos Oliva Campos and Harry E. Vanden, eds. *Social Movements and Leftist Governments in Latin America: Confrontation or Co-optation?* London: Zed Books, 2012.

Prevost, Gary and Harry E. Vanden, eds. The *Undermining of the Sandinista Revolution.* New York: St. Martin's Press, 1997.

Rabe. Stephen G. *The Killing Zone: The United States Wages Cold War in Latin America.* New York: Oxford University Press, 2011.

———. *Kissinger and Latin America: Intervention, Human Rights, Diplomacy.* Ithaca: Cornell University Press, 2020.

———. *The Most Dangerous Area in the World: John F. Kennedy Confronts Communist Revolution in Latin America.* Chapel Hill: University of North Carolina Press, 1999.

Ramírez, Sergio. *Adios Muchachos: A Memoir of the Sandinista Revolution.* Translated by Stacey Alba D. Skar. Durham: Duke University Press, 2012.

Randall, Margaret. *Exporting Revolution: Cuba's Global Solidarity.* Durham: Duke University Press, 2017.

Reid, Michael. *The Forgotten Continent: History of the New Latin America.* New Haven: Yale University Press, 2017.

Richmond, Douglas W. *Carlos Pellegrini and the Crisis of the Argentine Elites, 1880–1916.* New York: Praeger, 1989.

Rock, David. *Politics in Argentina, 1890–1930: The Rise and Fall of Radicalism.* Cambridge, UK: Cambridge University Press, 1975.

Rosen, Fred. *Empire and Dissent: The United States and Latin America.* Durham: Duke University Press, 2008.

Rosen, Jonathan D. and Hanna S. Kassab, eds. *Corruption in the Americas.* Lanham, MD: Lexington Books, 2020.

Rothenberg, Daniel, ed. *Memory of Silence: The Guatemalan Truth Commission Report.* New York: Palgrave Macmillan, 2012.

Ruíz, Ramón E. *The Great Rebellion: Mexico, 1905–1924.* New York: W. W. Norton, 1980.

Sabato, Hilda. *Republics of the New World: The Revolutionary Political Experiment in Nineteenth-Century Latin America*. Princeton, NJ: Princeton University Press, 2018.

Salas, Elizabeth. *Soldaderas in the Mexican Military: Myth and History*. Austin: University of Texas Press, 1990.

Sanford, Victoria. *Buried Secrets: Truth and Human Rights in Guatemala*. New York: Palgrave Macmillan, 2003.

Sarmiento, Domingo F. *Life in the Argentine Republic in the Days of the Tyrants or, Civilization and Barbarism*. New York: Collier Books, 1961.

Scheman, L. Ronald, ed. *The Alliance for Progress: A Retrospective*. New York: Praeger, 1988.

Schlesinger, Stephen and Stephen Kinzer. *Bitter Fruit: The Story of the American Coup in Guatemala*. rev. and expanded ed. Cambridge: David Rockefeller Center for Latin American Studies, Harvard University, 2005.

Schneider, Ronald M. *Latin American Political History: Patterns and Personalities*. Boulder: Westview Press, 2007.

Schoultz, Lars. *National Security and United States Policy Toward Latin America*. Princeton: Princeton University Press, 1987.

————. *That Infernal Little Cuban Republic: The United States and the Cuban Revolution*. Chapel Hill: University of North Carolina Press, 2009.

Schultz, Jim and Melissa Crane Draper. *Dignity and Defiance: Stories from Bolivia's Challenge to Globalization*. Berkeley: University of California Press, 2008.

Servicio Paz y Justicia, Uruguay. *Uruguay Nunca Más: Human Rights Violations, 1972–1985*. Translated by Elizabeth Hampsten. Philadelphia: Temple University Press, 1992.

Sigmund, Paul E. *The Overthrow of Allende and the Politics of Chile, 1964–1976*. Pittsburgh: University of Pittsburgh Press, 1977.

Silva, Eduardo and Federico M. Rossi, eds. *Reshaping the Political Arena in Latin America: From Resisting Neoliberalism to the Second Incorporation*. Pittsburgh: University of Pittsburgh Press, 2018.

Skidmore, Thomas E. *Politics in Brazil, 1930–1964*. New York: Oxford University Press, 1967.

————. *The Politics of Military Rule in Brazil, 1964–1985*. New York: Oxford University Press, 1988.

Smale, Robert L. *"I Sweat the Flavor of Tin": Labor Activism in Early Twentieth-Century Bolivia*. Pittsburgh: University of Pittsburgh Press, 2010.

Smilde, David and Daniel C. Hellinger, eds. *Venezuela's Bolivarian Democracy: Participation, Politics, and Culture under Chávez*. Durham: Duke University Press, 2011.

Smith, Peter H. with Cameron J. Sells. *Democracy in Latin America: Political Change in Comparative Perspective*. Third ed. New York: Oxford University Press, 2017.

Smith, Peter H. with Ana Covarrubias. *Talons of the Eagle: Latin America, the United States, and the World*. Fifth ed. New York: Oxford University Press, 2022.

Solimano, Andrés. *Chile and the Neoliberal Trap: The Post-Pinochet Era*. New York: Cambridge University Press, 2012.

Soliz, Carmen. *Fields of Revolution: Agrarian Reform and Rural State Formation in Bolivia, 1935–1964*. Pittsburgh: University of Pittsburgh Press, 2021.

Sosnowski, Saúl and Louise B. Popkin, eds. *Repression, Exile, and Democracy: Uruguayan Culture*. Translated by Louise B. Popkin. Durham: Duke University Press, 1993.

Spooner, Mary Helen. *Soldiers in a Narrow Land: The Pinochet Regime in Chile*. Berkeley: University of California Press, 1994.

Stallings, Barbara. *Banker to the Third World: U.S. Portfolio Investments in Latin America, 1900–1986*. Berkeley: University of California Press, 1987.

Stein, Steve. *Populism in Peru: The Emergence of the Masses and the Politics of Social Control*. Madison: University of Wisconsin Press, 1980.

Stern, Steve J., ed. *Shining and Other Paths: War and Society in Peru, 1980–1995*. Durham: Duke University Press, 1998.

Stevens, Donald F. *Origins of Instability in Early Republican Mexico*. Durham: Duke University Press, 1991.

Stoner, K. Lynn. *From the House to the Streets: The Cuban Woman's Movement for Legal Reform, 1898–1940*. Durham: Duke University Press, 1991.

Suchlicki, Jaime. *University Students* and *Revolution in Cuba, 1920–1968*. Coral Gables: University of Miami Press, 1969.

Sweig, Julia E. *Inside the Cuban Revolution: Fidel Castro and the Urban Underground*. Cambridge: Harvard University Press, 2002.

Szulc, Tad. *Fidel Castro: A Critical Portrait*. New York: William Morrow, 1986.

———. *Twilight of the Tyrants*. New York: Holt, 1959.

Taffet, Jeffrey F. *Foreign Aid as Foreign Policy: The Alliance for Progress in Latin America*. New York: Routledge, 2007.

Tamarin, David. *The Argentine Labor Movement, 1930–1945: A Study in the Origins of Peronism*. Albuquerque: University of New Mexico Press, 1985.

Thomas, Hugh. *Cuba, or, the Pursuit of Freedom*. Second ed. New York: Da Capo Press, 1998.

Tillman, Ellen D. *Dollar Diplomacy by Force: Nation-Building and Resistance in the Dominican Republic*. Chapel Hill: University of North Carolina Press, 2016.

Timerman, Jacobo. *Prisoner without a Name, Cell without a Number*. Translated by Tony Talbott. New York: Vintage Books, 1988.

Tombs, David. *Latin American Liberation Theology*. Boston: Brill Academic Publishers, 2002.

Topik, Steven and Allen Wells. *Global Markets Transformed, 1870–1945*. Cambridge: The Belknap Press of Harvard University Press, 2014.

———. *The Second Conquest of Latin America: Coffee, Henequen, and Oil during the Export Boom, 1850–1930*. Austin: Institute of Latin American Studies, University of Texas Press, 1998.

Tutino, John, ed. *New Countries: Capitalism, Revolutions, and Nations in the Americas*. Durham: Duke University Press, 2016.

Valenzuela, Arturo. *The Breakdown of Democratic Regimes: Chile*. Baltimore: Johns Hopkins University Press, 1978.

Vanden, Harry E. and Gary Prevost. *Democracy and Socialism in Sandinista Nicaragua*. Boulder: Lynne Rienner, 1993.

———. *Politics of Latin America: The Power Game*. Seventh ed. New York: Oxford University Press, 2020.

Vanger, Milton I. *Uruguay's José Batlle y Ordóñez: The Determined Visionary, 1915–1917*. Boulder: Lynne Rienner, 2010.

Verbitsky, Horacio. *The Flight: Confessions of an Argentine Dirty Warrior*. Translated by Esther Allen. New York: New Press, 1996.

Walker, Thomas W., ed. *Revolution and Counterrevolution in Nicaragua, 1979–1990*. Boulder: Westview, 1991.

Walker, Thomas W. and Ariel C. Armony, eds. *Repression, Resistance, and Democratic Transition in Central America*. Wilmington: Scholarly Resources, 2000.

Webber, Jeffrey R. and Barry Carr, eds. *The New Latin American Left: Cracks in the Empire*. Lanham, MD: Rowman & Littlefield, 2013.

Weis, Michael W. *Cold Warriors and Coups D'État: Brazilian-American Relations, 1945–1964*. Albuquerque: University of New Mexico Press, 1993.

Wells, Allen. *Yucatán's Gilded Age: Haciendas, Henequen, and International Harvester, 1860–1915*. Albuquerque: University of New Mexico Press, 1985.

Whitfield, Teresa. *Paying the Price: Ignacio Ellacuria and the Murdered Jesuits in El Salvador*. Philadelphia: Temple University Press, 1995.

Wickham-Crowley, Timothy P. *Guerrillas and Revolution in Latin America: A Comparative Study of Insurgents and Regimes since 1956*. Princeton: Princeton University Press, 1992.

Williams, John Hoyt. *The Rise and Fall of the Paraguayan Republic, 1800–1870*. Austin: Institute of Latin American Studies, University of Texas, 1979.

Winn, Peter, ed. *Victims of the Chilean Miracle: Workers and Neoliberalism in the Pinochet Era, 1973–2002*. Durham: Duke University Press, 2004.

Wolfe, Joel. *Working Women, Working Men: São Paulo and the Rise of Brazil's Industrial Working Class, 1900–1955*. Durham: Duke University Press, 1993.

Womack, John. *Zapata and the Mexican Revolution*. New York: Vintage Press, 1968.

Wright, Thomas C. *Impunity, Human Rights, and Democracy: Chile and Argentina, 1990–2005*. Austin: University of Texas Press, 2014.

———. *Latin America in the Era of the Cuban Revolution and Beyond*. Third ed. Santa Barbara: Praeger, 2018.

———. *State Terrorism in Latin America: Chile, Argentina, and International Human Rights*. Lanham, MD: Rowman & Littlefield, 2007.

Wright, Thomas C. and Rody Oñate. *Flight from Chile: Voices of Exile*. Albuquerque: University of New Mexico Press, 1998.

Yashar, Deborah J. *Contesting Citizenship in Latin America: The Rise of Indigenous Movements and the Post-Liberal Challenge*. New York: Cambridge University Press, 2005.

Index

220 *Index*

220 *Index*

United Fruit Company (UFCO), 57, 74, 75
United Nations (UN), 66–67
United Socialist Party of Venezuela (PSUV), 176
United States Agency for International Development (USAID), 179
urban guerrillas, 123, 125–26, 132, 133
Uriburu, José Félix, 33, 44
Urrutia, Manuel, 87–88
Uruguay, 7, 36, 58, 85, 123, 129, 135, 160, *165*, 174, 192; Blanco Party, 29, 44; democracy in, 63, 65, 110, 132; dictatorship of, 44, 106, 151; oligarchy in, 24, 28–31, 34, 41, 43; socioeconomic democratization efforts, 33, 126, 159; state terrorism in, 115, 126–27, 133, 139–42, 147, 150, 163; women's representation in government, 61, *62, 167;* working classes of, 22, 41
U.S. Agency for International Development (USAID), 68, 179

Vargas, Getúlio, 48–49, 54, 62, 96, 125
Vargas Llosa, Mario, 148
Vásquez, Tabaré, 174
Velasco Alvarado, Juan, 105–10
Venezuela, 4, 85, 95, 124, 155, *165*, 174, 179; Chávez as ruler of, 176, 178, 181; democracy in, 58, 69–70, 99–100, 102, 111, 175; dictatorship in, 57, 65, 99, 175, 177, 182–84; women's representation in government, *62, 167*

Vicaría de la Solidaridad, 130–31, 135
Videla, Jorge Rafael, 132–33, 134
Villa, Pancho, 26–27
Villa Grimaldi facility, 129
Villarroel, Gualberto, 56, 77, 80
La Violencia period, 61, 70

War of Texas Secession, 6
War of the Thousand Days, 70
War of the Triple Alliance, 7
Waynick, Capus, 68
women's suffrage, 45, 61–62, 63, 65, 76, 78, 166, 191
Workers' Assembly of National Nutrition, 33, 34
Workers' Party (PT), 177, 178
World Bank, 156, 158, 159, 172, 173, 179
World War I, 10, 24, 33, 34, 36, 40, 58, 61
World War II, 1, 49, 62, 65, 66, 67, 69, 81, 89, 111, 146

Yacimientos Petrolíferos Fiscales (YPF), 32
Yon Sosa, Marco Antonio, 139
Yrigoyen, Hipólito, 32, 33, 44

Zapata, Emiliano, 26–27, 28
Zapatista National Liberation Army (EZLN), 149, 159
Zelaya, José Manuel, 170
Zero Hunger *(Fome Zero)* program, 177–78

www.ingramcontent.com/pod-product-compliance
Lightning Source LLC
Chambersburg PA
CBHW030314270326
41926CB00010B/1365